SharePoint

Interview Questions and Answers

(A ready reckoner for freshers, intermediaries and experts who are appearing for a SharePoint interview)

By

Shivprasad Koirala

BPB PUBLICATIONS
B-14 Connaught Place, New Delhi-110 001

FIRST EDITION 2009 REPRINTED 2013

ISBN –978-81-8333-309-2

Distributors:

COMPUTER BOOK CENTRE
12, Shrungar Shopping Centre, M.G. Road,
BANGALORE-560001 Ph: 25587923, 25584641

MICRO BOOKS
Shanti Niketan Building, 8, Camac Street
KOLKATTA-700017 Ph: 22826518/9

BUSINESS PROMOTION BUREAU
8/1, Ritchie Street, Mount Road,
CHENNAI-600002 Ph: 28410796, 28550491

BPB PUBLICATIONS
B-14, Connaught Place, NEW DELHI-110001
Ph : 23325760, 23723393, 23737742

BPB BOOK CENTRE
376, Old Lajpat Rai Market, DELHI-110006
Ph: 23861747

MICRO MEDIA
Shop No.5, Mahendra Chambers, 150 D.N. Rd,
Next to Capital Cinema V.T. (C.S.T.) Station,
MUMBAI-400001 Ph: 22078296, 22078297

DECCAN AGENCIES
4-3-329, Bank Street,
HYDERABAD-500195 Ph: 24756400, 24756967

INFO TECH
G-2, Sidhartha Building , 96, Nehru Place,
NEW DELHI-110019
Ph: 26438245, 26415092, 26234208

INFO TECH
Shop No. 2, F-38, South Extention Part-I
NEW DELHI-110049
Ph: 24691288

Published by **Manish Jain** for BPB Publications, B-14, Connaught Place, New Delhi-110001 and Printed by him at Akash Press, New Delhi.

Dedication

First of all I would like to thank my mom and dad for bringing me to life and tolerating me. I would like to apologize to my two kids Sanjana and Simran, whose dad's play time has been stolen and given to this book…Sorry Bacchus, I am so selfish. Then comes my best friend that's my wife who trusted me and I still wonder why she trusts me so much. Without BPB Publications and Manish Jain, this author would have never existed. I am blessed to have Raju as my brother who always keeps my momentum going. I am grateful to Bhavnesh Asar who initially conceptualized the idea as I believe concept thinking is more important than execution. Thanks to Shaam and Khadak for all the effort they have put in day and night. It was their tiresome three months of continuous writing that we have finally made it.

Finally, without you readers, Shivprasad Koirala does not exist, thanks for accepting me as an author.

About the author

The author works in a big multinational company and has good experience in software industry. He is presently working as project lead and in past has led projects in banking, travel and financial sectors. But on top of all, he is a simple developer like you all guys, doing an 8-hour job.

"Writing is something extra I do as I love doing it. No one is perfect and same holds true for me.So anything you want to comment, suggest, and point typo/grammar mistakes or technical mistakes regarding the book, you can mail me at bpb@vsnl.com. Believe me guys, even your harsh words would be received with love and treated to the top most priority. Without you guys, I am not an author. Writing an interview question book is really a great deal of responsibility. I have tried to cover maximum questions as I always think probably leaving one silly question will cost someone's job there. But huge natural variations in an interview are something difficult to cover in this small book. So if you have come across such questions during interview which are not addressed in this book, do mail at bpb@vsnl.com.Who knows probably that question can save some other guys job."

Features of the book

- Around 400 plus interview questions from live SharePoint interviews.
- Full range of interview questions right from junior SharePoint developer to a senior people.
- Covers major sections in SharePoint like WSS, Webparts, custom controls, and workflow.
- In SharePoint, content types and custom data types are the most favorite topics; this book explains these concepts in a seamless manner.
- Workflow is most visited section during SharePoint interviews. This book dedicates 10 questions which explain how workflow is implemented step by step in SharePoint.
- Book covers important points like salary negotiations; resume making and general points to be remembered during interview.
- Ideal for SharePoint professionals who are looking for Quick reference and FAQ.

- ❑ Also recommended for SharePoint interviewers who are looking for what questions to be asked to get better and decent SharePoint professionals.
- ❑ Recommended for freshers and students who want to have a feel of what kind of questions are asked during SharePoint interviews.
- ❑ CD has all source code we have discussed in the book.
- ❑ CD provided with the book has 26 SharePoint questions and answers videos free. Do not miss to browse through them.
- ❑ We have provided an Excel sheet which can help you measure how much you are ready for SharePoint interviews.

I am sure after reading this book, reader will have extra confidence and a better approach for SharePoint interviews.

Foreword

Changing job is one of the biggest events for any IT professional. When he starts the search, he realizes that he needs much more than actual experience. Working on a project is one thing and cracking an interview is a different ball game, many may differ on this but that's my personal opinion. When you work on a project, you are doing a routine job and you tend to forget the basic fundamentals. For instance, you are working on a highly technical project which uses SharePoint workflows in project, it's very much possible that you can crack workflows like anything but you may fail in simple SharePoint user control questions. It does not mean you do not know the fundamentals; it's only that you need to revise the same.

This book will give you bird eye view of what is needed in SharePoint interviews. It will help you in doing quick revision so that you can be ready for the interview in a day or two. The best way to read this book is not from start to end rather just read the index and then go in details if needed.

It's really good to see emails saying 'We got a job,' which just makes us feel better, please do share your experiences on shiv_koirala@yahoo.com. I hope this book takes you to a better height and gives you extra confidence boost during interviews.

Best of Luck and Happy Job-Hunting....

Do not miss the 26 SharePoint videos and 200 Demo videos in CD!

In the CD, we have provided 26 SharePoint questions and answer videos. You need to install flash to see the video. In case you are feeling too bored to read this whole book, you can just plug in your ear phones, relax and hear the 26 videos. It's like reading this whole book. You can also see 200 demo videos for LINQ, WCF, WPF, WWF, Silverlight, Design patterns, UML and lot more.

Contents

Dedication ii
Features of the book iii
Foreword iv
Do not miss the 26 SharePoint videos and 200 Demo videos in CD iv
SharePoint in Software Company hierarchy 1
Resume Preparation Guidelines 3
The salary slip (CTC, Gross and Net) 4
Salary Negotiation 6
Points to remember 8
Interview rating Sheet 10
What is SharePoint? 10
What is WSS and MOSS? 11
How does WSS actually work? 11
What is site and site collection? 12
What is the main advantage of using site collections? 12
What is the use of SQL Server in SharePoint? 13
What is the concept of virtual path provider? 13
What is the concept of ghosting and unghosting in SharePoint? 15
What is the concept of safemodeparser in ASP.NET? 16
How can I create my first site in SharePoint? 16
What is Quick Launch menu? 19
We have heard that we can customize SharePoint sites how do we do that? 19
We have heard it has readymade functional modules for collaboration? 20
How can we enable these reusable components in my site? 22
How can we display a simple custom page in SharePoint? 24
The above page does not look like a standard SharePoint page? 25
Above code is completely inline, how can we implement behind code in SharePoint? 27
What is the concept of features in SharePoint? 30
Can you explain the broader steps for deploying/activating a feature? 32
I want that the feature should be only displayed to admin? 37
How can we provision page template and page instances? 38

Why customized pages are parsed using no-compile mode? 41
What is safe mode processing and Safe Controls? 42
Can you explain WSS model? 43
How can we use custom controls in SharePoint? 46
How can you view a detail error in SharePoint? 48
How can we display ASCX control in SharePoint pages? 49
What are WebParts and in what ways does it vary in SharePoint environment? 51
What are the different life cycle events that WebPart goes through? 53
What's the difference between WebParts in WSS 2.0 and 3.0? 53
Can you explain the 6 steps we need to create a WebPart in SharePoint? 54
How can we implement customization and personalization in WebParts? 58
How can we create a custom editor for WebPart? 63
SharePoint is about centralizing documents, how similar is to the Windows folder? 66
Can we add custom fields to our document library documents? 70
What are content types in SharePoint? 73
What's the difference between content and custom columns, they do the same thing? 76
Can you elaborate more on List and Content Types in SharePoint? 77
Which are the various readymade list types that SharePoint provides currently? 79
What is Windows Workflow Foundation? 79
What is a Workflow? 79
What are different types of Workflow in Windows Workflow foundation? 80
Is SharePoint workflow same as Windows workflow? 81
What are the different stages of SharePoint workflow life cycle? 82
What is a three-state workflow in SharePoint? 83
Does SharePoint only have three-state workflow? 91
How can we create SharePoint workflow using SharePoint designer? 91
What is Infopath? 97
In what format is the Infopath form design saved? 97
Reference 97
.NET Interview questions 101
SQL Server Interview questions 117
Project Management Interview questions 127
Software Architecture Interview Questions 132
JAVA Interview questions 135

SharePoint in Software Company Hierarchy

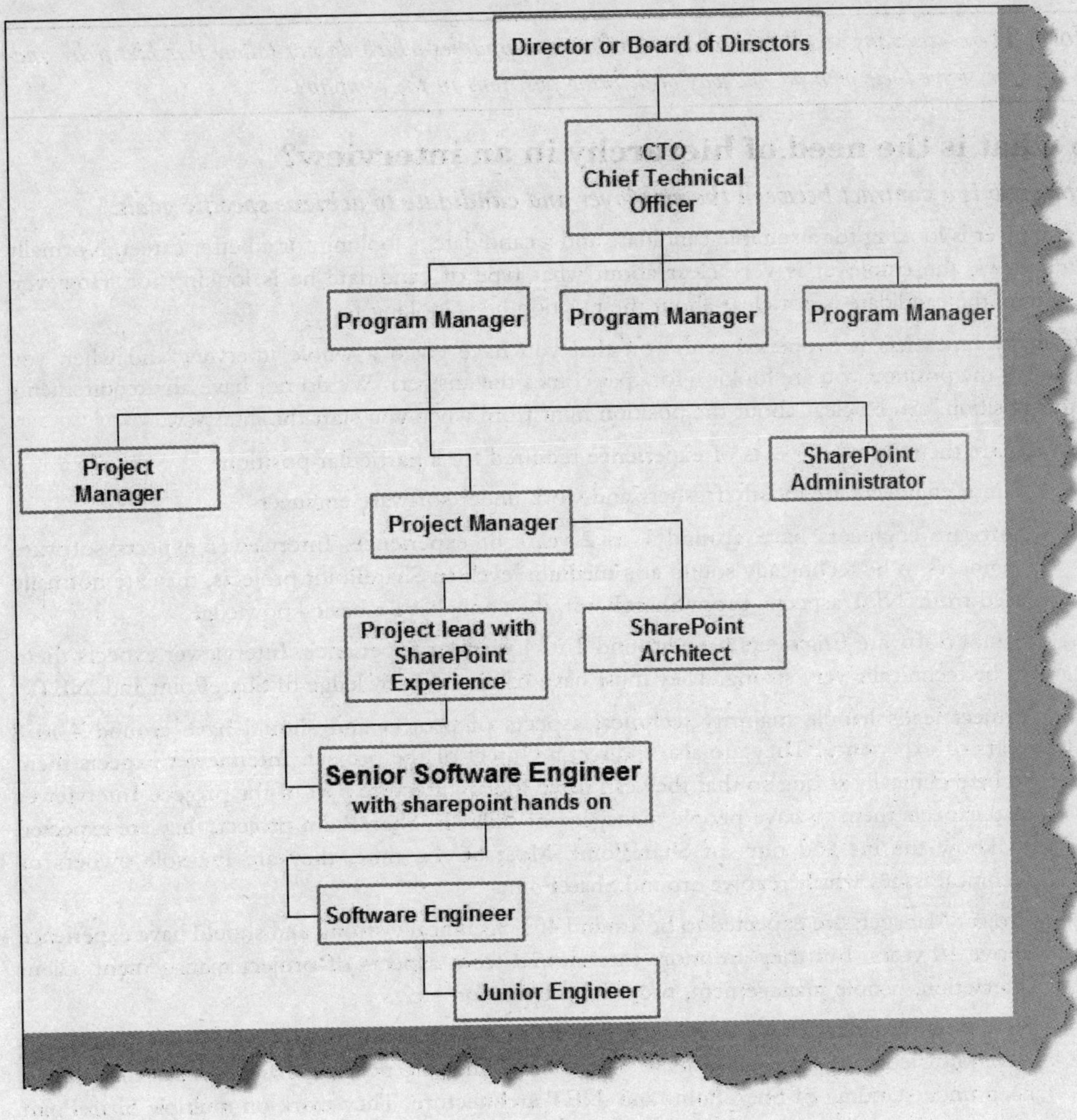

Figure: 0.2 IT Company hierarchy

It's very important during interview to be clear about what position you are targeting. Depending on what position you are targeting, the interviewer will shoot you questions. For example, if you are looking for a SharePoint Administrator position, you will be asked around 20% programming questions and 80% SharePoint administrator questions.

Above is a figure of a general hierarchy across most IT companies and how SharePoint administrator, developers and architects fit in the same.

> **Note:** *There are many small and medium software companies which do not follow this hierarchy and they have their own ad hoc way of defining positions in the company.*

So what is the need of hierarchy in an interview?

"Interview is a contract between the employer and candidate to achieve specific goals."

An employer is looking for a suitable candidate and a candidate is looking for a better career. Normally in interviews, the employer is very clear about what type of candidate he is looking for. However, 90% times, the candidate is not clear about the position he is looking for.

How many times has it happened with you that you have given a whole interview and when you mentioned the position you are looking for...pat comes the answer, "We do not have any requirements for this position." So be clear about the position right from when you start the interview.

Following are the number of years of experience required for a particular position:

- Junior engineers are mostly freshers and work under software engineers.
- Software engineers have around 1 to 2 years of experience. Interviewer expects software engineers to be technically sound at a medium level. In SharePoint projects, they are normally used from .NET aspects. From SharePoint, they only have a basic knowledge.
- Senior Software Engineers have around 2 to 4 years of experience. Interviewer expects them to be technically very strong. They must have hands-on knowledge of SharePoint and .NET.
- Project leads handle majority technical aspects of project and should have around 4 to 8 years of experience. They are also indirect architect of the project. Interviewer expects them to be technically strong so that they can drive the architecture part of the project. Interviewer also expects them to have people management skills. In SharePoint project, they are expected to know the ins and outs of SharePoint. Most of the time, they are the sole owners of technical issues which revolve around SharePoint.
- Project Managers are expected to be around 40% technically strong and should have experience above 10 years. But they are more interviewed from aspects of project management, client interaction, people management, proposal preparation etc.
- SharePoint architects have more than 8 years of experience in SharePoint. They should also have knowledge of older versions of SharePoint. They are not only hands on but they have a deep understanding of SharePoint and .NET architecture. They work on multiple SharePoint projects where they do activities like defining architecture, solving critical SharePoint issues and ensuring that the project team does not face technical SharePoint problems.

- ❑ SharePoint administrators maintain SharePoint portal. They do not work on projects as such. Normally you will find SharePoint administrators working directly with the top management. They normally conduct activities like role management, site creation, backup, etc.

So now judge where you stand, and where you want to go....

Resume Preparation Guidelines

It is wisely said, "First impression is the last impression."

> **Note:** *A sample resume is provided in "SampleResume" folder.*

Before the interviewer meets you, he will first meet your resume. Interviewer looking at your resume is almost a 20% interview happening without you knowing it. I was always a bad guy when it comes to resume preparation. But when I looked at my friends' resume, they were really good. Now that I am writing series of book on interviews, I thought this will be a good point to put in. You can happily skip it if you are confident about your resume. There is no hard and fast rule that you have to follow the same pattern but just see if all points in the check list are attended:

- ❑ Use plain text when you are sending resumes through email. For instance, you sent your resume using Microsoft Word and what if the interviewer is using Linux, he will never be able to read your resume. Or, you sent your resume in Word 2000 and the guy has Word 97…ouch.
- ❑ Attach a covering letter as it really impresses and makes you look traditionally formal. Yes, even if you are sending your CV through email, send a covering letter.

Check list of content you should have in your resume:

- ❑ Start with an objective or summary, for instance, "Working as a SharePoint administrator for more than 4 years. Implemented customer portal using SharePoint. Followed industry best practices and adhered and implemented processes, which enhanced the quality of technical delivery. Pledge to deliver the best technical solutions to the industry."
- ❑ Specify your core strengths at the start of the resume by which the interviewer can make a quick decision whether you are eligible for the position or not. For example:
    - Looked after SharePoint intranet portal independently. Played a major role in SharePoint administration.
    - Worked extensively on SharePoint webparts and BDC.
    - Well versed with SharePoint workflows and security.
    - Looking forward to work on project manager or senior manager position.

This is also a good position to specify your objective or position which makes it clear to the interviewer that should he call you for an interview or not. For instance, if you are looking for senior positions specify it explicitly 'looking for this job profile.' Any kind of Microsoft certification you have, make it visible in this section.

Once you have specified briefly your goals and what you have done, specify what type of technology you have worked with. For instance InfoPath, TOOLS, Languages, Web servers, process (Six sigma, CMMI), etc.

- After that you can make a run through of your experience company wise that is which company you have worked with, year/month joining and year/month of leaving. This will give an overview to the interviewer what type of companies you have associated yourself.

Then, mention all your projects you have worked till now. Best is to start in descending order that is from your current project and go backwards. For every project, try to put these things:

- Project Name/Client name (It's sometimes unethical to mention clients name; I leave it to the readers).
- Number of team members.
- Time span of the project.
- Tools, language, RDBMS and technology used to complete the project.
- Brief summary of the project.

Senior people who have huge experience will tend to increase their CV with putting in summary for all projects. Best for them is to just put description of the first three projects in descending manner and rest they can say verbally during interview. I have even seen CV above 15 pages…I doubt who can read it.

- Finally comes your education and personal details.
- Trying for onsite, do not forget to mention your passport number.
- Some guys tend to make their CV long. I think an optimal size should be not more than 4 to 5 pages.
- Do not mention your salary in CV. You can talk about it during interview with HR or the interviewer.
- When you are writing your summary for project, make it effective by using verbs like managed a team of 5 members, architected the project from start to finish etc. It puts huge weight on your CV.
- This is essential very essential take 4-5 Xerox copies of your resume as you will need it now and then.
- Just in case take at least 2 passport photos with you. You can escape it but many times you will need it.
- Carry all your current office documents, specially your salary slips and joining letter.

The salary slip (CTC, Gross and Net)

Mr. Raju left his old organization where he had a package of 4,00,000 INR and joined a new organization with a package of 6,00,000 INR. In his old company, he was getting 40,000 INR on hand. At the first glance, Mr. Raju felt like he has received a 50% hike. When he received the first salary in the new company, he got 36,000 INR on hand, SHOCKED! We are sure many will feel cheated, but it's not the organization, it's your mistake not to analyze your salary slip properly.

It's a psychology of every employee to look at what he gets on hand. First thing when you get your salary do not accept it, take it home and dissect it. Try to extract what you will get on hand rather than looking at the CTC.

Note: *We have written this tutorial according to Indian corporate industry. But the basic concept will hold true even for other geographical corporates.*

Here's a simple methodology by which we can conclude our on-hand component easily. Every salary slip has lot of components like basic, HRA, PF etc. Every salary slip component falls in to five categories as shown in figure 'Five categories.'

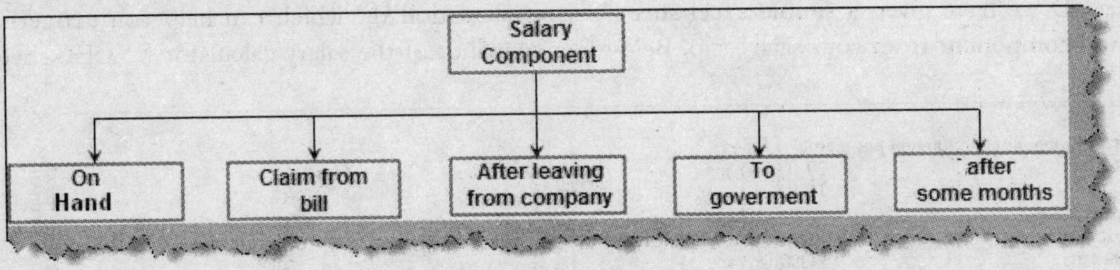

Figure: Five categories

On hand: Salary components which you get on hand needs to be pushed in to this category. Some of the examples are basic, HRA etc. This component is something which you get fixed every month and directly in to your hand.

Claim from bill: There are some salary components which we get after submitting bills. Please note this is not a monthly on-hand component, rather it's a claim which you get after submitting bills. Some of the examples of this category are LTA and phone bills.

After some months: There are salary components like bonus or some organization call them as retention bonus which is received after some months. This can be in a form of yearly or quarterly bonus. Bonuses depend on company policies and many companies add this to your CTC. Again this amount is not received in the same month itself and they do not form the monthly on-hand component.

After leaving company: There are some salary components which we get after leaving the company. For example provident fund (PF). Again this component does not add to your on-hand monthly, rather it's something you will get after resignation.

To government: Some of the salary components go to the government like PT (professional tax), IT (Income tax) etc. You will never get this amount. It's something you pay to the government for the facilities they provide or you can say for running the country.

Now that we have segregated our components in to the above five categories, its time to understand three principles - CTC, Gross and Net.

CTC is everything that company spends on us. Many professionals get carried by the CTC figure and hop the jobs. CTC is the addition of all the five components. Yes, you guessed it right it also has the salary component which you will not get on hand.

CTC = on hand + Claim from bill + after leaving company + to government + after some months.

Gross is only on hand. This is the figure on which you should negotiate. Many times company try to shuffle the salary components in the above categories to come to this figure, be careful and alert when they do so.

Gross = on hand

Net is what you get exactly on hand after Income tax deduction.

Net = Gross - Tax on gross.

In the CD we have given a simple excel sheet 'SalaryCalculation.xls' which can help you extract the on-hand component from your salary slip. Below is a snapshot of the salary calculator EXCEL sheet.

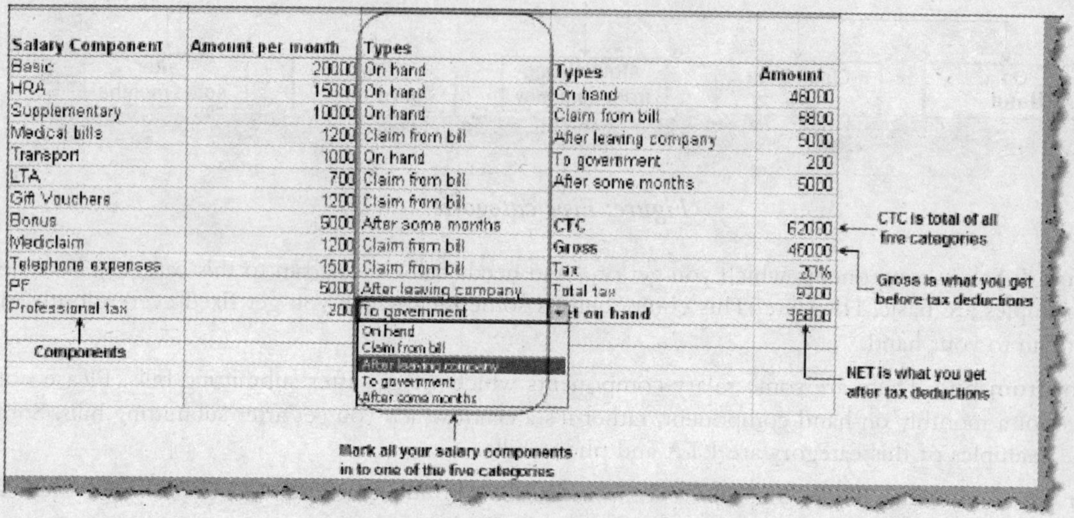

Figure: Salary calculator

You just need to enter all components and select from the combo box in which category the components belong. This sheet is a sample sheet, so probably you will need to add and remove some components according to your slip. Also you need to adjust the tax value according to your salary range.

Salary Negotiation

Ok that's what we all do it for MONEY… not everyone but still money means a lot. This is probably the weakest area for techno savvy guys. They are not good negotiators. I have seen so many guys at the first instance they will smile and say "NEGOTIABLE SIR".

So here are some points:

- ❑ Do a study of what is the salary trend? For instance have some kind of baseline. For example what is the salary trend on number of years of experience? Discuss this with your friends.
- ❑ Do not mention your expected salary on the resume.
- ❑ Let the employer first make the salary offer. Try to delay the salary discussion till the end.
- ❑ If they say what you expect, come with a figure with a little higher end and say negotiable. Remember never say negotiable on something which you have aimed, HR guys will always bring it down. So negotiate on AIMED SALARY + something extra.

- The normal trend is that they look at your current salary and add a little to it so that they can pull you in. Do your home work - "my salary is this much and I expect this much so whatever it is now, I will not come below this."
- Do not be harsh during salary negotiations.
- It's good to aim high. For instance I want 1 billion dollars/month but at the same time, be realistic.
- Some companies have those hidden costs attached in salary, clarify it rather to be surprised at the first salary package.
- Many of the companies add extra performance compensation in your basic which can be surprising at times. So have a detail break down. Best is to discuss on hand salary rather than NET or CTC.
- Talk with the employer in what frequency does the hike happen.
- Take everything in writing, go back to your home and have a look once with a cool head is the offer worth it of what your current employer is giving.
- Do not forget once you have job in hand, you can come back to your current employer for negotiation.
- Remember the worst part is cribbing after joining the company that your colleague is getting more. So be careful while interview or be sportive to be a good negotiator in the next interview.
- One very important thing is that the best negotiation ground is not the new company where you are going but the old company which you are leaving. So once you have offer on hand get back to your old employee and show them the offer and then make your next move. It's my experience that negotiating with the old employer is easy than the new one....Frankly if approached properly rarely any one will say no as you have spent quiet an amount of time with them. Just do not be aggressive or egoistic that you have an offer on hand.
- Sometimes, some things are worth above money: JOB SATISFACTION. So whatever you negotiate, if you think you can get JOB SATISFACTION aspect on higher grounds, go for it. I think its worth more than money.

Applicable to Only India	
Years of experience	Amount in Rupees CTC (Monthly)
Fresher's	15000 to 20000
1 to 2 yrs	25000 to 30000
3 to 4 yrs	35000 to 45000
4 to 6 yrs	45000 to 50000
6 to 8 yrs	55000 to 65000
8 to 10 yrs	75000 to 85000
10 to 15 yrs	90000 to 100000
15 yrs and above	100000 and above. Mostly depends on negotiations.

Table: 0.3 Salary Card for India

We have taken bonus as a part of CTC.

Applicable to US Only	
Years of experience	Amount in Dollars (Yearly)
Fresher's	45000 to 55000
2 to 4 yrs	55000 to 60000
4 to 6 yrs	60000 to 65000
6 to 8 yrs	70000 to 80000
8 to 12 yrs	80000 to 90000
12 and above	Depends on negotiations

Table: 0.4 US Salary Card

> **Note:** *The above Salary card is based on my experience and some talk which I had with my friends who are in IT industry. In case you are finding discrepancies please do mail me at shiv_koirala@yahoo.com, probably we can standardize it better for the community.*

The score card shown above is completely derived from author's experience and interaction he had in his circle. It is not an approved score card by any authorized body as such and should be taken only has benchmark to measure your success. Also note that these rates are applicable for medium and large software companies. Small company rate cards are very irregular and governed by a single owner of the company. So the above rate card is not applicable for small companies. Many people do get mind blowing salaries even with small experience which again the score card does not reflect.

Points to remember

- ❑ One of the first questions asked during interview is "Can you say something about yourself"?
- ❑ Can you describe yourself and what you have achieved till now?
- ❑ Why do you want to leave the current company?
- ❑ Where do you see yourself after three years?
- ❑ What are your positive and negative points?
- ❑ How do you rate yourself in SharePoint workflows in one out of ten?
- ❑ Are you looking for onsite opportunities? (Be careful do not show your desperation of abroad journeys.)
- ❑ Why have you changed so many jobs? (Prepare a decent answer do not blame companies and individuals for your frequent change.)
- ❑ Never talk for more than 1 minute straight during interview.
- ❑ Have you worked with previous version of SharePoint InfoPath?
- ❑ Would you be interested in a full time SharePoint administrator job?
- ❑ Do not mention client names in resume. If asked, say that it's confidential which brings ahead qualities like honesty.

- ❑ When you make your resume keep your recent projects at the top.
- ❑ Find out what the employer is looking for by asking him questions at the start of interview. Example if a company has projects on SharePoint administration, employer will not be looking for SharePoint developers.
- ❑ Can you give a brief about your family background?
- ❑ As you are fresher, do you think you can really do this job?
- ❑ Have you heard about our company? Say five points about our company? Just read at least once what company you are going for?
- ❑ Can you describe your best project you have worked with?
- ❑ Do you work on Saturday and Sunday?
- ❑ Which is the biggest team size you have worked with?
- ❑ Can you describe your current project you have worked with?
- ❑ How much time will you need to join our organization? What's notice period for your current company?
- ❑ What certifications have you cleared?
- ❑ Do you have passport size photos, last year mark sheet, previous companies employment letter, last month's salary slip, passport and other necessary documents?
- ❑ What is the most important thing that motivates you?
- ❑ Why you want to leave the previous organization?
- ❑ Which type of job gives you greatest satisfaction?
- ❑ What is the type of environment you are looking for?
- ❑ Do you have experience in project management?
- ❑ Do you like to work as a team or as individual?
- ❑ Describe your best project manager you have worked with?
- ❑ Why should I hire you?
- ❑ Have you been ever fired or forced to resign?
- ❑ Can you explain some important points that you have learnt from your past project experiences?
- ❑ Have you gone through some unsuccessful projects, if yes, can you explain why did the project fail?
- ❑ Will you be comfortable with location shift? If you have personal problems, say no right at the first stage.... or else within two months you have to read my book again.
- ❑ Do you work late nights? Best answer is if there is project deadline, yes. Do not show that it's your culture to work during nights.
- ❑ Any special achievements in your life till now...tell your best project which you have done best in your career.
- ❑ Any plans of opening your own software company....Beware do not start pouring your Bill Gate's dream to him...can create a wrong impression.

Interview rating Sheet

We have provided a self assessment rating sheet in the book for Sharepoint, .NET, Java, Networking, Project management, Architecture, SQL Server and lot more. If you are able get 80% in the assessment, we are sure you can crack any Interview. You can find the assessment sheet in CD as an excel file (InterviewRating.xls). So take the self test again and again to improve your confidence.

What is SharePoint?

SharePoint helps team members to connect and exchange information in a collaborative manner. It helps to centralize enterprise information for efficient functioning. For instance below is how a normal organization works. Files and documents scattered in individual PC and data is transported according to custom protocols. The communication protocol for sending these data is also person dependent. Somebody would use an email; somebody would share a drive etc.

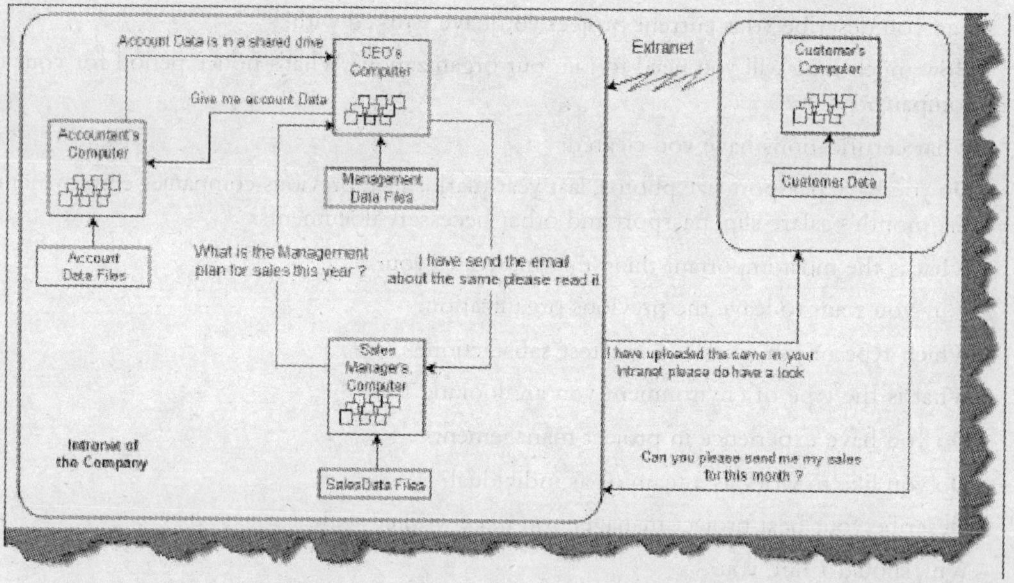

Sharepoint unites all the documents into one centralized place and unifies the data transport mechanism. In one sentence, it is a central enterprise information portal.

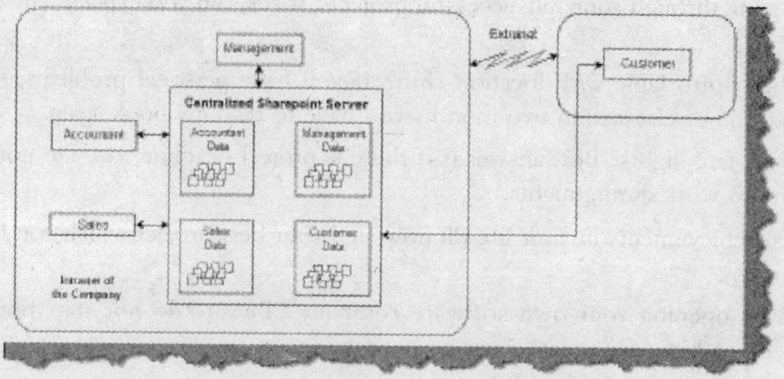

What is WSS and MOSS?

Microsoft has divided SharePoint products in two parts. One is called as WSS (Windows SharePoint services) and the other is MOSS (Microsoft Office SharePoint server). WSS is the platform on which MOSS is built. The WSS part is licensed through Windows 2003 server and it does not cost. MOSS is separate product by itself and it needs licensing and it has a good amount of cost associated with it. WSS is good for small team and small projects. MOSS has extra functionalities in other words value added services. So the choice between WSS and MOSS will depend on budget of the project and the VAS provided by MOSS.

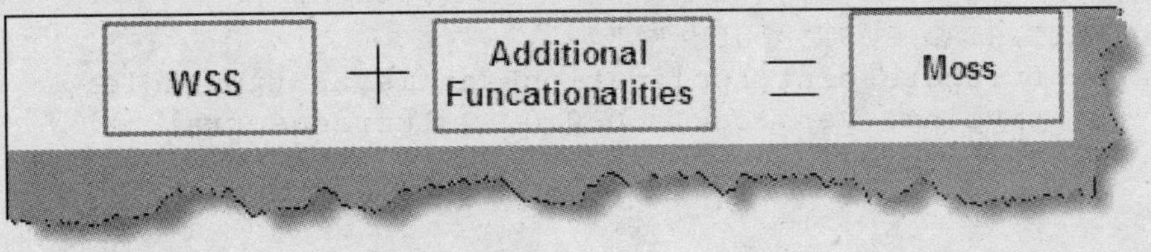

How does WSS actually work?

WSS does not work in an isolated fashion. It needs help of two more products, which include IIS (Internet Information Server) and SQL Server.

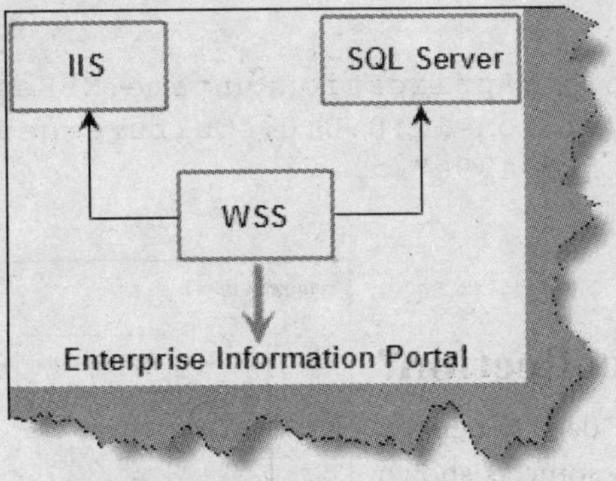

In order to understand how WSS works with IIS, we first need to understand the concept of "HttpHandlers and HttpModules". If you are not aware of it you can refresh about the same from the reference section provided in the book.

Using the HttpHandlers and HttpModules request is first passed through the SharePoint runtime and then passed to the ASP.NET runtime (aspnet_isapi.dll).

If we open the web.config file of a WSS enabled IIS web application, we can see the application run time handlers and modules.

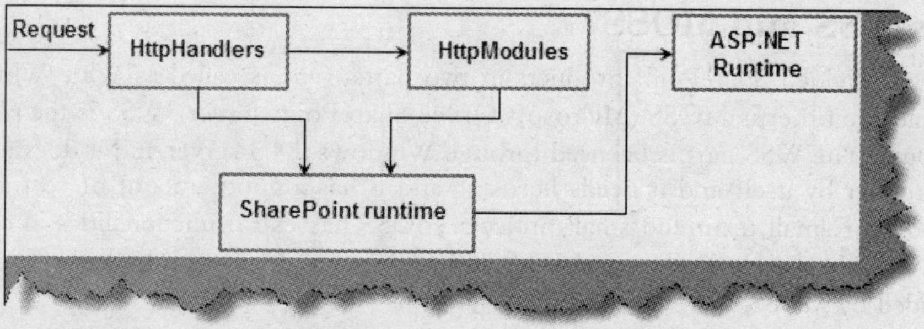


```
<httpHandlers>
<add verb="GET,HEAD,POST" path="*"
type="Microsoft.SharePoint.ApplicationRuntime.SPHttpHandler,
Microsoft.SharePoint, Version=12.0.0.0, Culture=neutral,
PublicKeyToken=71e9bce111e9429c"/>
....
...
</httpHandlers>
```

We have highlighted the application runtime module.

```
<httpModules>
<add name="SPRequest"
type="Microsoft.SharePoint.ApplicationRuntime.SPRequestModule,
Microsoft.SharePoint, Version=12.0.0.0, Culture=neutral,
PublicKeyToken=71e9bce111e9429c"/>
...
...
</httpModules>
```

What is site and site collection?

SharePoint is all about enterprise data. When we talk about enterprise data it looks some as shown in the figure below. In other words, it means grouping and sub groupings of data.

SharePoint extends the IIS web application structure to accommodate the above defined data structure using site and site collections. We will see in the later section how to create site collections.

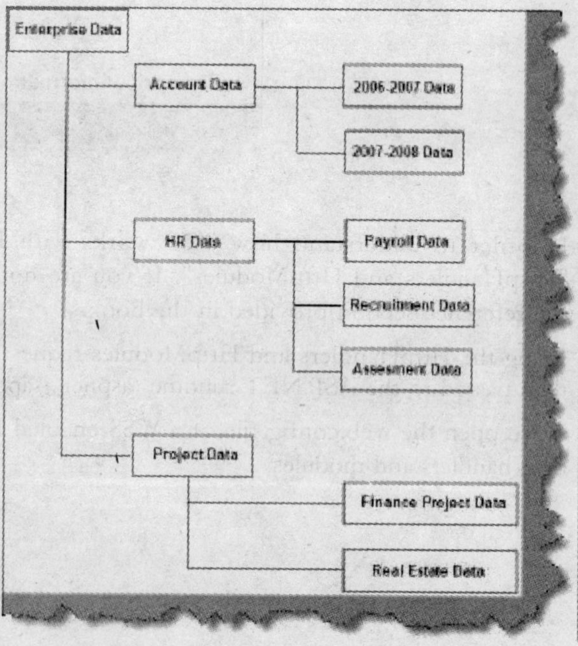

What is the main advantage of using site collections?

As said previously, SharePoint is all about data and data should properly be authenticated/authorized to proper users. By defining the structure in site and site collection, we can now define roles and responsibilities according to data. For instance in the previous figure we will assign all HR user to payroll, recruitment and assessment site. These users will not be assigned to account site collection. Same holds true for accounts user.

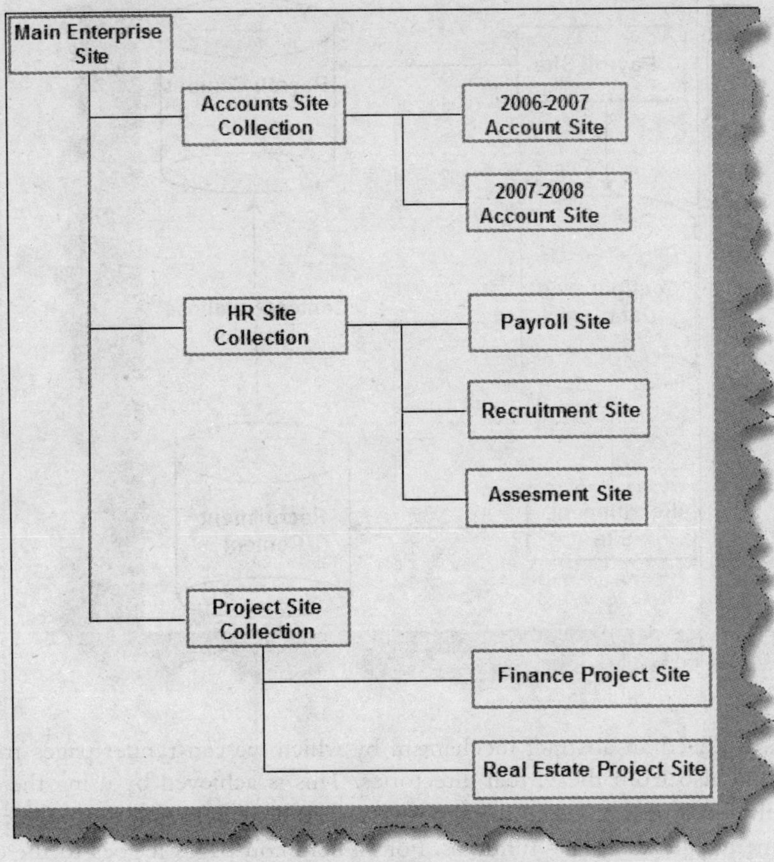

So when you design your hierarchy of site and site collection, you need to keep in mind the enterprise hierarchy structure and design the same accordingly.

What is the use of SQL Server in SharePoint?

SQL Server is used to store content and configuration information. We have two types of databases: one is the content database and the other is the configuration database. As previously said, content is according to every site. So every site has its own content database. For instance, if we have a payroll site and recruitment site, they have their own content database. Configuration database is for the entire site as they are used in web farms, site configuration and lot of other things which are generic and common across all the sites.

What is the concept of virtual path provider?

Any project has two parts - one is the standard and common part and the other is the customized version. In ASP.NET, we have two types of pages for any project - one is common ASPX pages and the other is customized ASPX pages. Common pages are stored on file directories while customized versions of pages are stored in content database.

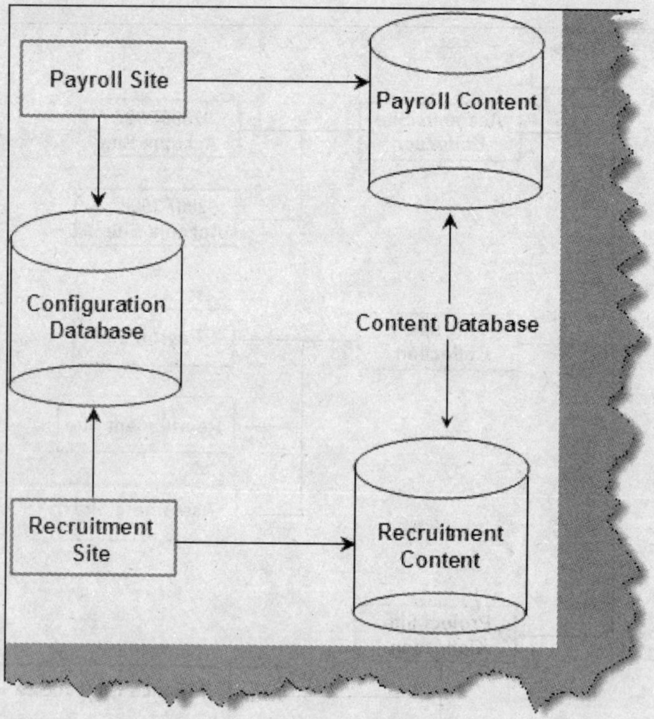

So in other words we need an abstract mechanism by which we can render pages from SQL Server content database and also from the virtual directories. This is achieved by using the virtual provider provided by SharePoint. So for all customized pages, virtual provider reads from the content database and passes the same to the ASP.NET runtimes. For all common pages it goes to the directory, parses it and the passes the same across to the ASP.NET runtime.

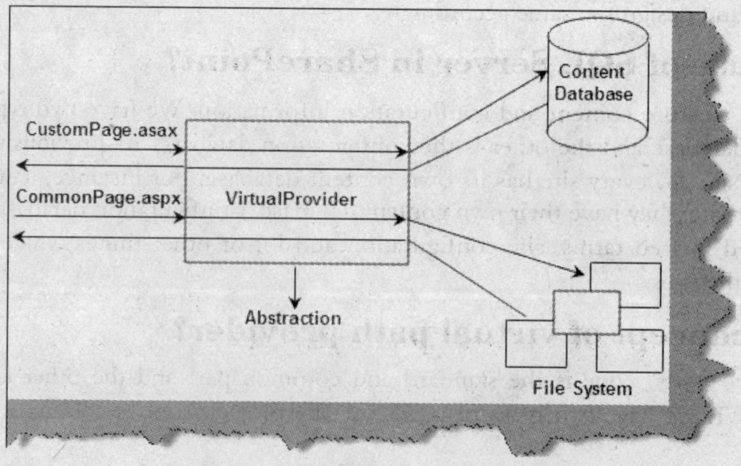

Virtual provider is an abstraction which loads the page from the content or the file system depending on whether it's customized or common pages and passes the same to the ASP.NET runtime.

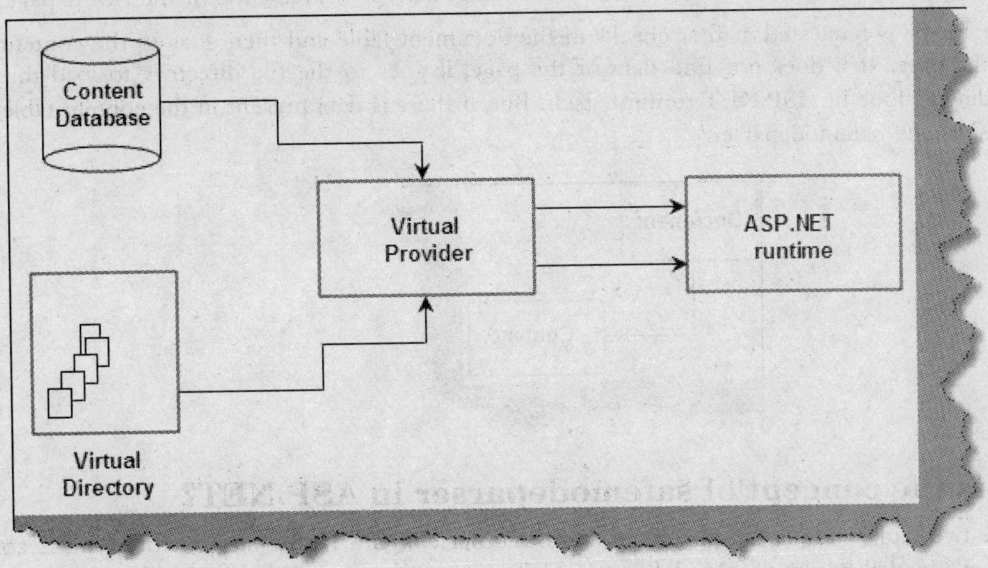

What is the concept of ghosting and unghosting in SharePoint?

In SharePoint, most of the site pages derive from templates. The custom pages only store the difference between them. The template is loaded in memory and applied to the custom pages on the fly. In other words, the template is stored in a cache. This definitely brings in performance and flexibility. Flexibility is in terms that when we change the template page, it's applied to all custom pages. These pages are loaded from the file system. So pages which are loaded from the file system are termed as ghosted pages.

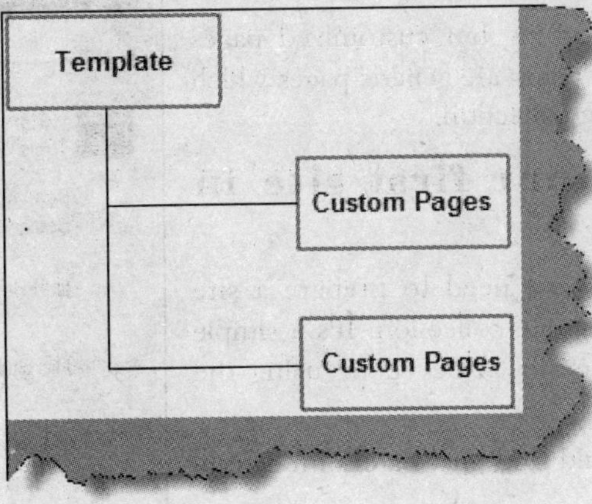

If the page data is loaded from the content database, it's termed as unghosted pages.

As a note, let me clarify the concept of document and content table as well. SharePoint stores all pages in the database. Looking from a 50,000 feet it has two tables one is the document table which has the entry of page and the other is the content which has the source code of the ASPX page.

So when a page is requested, it first checks in the document table and then goes to the content table to load the page. If it does not find data of the page, it goes to the file directory to load the page. This loading is done by ASP.NET runtime itself. But, if there is data present in the content table, then it's loaded by the 'safemodeparser.'

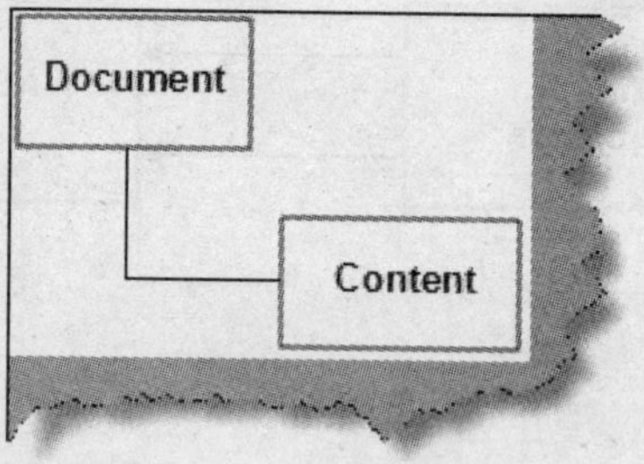

What is the concept of safemodeparser in ASP.NET?

There are two tables: one is the document and the other content. If the page is stored in the content database, it's loaded by the SafeModeParser which is page parser provided by SharePoint. If there is no data found in the content, it's loaded from the file directory by simple ASP.NET runtime.

What is the concept of Site pages and Application pages?

Site pages are customized pages and are saved into content database. So when you use the SharePoint designer to make custom changes, it saves the changes into content database. If you want to make generic pages in a site collection which will be used by everyone, like for instance, the 'Settings.aspx' page then you need to use application pages.

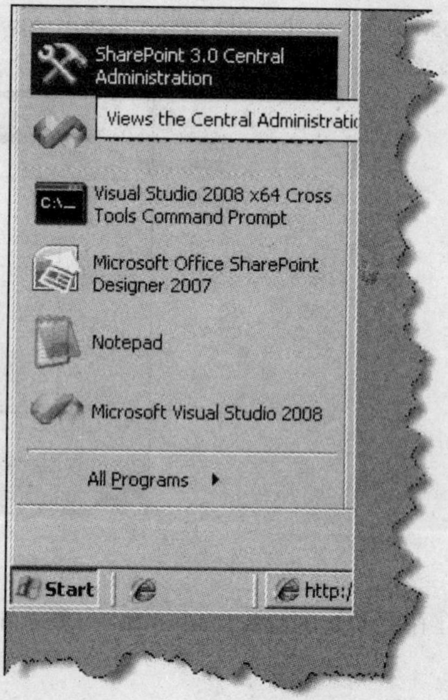

In other words, Site pages are nothing but customized pages stored in content, while application pages are generic pages which will be used by all the sites in a site collection.

How can we create our first site in SharePoint?

To create any site in SharePoint, we need to prepare a site collection and define site inside the site collection. It's a simple four-step procedure and can be easily achieved by using the SharePoint central administration.

Step 1: Click on start and we should find the SharePoint central administration menu.

Step 2: Once we click on the central administration menu, we need to click on the 'application management' tab and then click 'Create site collection.'

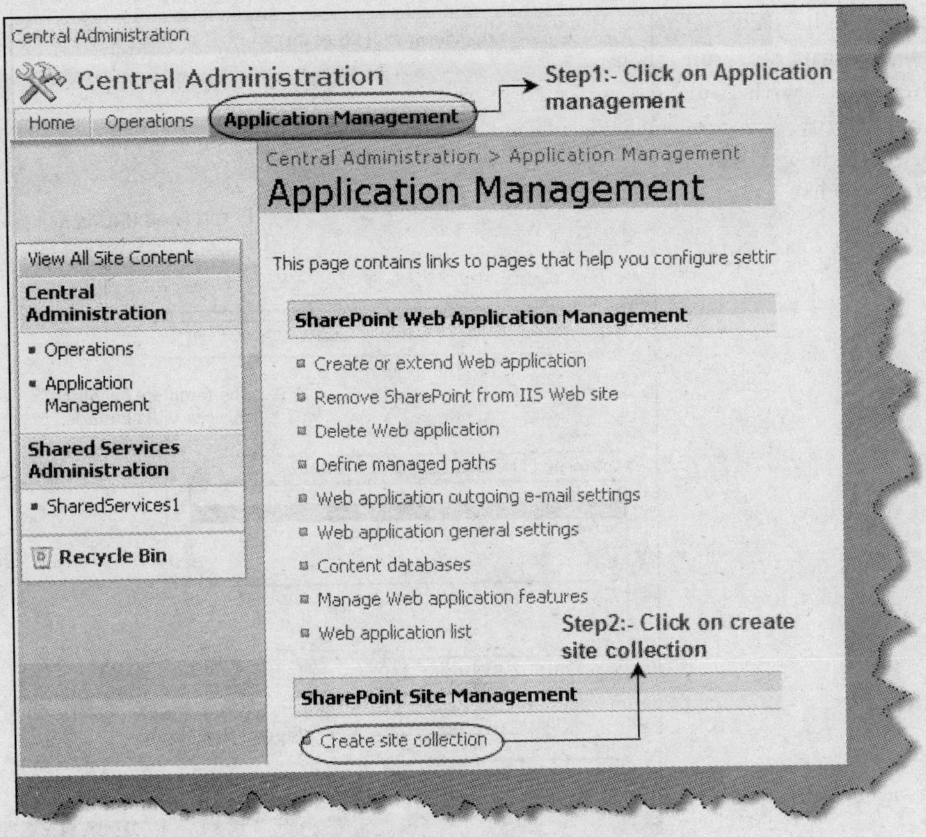

Step 3: Once we click 'Create site collection,' we would see a form which needs all necessary details to create a site. All details are almost self-understandable, the important ones being the site name, the template and the username in which SharePoint will run. All sites in SharePoint need to be inherited from some master as they cannot stand on their own.

Step 4: Once you have clicked 'Ok' we can now run the URL with our SharePoint name. Below is how a blank site looks like.

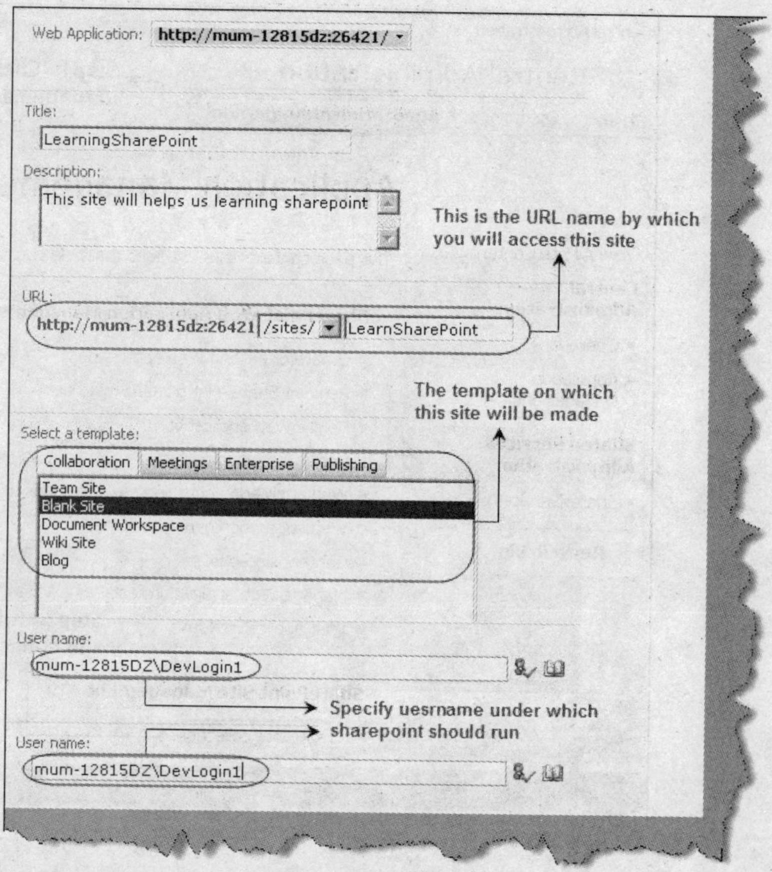

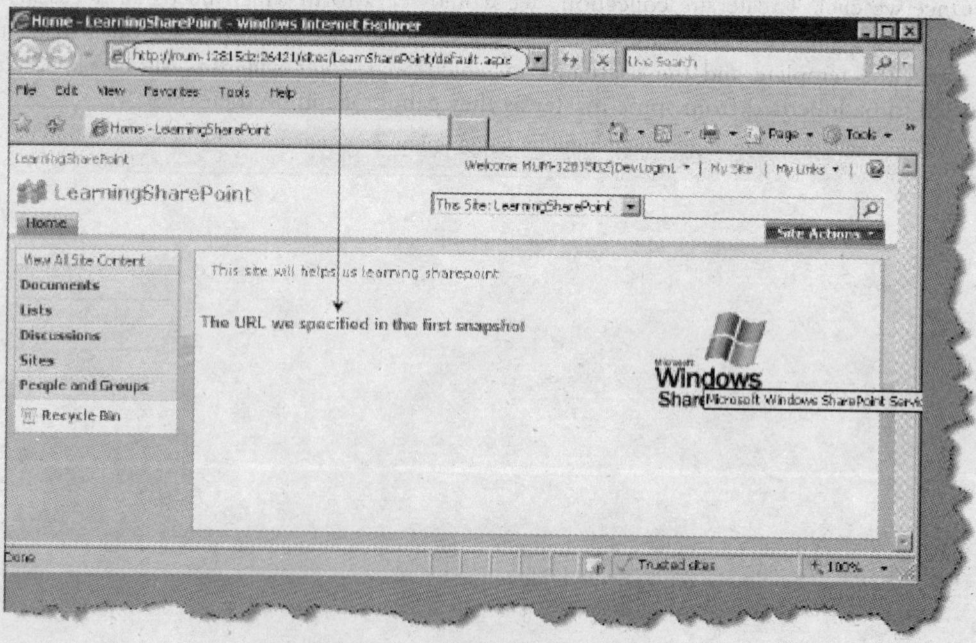

What is Quick Launch menu?

It's the menu on the left side under the 'Home' tab.

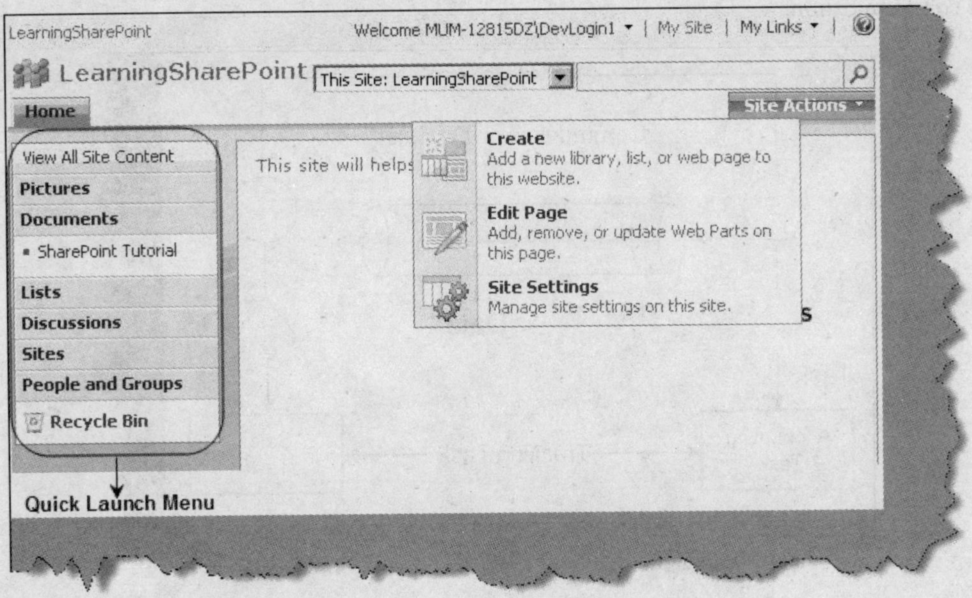

How can we customize SharePoint sites?

On the left hand side corner, there is a site actions menu. Click on the site action menu and click on site settings menu link. Once we click on the link, we will be popped with different settings by which we can customize the site.

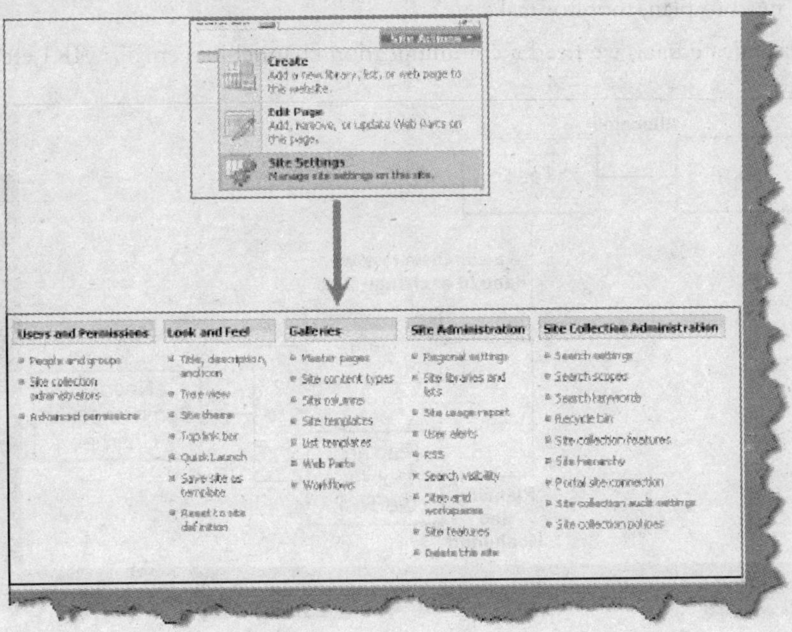

What about the readymade functional modules for collaboration?

The best part about SharePoint is collaboration. Collaboration has four major entities: people, task, data and communication.

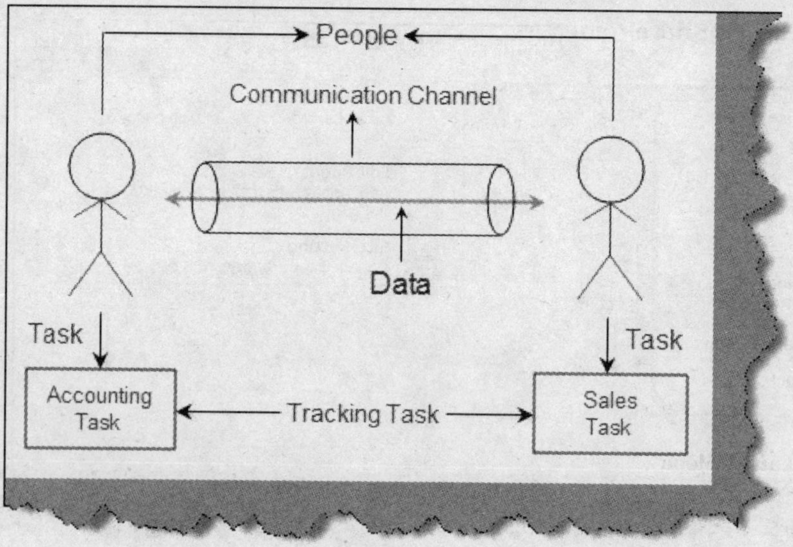

Some of the key points of enterprise include:

- We have people in our organizations.
- People are assigned task.
- To complete task, we need to exchange data.
- We also need to plan/monitor tasks.
- To communicate data, we need a communication channel like email, WIKI etc.

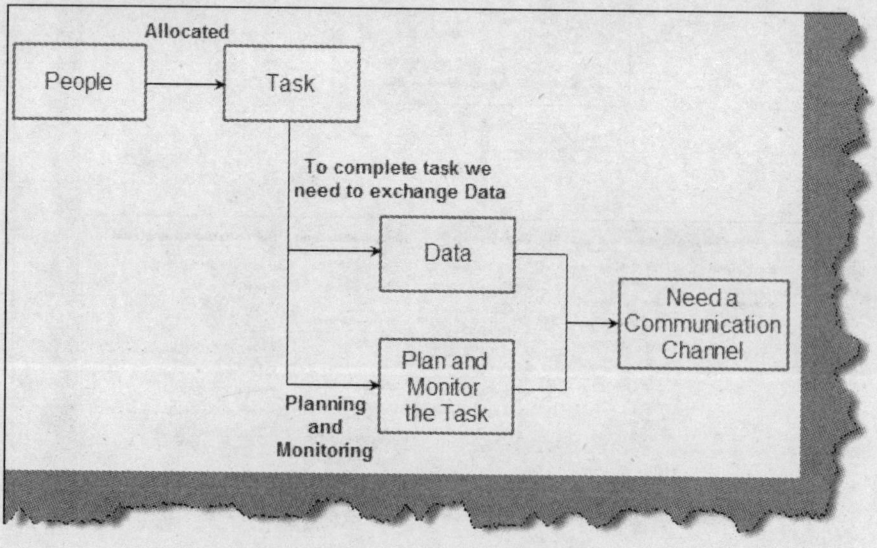

SharePoint has lot of readymade functions which can help us to accommodate all the requirements of collaboration. To see the readymade functionalities, we click on site actions and click on create. We are popped with a list of reusable functionality page which we can pick up and achieve collaboration.

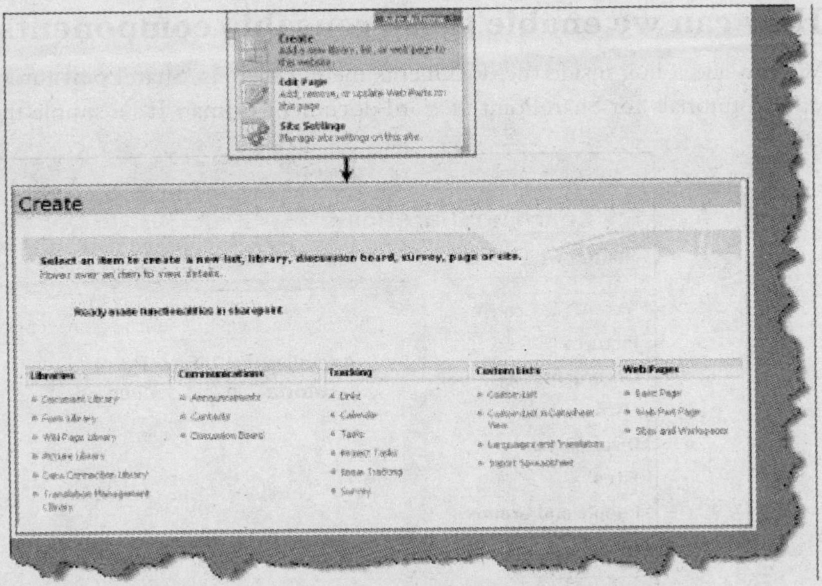

We can map the readymade functionalities with collaboration requirements.

Readymade functionalities in SharePoint		
People	Contacts	We can get this section in the communication section of the create page. It creates page which can help us to maintain contact information about people.
Task	Tasks	We can get this in the tracking section of the create page. It helps us to track task which our team member needs to complete.
Data	Document library	Helps to share, edit and version documents.
	Picture Library	Helps to share picture documents.
	Translation management	Helps to create document in multilingual languages.
	Data connection library	Helps to share files that contain information about external data.
Monitoring	Project task	We can get this in the tracking section of the create page. It gives a Gantt chart view of tasks.
	Issue tracking	We can get this reusable functionality in the tracking section of create page. Is helps to manage/assign and prioritize issues from start to finish.
	Calendar	Helps to create calendar for deadlines and events
Communication	WIKI	Helps to create interconnected system like WIKI.
	Announcement	Helps to share news and status through announcements.
	Discussion board	Helps to create discussion board like the news group.

How can we enable these reusable components in our site?

We can add a link inside the documents menu called as 'SharePoint tutorial.' In this section, team can upload tutorials for SharePoint in word document format. It's a simple three-step process:

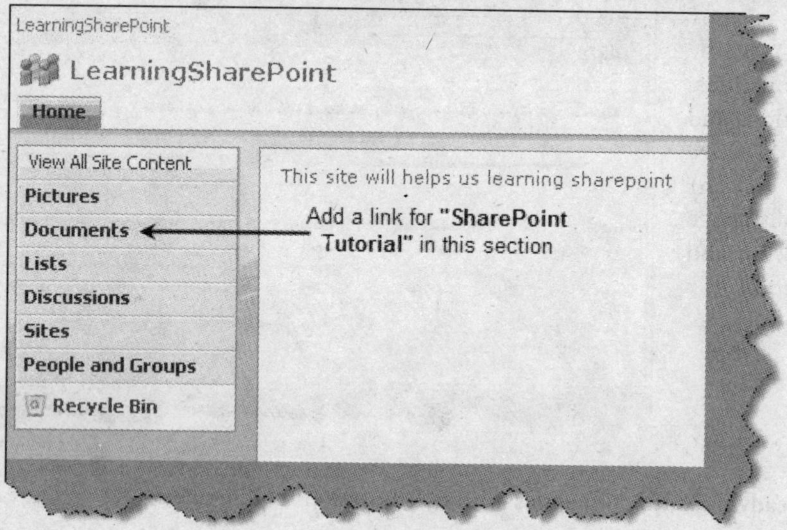

Step 1: Click on the site actions and then click on create link from the menu. It will display reusable functionalities provided by SharePoint. Select 'Document library' from the libraries section.

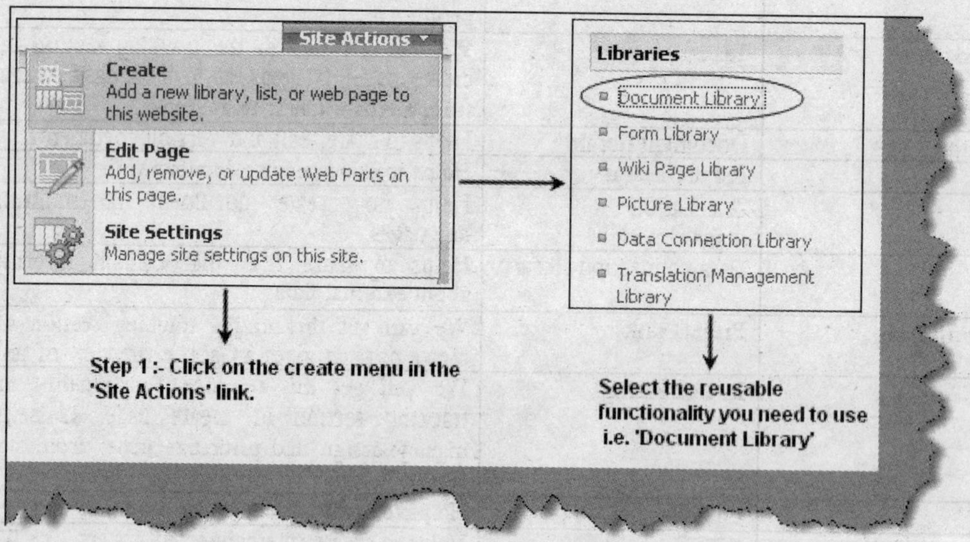

Step 2: Give the link name as 'SharePoint tutorial' and select document types to be unloaded as word format. For this we need to select the document template to be of type 'Microsoft word.'

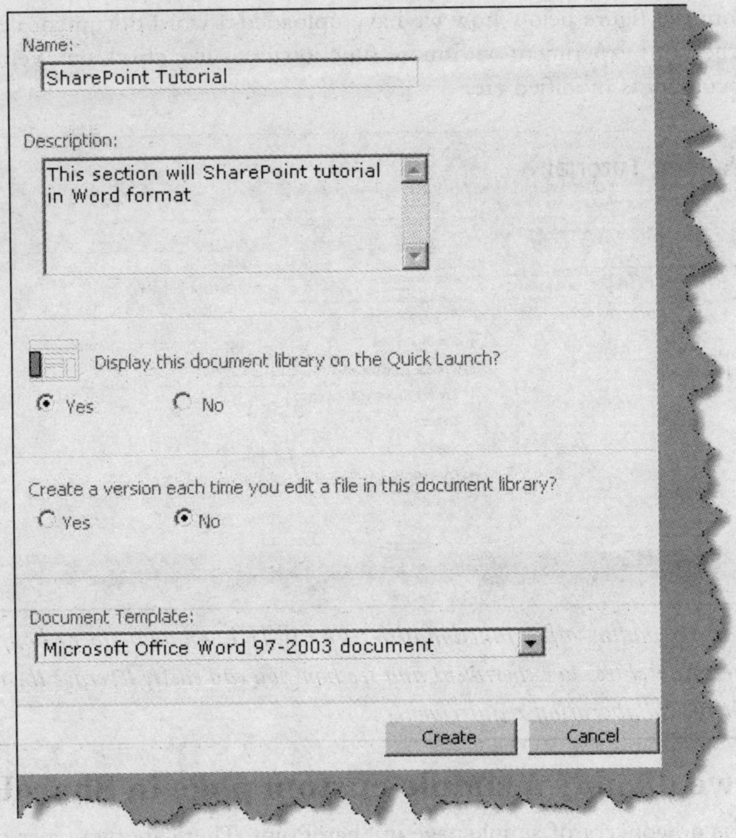

Step 3: We can now see the SharePoint tutorial link and we can click on upload to push in a word document inside this library collection.

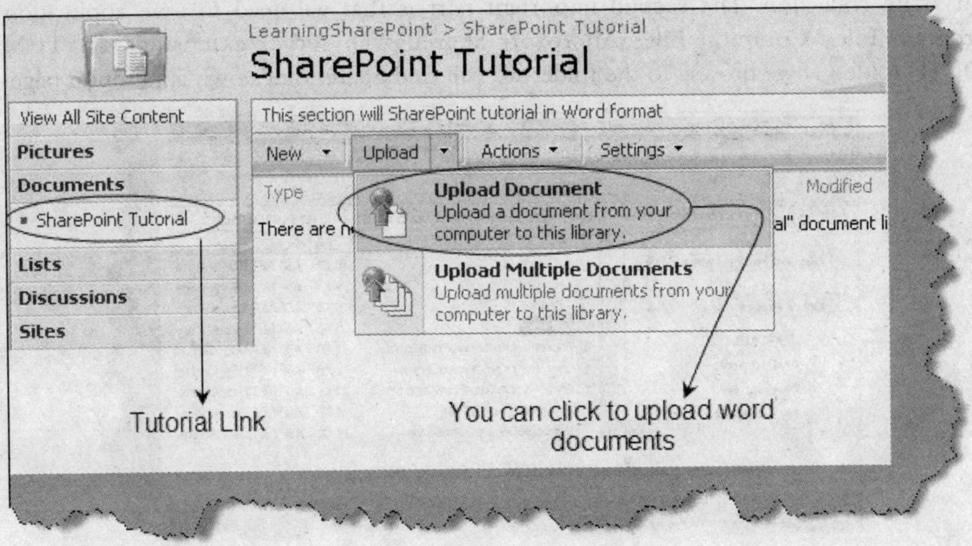

We can see from the figure below how we have uploaded a word document i.e. "SharePoint tutorial". We can right click and experiment with more functionalities like check out, versioning, workflow, send alerts when document is modified etc.

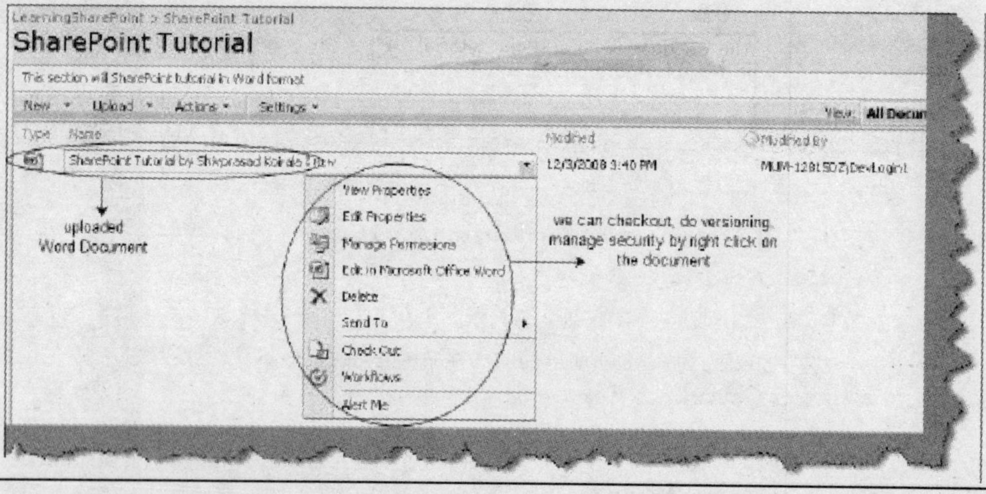

Note: *You can try adding other functionalities like WIKI, announcement board, picture library and lot more. So feel free to experiment and see how you can easily leverage the reusable functionalities to meet the collaboration requirements.*

How can we display a simple custom page in SharePoint?

Actually, there is no concept of simple page in SharePoint. There are two types of pages in SharePoint: one is an Application page and the other is the site page.

Application page is a generic page while site pages are custom to a website. Application pages are pages which are shared across sites like 'settings.aspx,' which will help us set generic properties across sites in a site collection. The second important part is that we need to save application pages in 'C:\Program Files\Common Files\Microsoft Shared\web server extensions\12\TEMPLATE\LAYOUTS' folder. If we browse to the folder we will find SharePoint's own application pages.

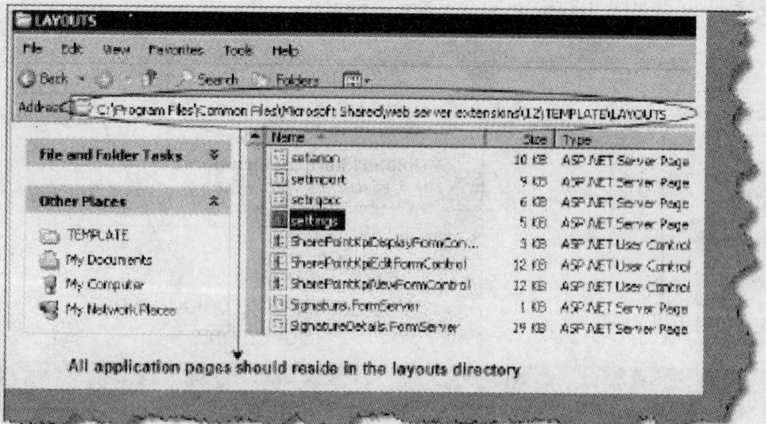

Let's make a simple page called as 'SimplePage.aspx.'

```
<b> Ohhhh I never Knew SharePoint is so easy </b>
```

Once we have saved the page, just browse to the IIS application and browse to the _layouts folder as shown in the figure below. If we open the page in browser we should see our display message.

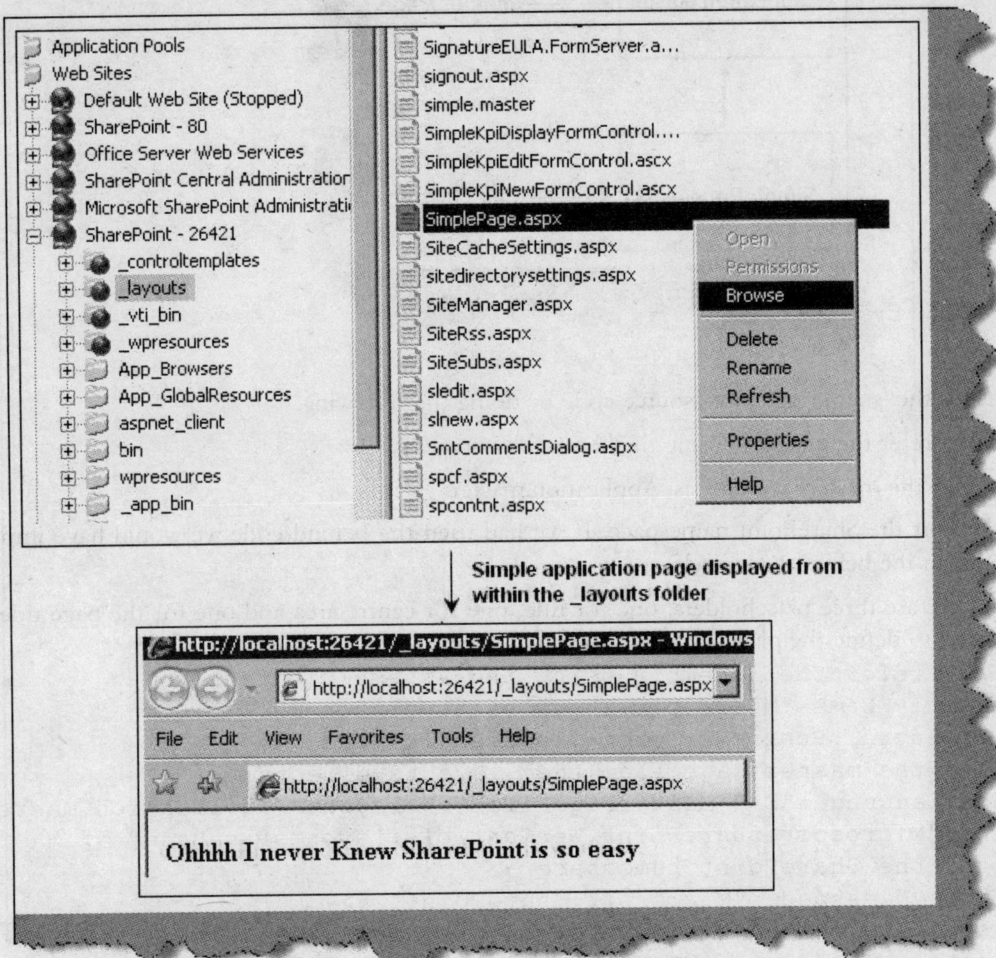

> **Note:** *For the next question you need to understand the concept of master pages. Consistent look and feel is one of the most important factors in enterprise portal and SharePoint achieves the same using Master pages.*

The above page does not look like a standard SharePoint page. How can we get that?

In order to get the SharePoint look and feel, we need to inherit from a SharePoint master page. As a rule, we should always inherit from a SharePoint master page so that our sites have a consistent look and feel. So let's modify our 'SimplePage.aspx.' To get the SharePoint style, we need to inherit from the SharePoint master page 'Application.Master.'

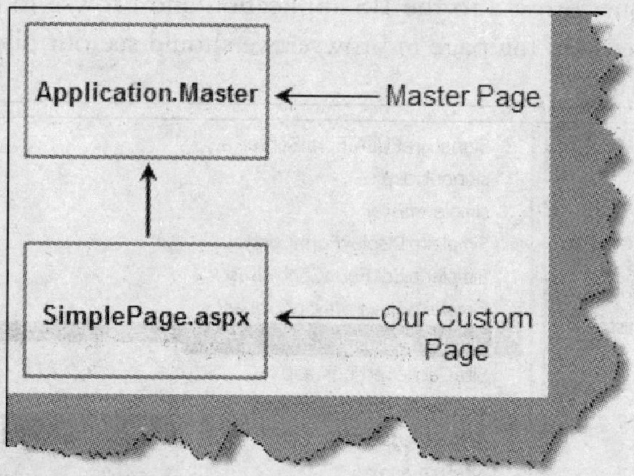

We can tailor the 'simplepage.aspx' source code by doing the following:

- First refer the assembly using the 'Assembly directive.'
- Refer the masterpage files as 'Application.master.'
- Import the SharePoint namespace. If we had used the behind code we would have imported this in the behind code itself.
- There are three placeholders: one for title, one for centre area and one for the page title. We need to define the placeholders in the child page.

```
<!- First refer the assembly using the Assembly directive ->
<%@ Assembly Name="Microsoft.SharePoint,Version=12.0.0.0,
Culture=neutral,PublicKeyToken=71e9bce111e9429c" %>
<!- Refer the master page from the _layouts directory ->
<%@ Page Language="C#" MasterPageFile="~/_layouts/application.master"
Inherits="Microsoft.SharePoint.WebControls.LayoutsPageBase" %>
<!-Import the SharePoint namespace ->
<%@ Import Namespace="Microsoft.SharePoint" %>
<!-This is the content holder for page title ->
<asp:Content ID="Content3" ContentPlaceHolderId="PlaceHolderPageTitle"
runat="server">
Let's learn SharePoint....
</asp:Content>
<!- This is the place holder for data for main page area ->
<asp:Content ID="Content1" ContentPlaceHolderId="PlaceHolderMain"
runat="server">
Oh its Damn Simple.....
</asp:Content>
<!- This is the placeholder for page title area ->
```

```
<asp:Content ID="Content2"
ContentPlaceHolderId="PlaceHolderPageTitleInTitleArea" runat="server">
SharePoint is Simple.....
</asp:Content>
```

LOL! Our SharePoint page now looks like a SharePoint page.

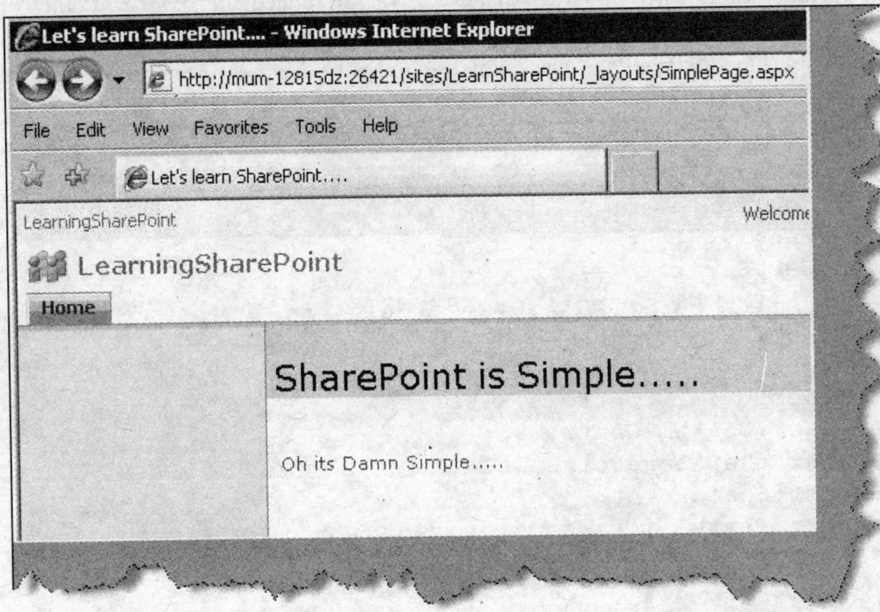

> **Note:** *You can get the source of the simple inline ASPX file in the CD in "SimpleSharePointASPXPage" folder.*

The above code is completely inline, how can we implement behind code in SharePoint?

We need to take care of the following regarding implementing behind code in ASP.NET:

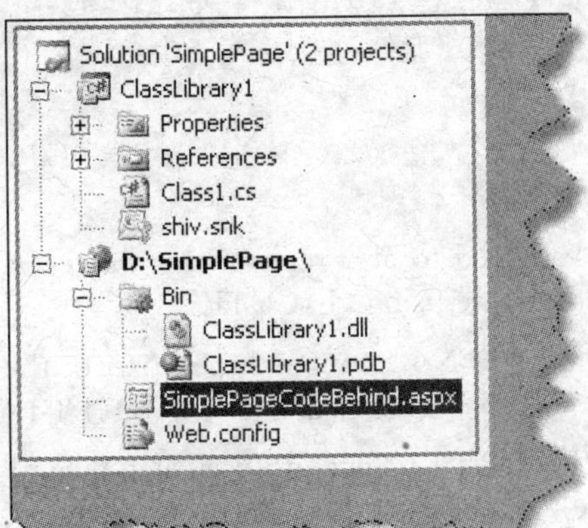

- ❑ The first and foremost requirement is that behind code should be registered into the GAC assembly. In other words, we need to code the behind code in a separate assembly/namespace and then compile the same in a DLL. Later we need to register the DLL in GAC.
- ❑ Second we need to use the assembly directive to refer the behind code.

Step 1: So the first step is to make two solution files: one is the behind code which goes in separate assembly 'ClassLibrary1' namespace and the other is the ASP.NET web project which has the

'SimplePageCodeBehind.aspx.' We also need to register this DLL in a GAC. So we need to generate a strong name to give to the assembly and register the same using the 'GACUTIL' provided by the .NET framework.

Step 2: The behind code is in a separate assembly as we need to register the same in the GAC. Let's keep the behind code simple. We have created two label objects and set the value. One of the important points to be noted is that we have referenced the 'System.Web.UI' namespace DLL and 'Microsoft.SharePoint' namespace DLL. The other point to be noted is that the class inherits from 'LayoutsPageBase' class which belongs to 'Microsoft.SharePoint' namespace.

```
using System;
using System.Data;
using System.Configuration;
using System.Web;
using System.Web.Security;
//need to refer the UI objects of ASP.NET
using System.Web.UI;
using System.Web.UI.WebControls;
using System.Web.UI.WebControls.WebParts;
using System.Web.UI.HtmlControls;
//Need to refer the SharePoint DLL
using Microsoft.SharePoint;
using Microsoft.SharePoint.WebControls;
namespace ClassLibrary1
{
//Inherit the behind code from 'LayoutsPageBase' class of SharePoint
 public partial class _Default : LayoutsPageBase
 {
 protected Label lblSiteQuestion;
 protected Label lblSiteAnswer;
 protected override void OnLoad(EventArgs e)
 {
 lblSiteQuestion.Text = " How can we implement behind code in
SharePoint ?";
 lblSiteAnswer.Text = " We need to register the behind DLL in GAC";
 }
}
}
```

We need to also register the above DLL in GAC. So we need to generate a strong name and register the same using GACUTIL.

Step 3: Now comes the UI part of the ASP.NET i.e. the ASPX page. Below is the code snippet which shows how the ASP.NET UI looks like.

The first thing to note is that behind code is not referred as code behind but is referred using the GAC public token key. In order to refer it using GAC key, we need to use the 'Assembly' attribute for the same.

We have also inherited from the master page file i.e. 'Application.Master' so that we have a consistent look and feel.

```
<!-Refer the SharePoint assembly ->
<%@ Assembly Name="Microsoft.SharePoint,Version=12.0.0.0,
Culture=neutral,PublicKeyToken=71e9bce111e9429c" %>
<!-Refer the behind code, Note that the behind code is coded in a
different assembly and registered in the GAC ->
<%@ Assembly Name="ClassLibrary1, Version=1.0.0.0,
Culture=neutral,PublicKeyToken=af6d081bf267e17e" %>
<!- In order to maintain consistent look and feel we need to inherit
from the Application.Master page ->
<%@ Page Language="C#" MasterPageFile="~/_layouts/application.master"
Inherits="ClassLibrary1._Default" EnableViewState="false"
EnableViewStateMac="false" %>
Once we have referred the Assembly and set the Page attributes, it's
time to fill the content in the placeholders defined in the master
page 'Application.Master.'
<asp:Content ID="Main" contentplaceholderid="PlaceHolderMain"
runat="server">
 <table border="1" cellpadding="4" cellspacing="0" style="font-
size:12">
 <tr>
 <td>Question</td>
 <td><b><asp:Label ID="lblSiteQuestion" runat="server"/></b></td>
 </tr>
 <tr>
 <td>Answer</td>
 <td><asp:Label ID="lblSiteAnswer" runat="server"/></td>
 </tr>
 </table>
</asp:Content>
<asp:Content ID="PageTitle" runat="server"
 contentplaceholderid="PlaceHolderPageTitle" >
 SharePoint Behind code implementation
</asp:Content>
<asp:Content ID="PageTitleInTitleArea" runat="server"
 contentplaceholderid="PlaceHolderPageTitleInTitleArea" >
 When we want to implement behind code we need to register the same in
GAC.
</asp:Content>
```

> **Note:** *Do not try to compile the project in VS.NET IDE. You can only compile the class assembly. The ASPX file you need to later paste it to the '_layout' directory i.e. 'C:\Program Files\Common Files\Microsoft Shared\web server extensions\12\TEMPLATE\LAYOUTS.'*

Once we have copied the ASPX file and registered the behind code assembly in GAC, we can run and enjoy how it looks like.

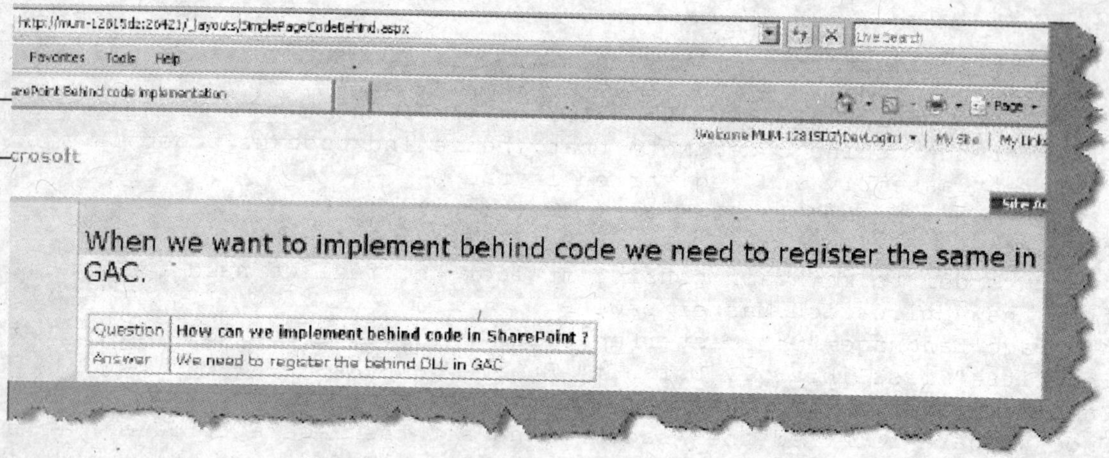

If you are thinking that behind code pages implementation is lot of pain in SharePoint. Hang on as we move ahead, you will see better way of implementation. Second we cannot rule out the benefits as compared to the pain incurred in implementing behind code pages in ASP.NET.

Note: *You can get the behind code in CD in folder 'SimpleSharePointBehindCode.'*

What is the concept of features in SharePoint?

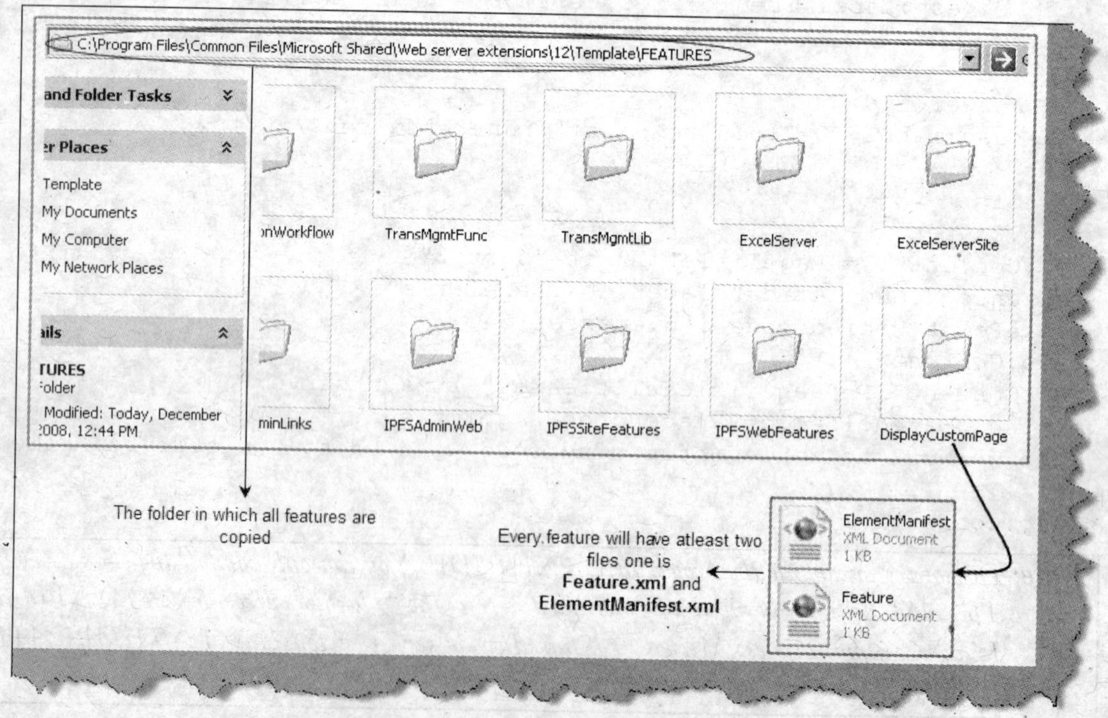

Whenever we think about SharePoint, we think in terms of collaboration. One of the much needed features in collaboration is on-demand functionality/feature activation. Feature makes it easier to activate and deactivate functionality in SharePoint.

Some points to be considered about features include:

- All features needs to be copied in "C:\Program Files\Common Files\Microsoft Shared\Web server extensions\12\Template\FEATURES\" directory. Microsoft Share reads the features from this directory. If we open the directory, we can find pre-installed features by SharePoint as shown below.
- Every feature will have two XML files: one is the 'Feature.xml' and the other is 'ElementManifest.xml.'

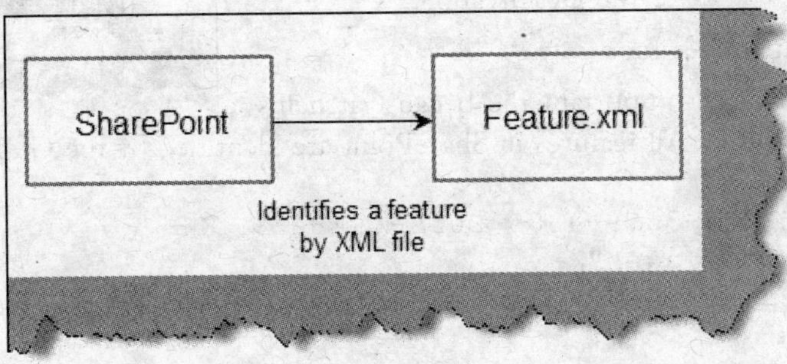

- SharePoint understands there is a feature by reading the feature XML file from the features folder.
- All features are identified by a unique GUID number.
- Features emit events which can be captured to write custom code. These events are captured in assembly, which needs to be registered in a GAC.

Summarizing what we discussed, we have a 'feature.xml' which points to an assembly, which captures the feature events for custom code. It also has another XML file which defines what exactly this feature will do.

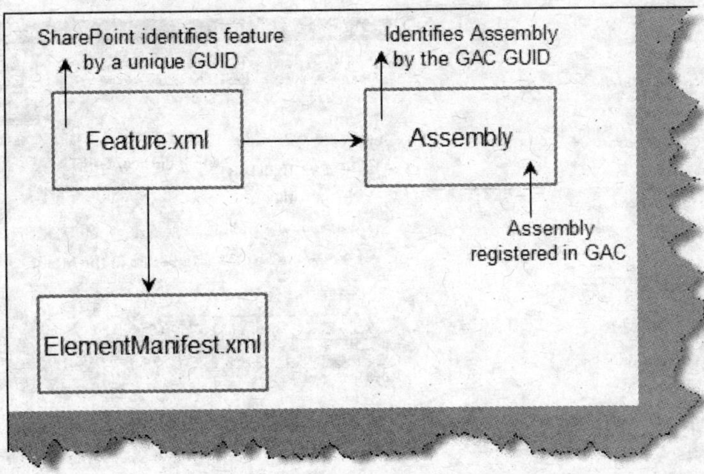

Can you explain the broader steps for deploying/activating a feature?

In order to understand the feature concepts, practically lets deploy the simple application page i.e. 'SimplePageCodeBehind.aspx' as feature. So when the user activates this feature, he will be able to browse the 'SimplePageCodeBehind.aspx.'

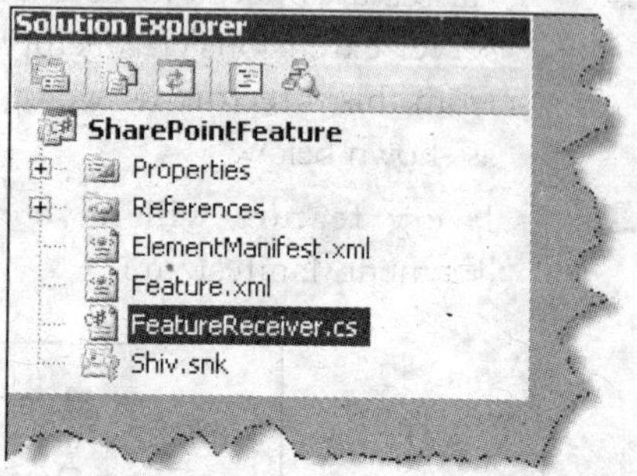

Step 1: Let's create a project 'SharePointFeature.' We can find the source code of the same attached in the CD. So below is the project tree which has the two XML files and a class file which will process the four events i.e. 'FeatureInstalled,' 'FeaturesUnInstalling,' 'FeatureActivated' and 'FeatureDeactivating.'

Let's understand these three files first.

Feature.XML: This is the most important file because it helps SharePoint identify the feature. All features in SharePoint are identified by the GUID key.

```
<Feature Id="48DEF2C4-33F9-4885-B0DE-6FE82E9FDCD8"
 Title="Go to Custom Pages"
 Description="This features enables us to go to Custom Page"
 Scope="Web"
 Hidden="FALSE"
 ImageUrl="menuprofile.gif"
 ReceiverAssembly="SharePointFeature, Version=1.0.0.0,
Culture=neutral, PublicKeyToken=af83741e324f585c"
 ReceiverClass="SharePointFeature.clsFeatureReceiver"
 xmlns="http://schemas.microsoft.com/SharePoint/" >
      <ElementManifests>
            <ElementManifest Location="ElementManifest.xml"/>
      </ElementManifests>
</Feature>
```

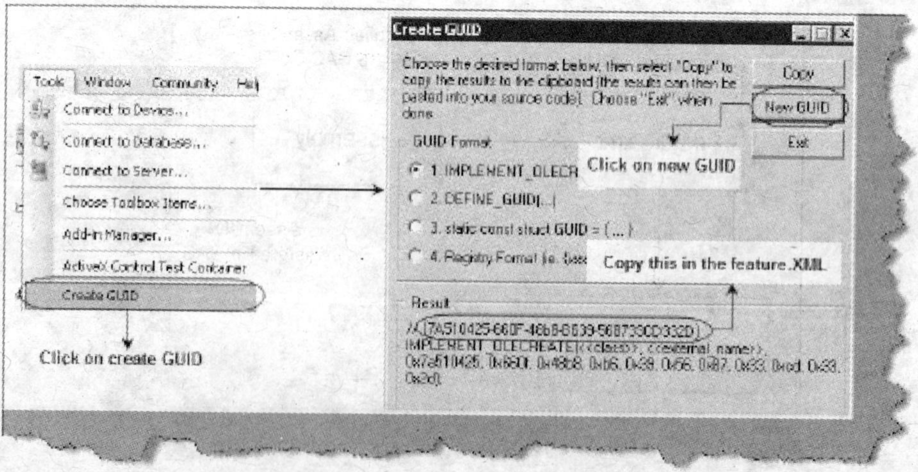

To generate a new GUID, click on Tools ' Create GUID and click 'New GUID.' Tools menu will get from within the IDE. We have marked the GUID value which we need to copy and paste in the 'feature.xml 'file.

Other than feature description and title there are two important things in the XML file. The first it points towards some other XML file and second it points to an assembly which captures events.

ElementManifest.XML file: ElementManifest.xml file actually specifies how the implementation will look like. There are two important points to be noted for the ElementManiFest.XML file. The custom action tag specifies on which control the feature will be activated. The control we are targeting at this moment is the 'SiteActionsToolBar.' This tool bar is the one which we see on the right hand side corner of our SharePoint portal. There is also a URLaction property which specifies which URL it should redirect to.

```
<Elements xmlns="http://schemas.microsoft.com/SharePoint/">
      <CustomAction
       Id="SiteActionsToolbar"
       GroupId="SiteActions"
       Location="Microsoft.SharePoint.StandardMenu"
       Sequence="10"
       Title="Display Custom Pages"
       Description="This links helps to display Custom Page"
       ImageUrl="_layouts/images/menuprofile.gif">
      <UrlAction Url="_layouts/SimplePageCodeBehind.aspx"/>
      </CustomAction>
</Elements>
```

In other words 'ElementManifest.xml' specifies the location of the feature and which page it should redirect to.

FeatureReceiver.cs: This class listens and implements custom actions of the feature.

We need to first refer the SharePoint namespace as shown in the below code snippet.

```
using System;
using System.Collections.Generic;
using System.Text;
//Refer the SharePoint namespace
using Microsoft.SharePoint;
```

We need to implement the 'SPFeatureReceiver' class and implement all the events.

```
namespace SharePointFeature
{
//Inherit from the 'SPFeatureReceiver" class
 public class clsFeatureReceiver : SPFeatureReceiver
 {
//Implement the four events of SPFeatureReceiver class
 public override void FeatureInstalled(SPFeatureReceiverProperties
properties){}
 public override void FeatureUninstalling(SPFeatureReceiverProperties
properties) { }
 //This event fires when the feature is activated
```

```
 public override void FeatureActivated(SPFeatureReceiverProperties
properties)
 {
     ....
     ....
     ....
     ....
 }
//This event fires when the feature is deactivated
 public override void FeatureDeactivating(SPFeatureReceiverProperties
properties)
 {
     ....
     ....
     ....
     ...
 }
 }
}
```

As a sample in the 'FeatureActivated' event we have set the description and title of the website.

```
public override void FeatureActivated(SPFeatureReceiverProperties
properties)
{
//get the object of SharePoint Web
 SPWeb site = (SPWeb)properties.Feature.Parent;
//Set the description,properties, titile and update the SpWeb object
 site.Description = "Click on the SiteActions to See how the custom
page display";
 site.Properties["OriginalTitle"] = "Display CustomPage";
 site.Properties.Update();
 site.Title = "This Site now has the custom page display";
 site.Update();
}
```

In 'FeatureDeactivating' we have reverted back the title and description.

```
public override void FeatureDeactivating(SPFeatureReceiverProperties
properties)
{
//Get hold of the SharePoint web object and reset back the values
 SPWeb site = (SPWeb)properties.Feature.Parent;
 site.Description = "Custom Page display is disabled";
 site.Title = site.Properties["OriginalTitle"];
 site.Update();
}
```

Step 2: We need to register the compiled assembly in GAC and provide the token value in the 'Feature.XML' file. We need to use GACUTIL to register. We can get the token by browsing to 'c:\Windows\Assembly' and then viewing the properties of the assembly.

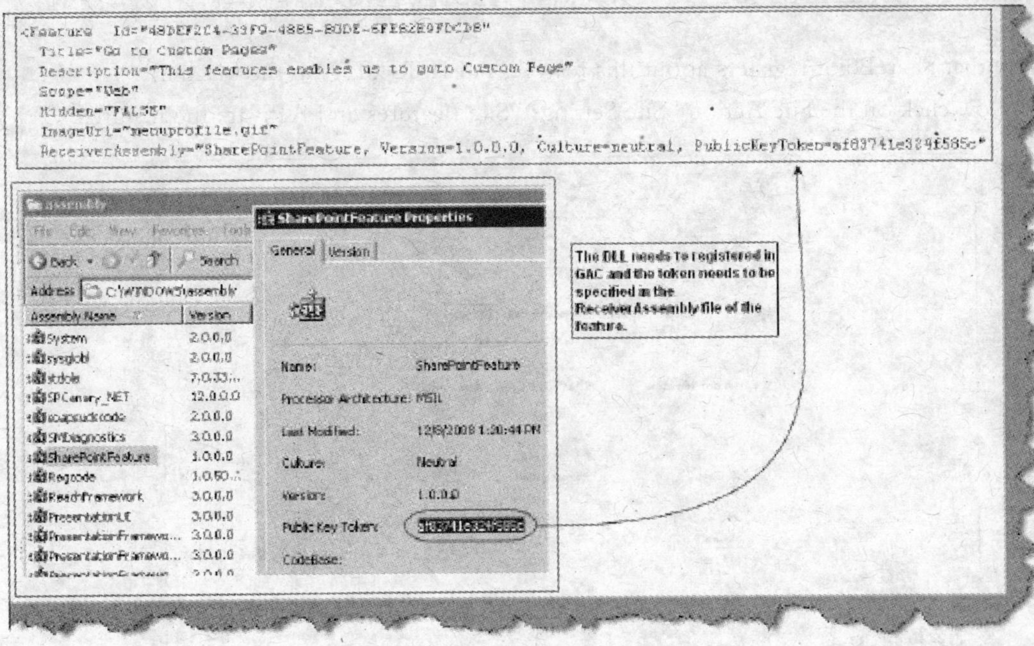

Step 3: Copy the two XML file i.e. 'Feature.xml' and 'ElementManisfest.xml' in the 'C:\Program Files\Common Files\Microsoft Shared\web server extensions\12\TEMPLATE\FEATURES\DisplayCustomPage' directory.

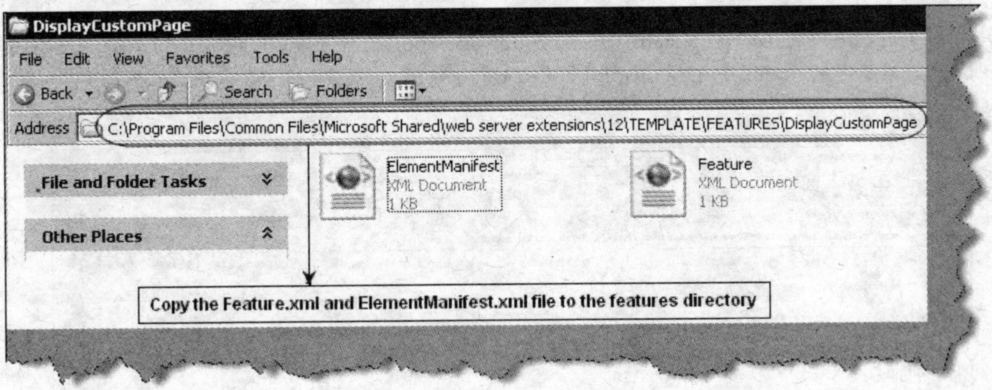

Step 4: Now we need to install the feature using STSADM.exe. So go to dos prompt ' and go to 'C:\Program Files\Common Files\Microsoft Shared\web server extensions\12\BIN' directory.>cd C:\Program Files\Common Files\Microsoft Shared\web server extensions\12\BIN

To install the feature, run the below command using 'STSADM.' Please note that we need to specify the relative directory path and not the physical path of 'Feature.xml' file.

```
>stsadm -o installfeature -filename DisplayCustomPage\Feature.xml
```

To ensure that SharePoint registers about this feature, run IISRESET on the machine.

Step 5: Now click on the Site Action ' Site Settings ' Site Features and Activate the feature.

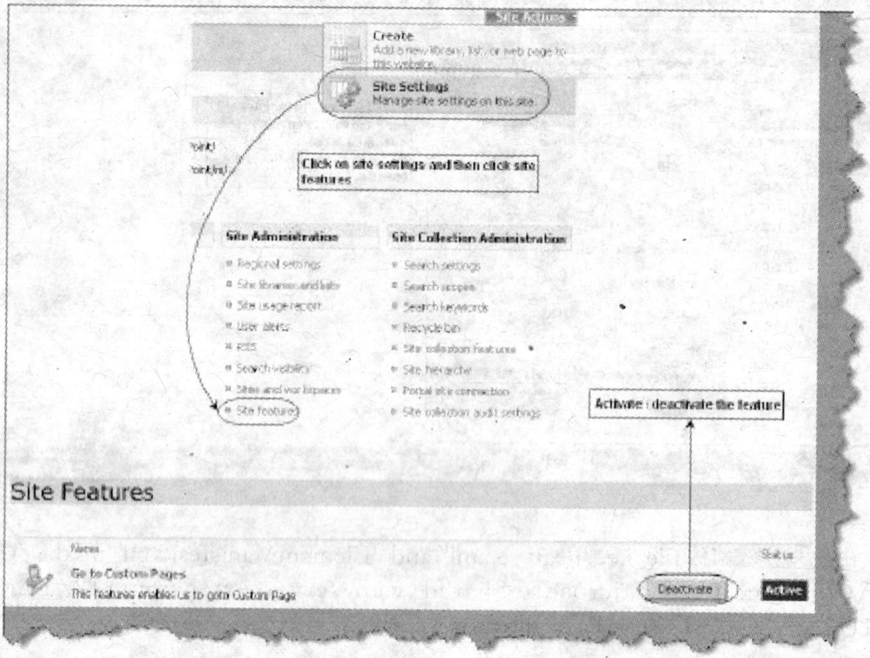

Now we can see our feature enabled in the site actions menu. If we click on the feature i.e. 'Display Custom Pages,' it will redirect us to 'SimplePageCodeBehind.aspx.'

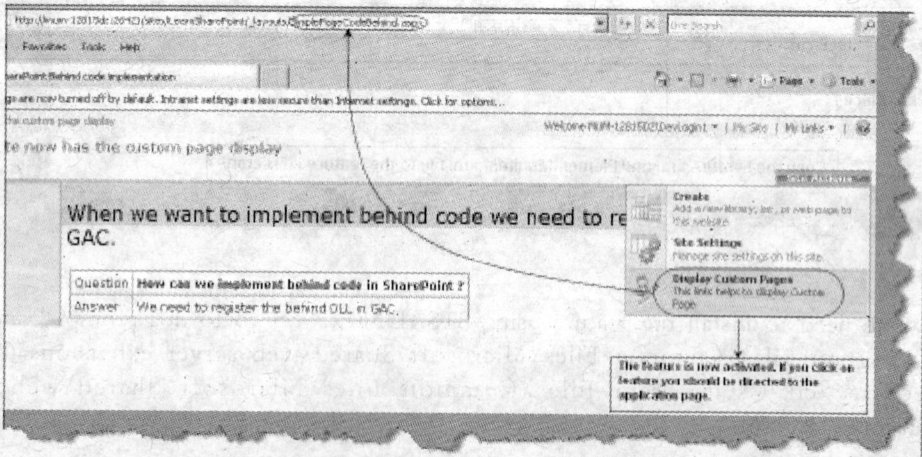

The other point to be noted is that the events have fired and set the title and description as described in the code.

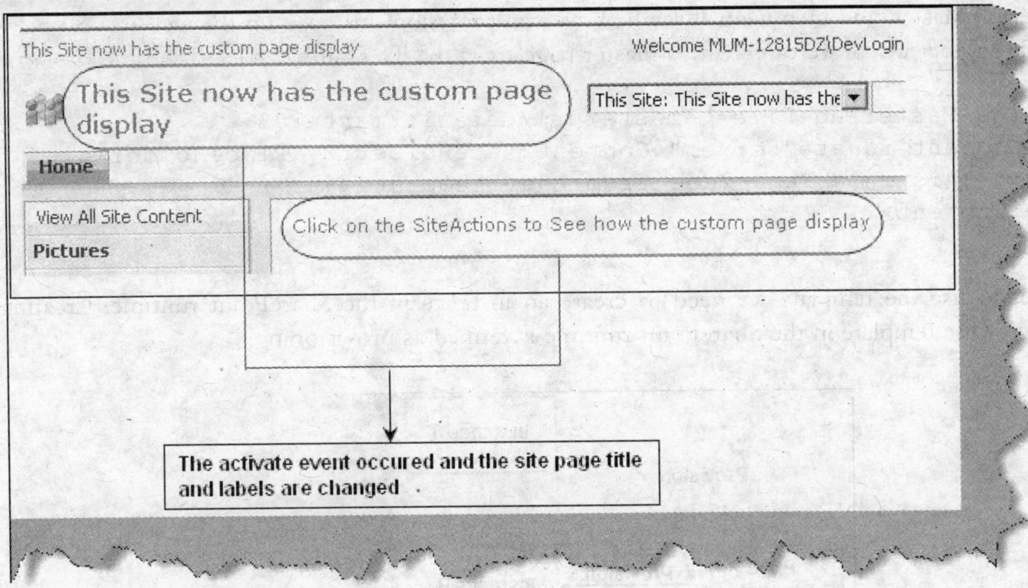

Try to experiment and deactivate the feature and we will see the title and description changing.

> ***Note:*** *You can get the source for the feature in CD.*

I want that the feature should be only displayed to admin. How is it possible?

If we want only administrators to view the features, set RequireSiteAdministrator="True" as shown in the below 'ElementManifest.XML' file.

```
<Elements xmlns="http://schemas.microsoft.com/SharePoint/">
     <CustomAction
      Id="SiteActionsToolbar"
      GroupId="SiteActions"
      RequireSiteAdministrator="True"
      Location="Microsoft.SharePoint.StandardMenu"
      Sequence="10"
      Title="Display Custom Pages"
      Description="This links helps to display Custom Page"
      ImageUrl="_layouts/images/menuprofile.gif">
     <UrlAction Url="_layouts/SimplePageCodeBehind.aspx"/>
     </CustomAction>
</Elements>
```

How can we provision page template and page instances?

Provisioning is a fancy name of making something available. So let's first create a page template using the 'Default.Master' and then we will see how we can provision this page on the website.. So below is the code snippet where we can create a master page from the 'Default.Master.'

```
<%@ Page MasterPageFile="~masterurl/default.master"%>
<asp:Content runat="server" ContentPlaceHolderID="PlaceHolderMain">
 <h3>Hi this is a Page made from Page template</h3>
</asp:Content>
```

In order to use the template we need to create an instance in the SharePoint runtime. Creating an instance of the template in the SharePoint runtime is termed as provisioning.

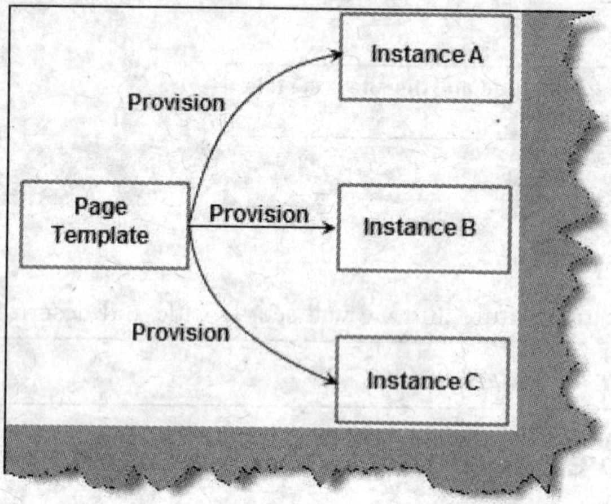

We need to use the 'Module' and 'File' tag to provision an instance of the template page. This is done in the 'ElementManifest.XML' file. Below is the code snippet of 'ElementManifest.XML' file which has the module tag with a file tag specifying what the URL page name is. This is the same template which we had shown on the top. 'PageA.aspx' is the instance name and 'MyPage.aspx' is the physical page name of the template page.

The type attribute has two values: 'Ghostable' and 'GhostableInLibrary.' If we want to provision a resource inside a document library, then we need to specify 'GhostableInLibrary.' If we do not want to provision a resource inside a document library then we need to specify 'Ghostable' value. For the current exercise, we have given the value as 'Ghostable.'

Note: *The path attribute has the page in the 'MyPath' folder.*

```
<Elements xmlns="http://schemas.microsoft.com/SharePoint/">
 <Module Path="MyPage" Url="SitePages">
 <File Url="MyPage.aspx" Name="PageA.aspx" Type="Ghostable"/>
 </Module>
</Elements>
```

We also need to define the feature.xml file which has the receiver class and the element manifest pointing to the elementmanifest.xml file.

```
<Feature Id="701B7EA3-0816-4a5f-8FFE-AD15F0E5B562" Title="Provision"
 Scope="Web"
 Description="This features enables us to goto Custom Page"
 Hidden="FALSE"
 ImageUrl="menuprofile.gif"
 ReceiverAssembly="ClassLibrary1, Version=1.0.0.0, Culture=neutral,
PublicKeyToken=52bd1db23825a2e4"
 ReceiverClass="ClassLibrary1.clsFeatureActivator"
 xmlns="http://schemas.microsoft.com/SharePoint/">
 <ElementManifests>
 <ElementManifest Location="ElementManifest.xml"/>
 </ElementManifests>
</Feature>
```

In the receiver class, add menu items in the quick launch nodes and in the activation event, add a link which will activate this feature and in the deactivation event, remove this feature.

So in the activation event, we first need to get reference to the SpSite object using the URL.

```
SPSite ObjQuickLaunch = new SPSite("http://mum2815dz:2/sites/
LearnSharePoint");
```

From the SpSite object we get the 'SpWeb' object.

```
SPWeb ObjSpWeb = ObjQuickLaunch.OpenWeb();
From the 'SpWeb' object we get reference to all node collection of the
Quick launch menu.
SPNavigationNodeCollection QuickLauncNodes =
ObjSpWeb.Navigation.QuickLaunch;
```

Now, create a menu of the page.

```
SPNavigationNode objMenuItem = new SPNavigationNode("Quest",
"SitePages/PageA.aspx");

Add the menu to the quick launch node.

QuickLauncNodes.AddAsFirst(objMenuItem);
ObjSpWeb.Update();
```

In the deactivation event we will remove the link.

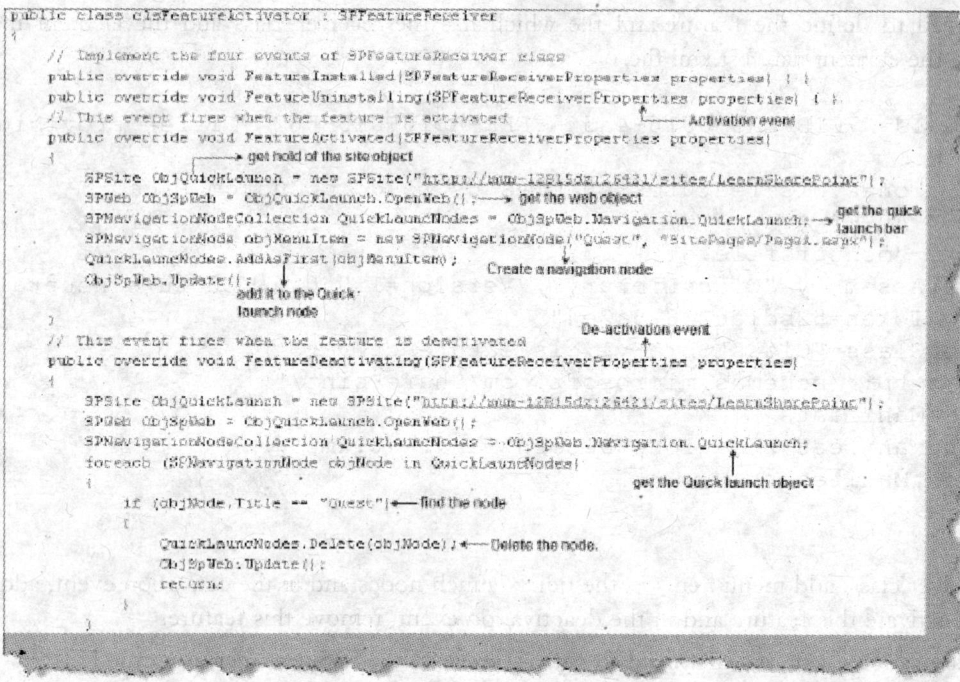

```
public class clsFeatureActivator : SPFeatureReceiver
{
    // Implement the four events of SPFeatureReceiver class
    public override void FeatureInstalled(SPFeatureReceiverProperties properties) { }
    public override void FeatureUninstalling(SPFeatureReceiverProperties properties) { }
    // This event fires when the feature is activated
    public override void FeatureActivated(SPFeatureReceiverProperties properties)
    {
        SPSite ObjQuickLaunch = new SPSite("http://mum-12815dz:26421/sites/LearnSharePoint");
        SPWeb ObjSpWeb = ObjQuickLaunch.OpenWeb();
        SPNavigationNodeCollection QuickLaunchNodes = ObjSpWeb.Navigation.QuickLaunch;
        SPNavigationNode objMenuItem = new SPNavigationNode("Quest", "SitePages/PageA.aspx");
        QuickLaunchNodes.AddAsFirst(objMenuItem);
        ObjSpWeb.Update();
    }
    // This event fires when the feature is deactivated
    public override void FeatureDeactivating(SPFeatureReceiverProperties properties)
    {
        SPSite ObjQuickLaunch = new SPSite("http://mum-12815dz:26421/sites/LearnSharePoint");
        SPWeb ObjSpWeb = ObjQuickLaunch.OpenWeb();
        SPNavigationNodeCollection QuickLaunchNodes = ObjSpWeb.Navigation.QuickLaunch;
        foreach (SPNavigationNode objNode in QuickLaunchNodes)
        {
            if (objNode.Title == "Quest")
            {
                QuickLaunchNodes.Delete(objNode);
                ObjSpWeb.Update();
                return;
            }
        }
```


After creating the two xml files and the class which will handle the feature events, use stsadm utility to register the feature. Once we have registered it, we should see the feature in the feature list display. We have named the feature as 'Provision' so we can see the 'Provision' feature.

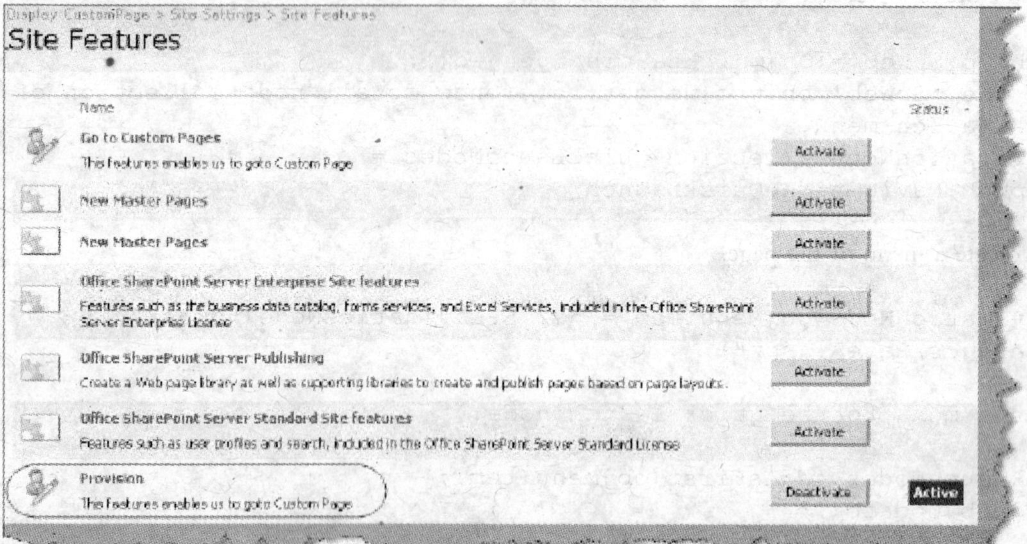

Once we activate the feature we should see the 'Quest' link which points to the template instance page 'PageA.aspx.' If we disable the feature we will not be able to browse the page instance.

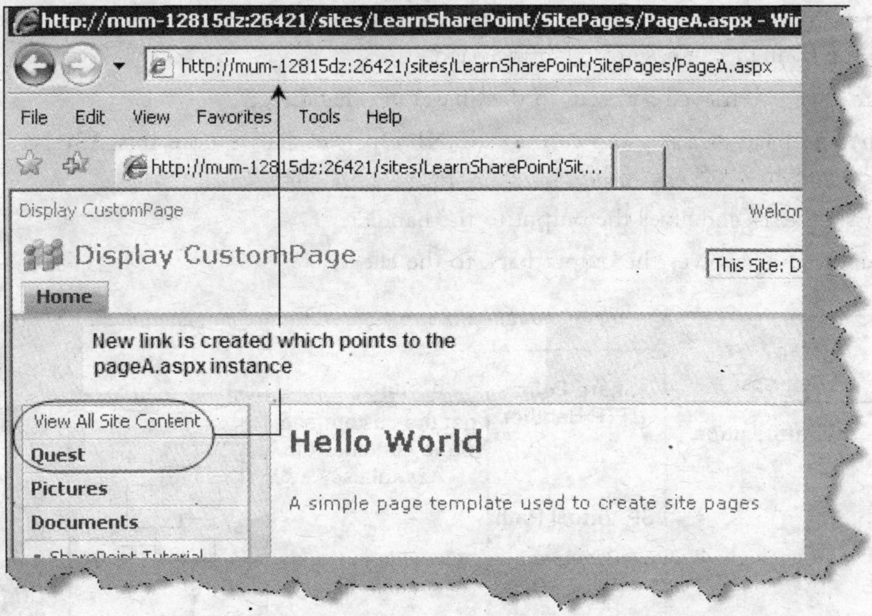

Why customized pages are parsed using no-compile mode?

Site pages can be customized while application pages are standard pages like 'settings.aspx' which is common across sites.

When a user customizes a site page, a customized version of the site page is saved in the content database. This provides lot of flexibility but it has its own disadvantages. We can customize site pages using 'SharePoint Designer.'

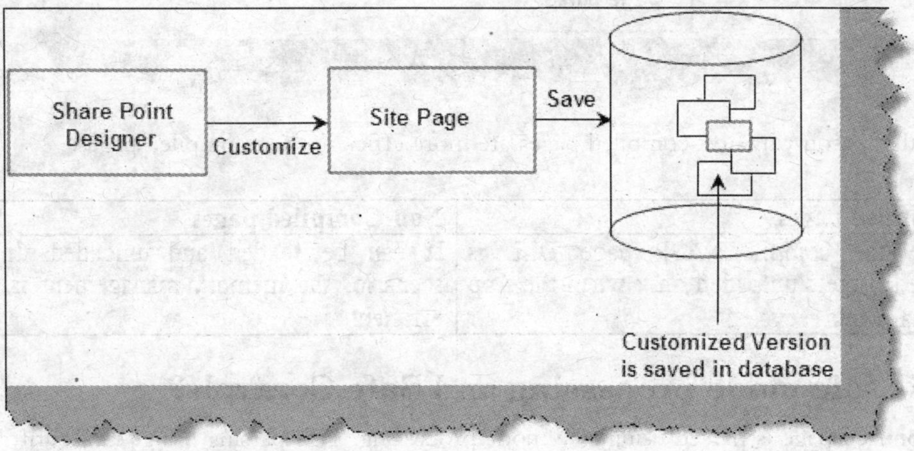

Now let's try to understand how a customized site page, which is saved content, is processed. Customized site pages are processed in six steps:

Step 1: The user requests a customized page.

Step 2: SharePoint HTTP handler i.e. 'SPVirtualPathProvider' picks the request and shoots a query to the content database to fetch the page.

Step 3: Site page is retrieved and sent to the SharePoint handler.

Step 4: The site page data is given to the ASP.NET parser. Please note this ASP.NET parser is not the one which IIS uses. This is made especially for SharePoint.

Step 5: Parser parses and gives the output to the handler.

Step 6: Handler finally gives the output back to the client.

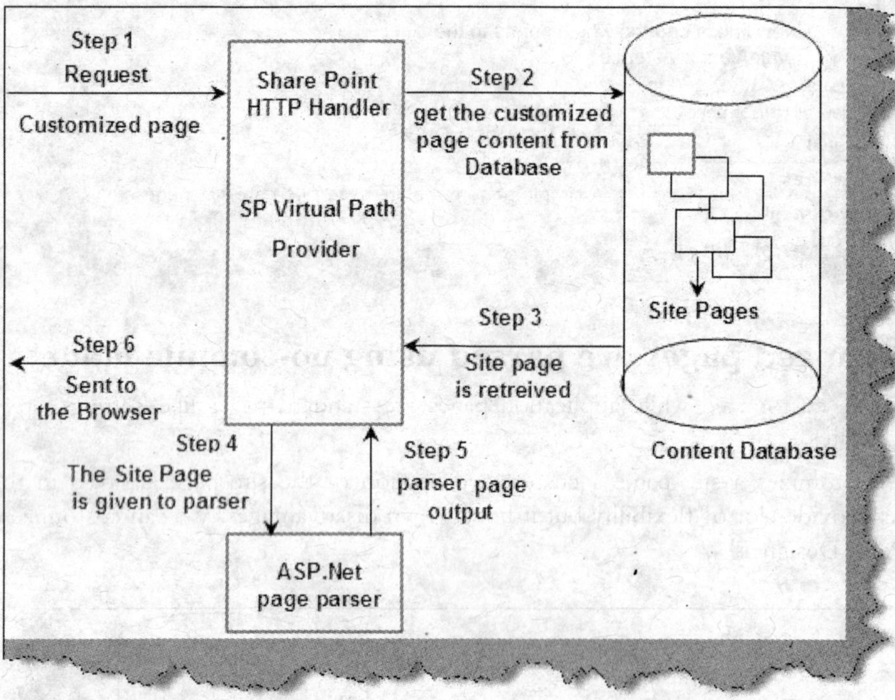

Below is the reason why non-compiled pages are more efficient then compiled pages.

Compiled pages	Non-Compiled pages
Once the compiled ASP page DLL is loaded, it gets unloaded only when the App Domain gets recycled.	It can be loaded and unloaded. In this scenario, the memory management is more efficient.

What is safe mode processing and Safe Controls?

Any customized page is parsed using safe mode processing. This parsing brings in security. Safe mode processing guarantees that there is no inline script in the customized page. In other words, safe mode processing disallows in-line script because a hacker can mount attack using in-line script. If we try to run in-line script on customized page we will get error 'Code blocks are not allowed in this file.'

In case we still want to run in-line script in customized pages, we need to specify 'AllowServerSideScript=true' in the 'SafeMode' tag section in web.config file.

```
<SharePoint>
<SafeMode... >
<PageParserPaths>
<PageParserPath
VirtualPath="/sites/MySite/SitePages/*"
IncludeSubFolders="true"
CompilationMode="Always"
AllowServerSideScript="true"/>
</PageParserPaths>
</SafeMode>
</SharePoint>
```

Safe controls help us define which controls the customized pages will have. Customized pages can only have controls which are defined in the web.config file in the 'SafeControls' tag. For instance in the below code snippet, we have defined that customized pages can use controls from 'Microsoft.SharePoint.WebControls.'

```
<SafeControls>
 <SafeControl
 Assembly="Microsoft.SharePoint"
 Namespace="Microsoft.SharePoint.WebControls"
 TypeName="*"
 AllowRemoteDesigner="True"/>
</SafeControls>
```

Can you explain WSS model?

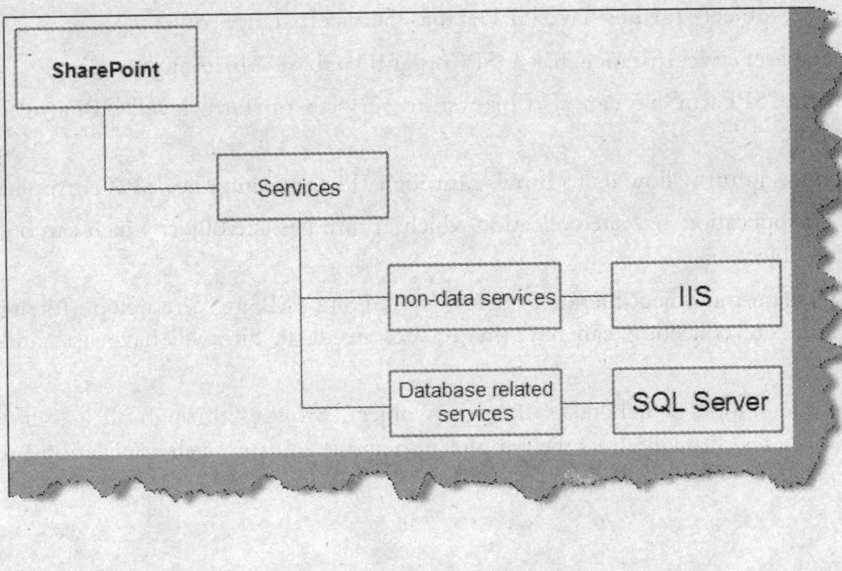

In order to understand WSS model, we need to first understand different types of services used by SharePoint. SharePoint uses two major services in IIS which is a non-data service and the other is SQL Server i.e. database related services.

SharePoint was designed from the view point that it can be used in web farms. Below figure shows two aspects: one a normal visualization of a web farm and other the SharePoint view point. In our normal view (i.e. the left hand side of the image), we can think of farms having servers and servers having the two services (i.e. IIS and DB service). When SharePoint visualizes the farm infrastructure, it's a bit different.

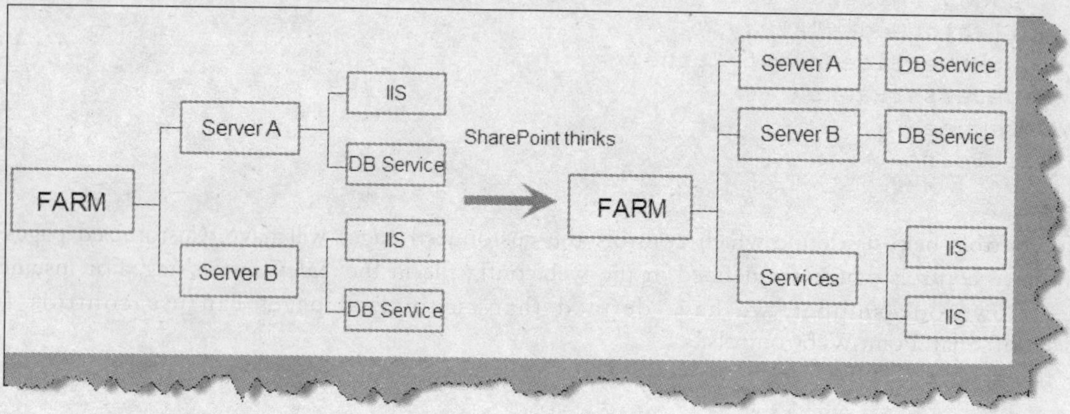

SharePoint visualizes the farm infrastructure in terms of database services and non-database services. So it visualizes database services attached to servers and non-database services like IIS differently.

Note: We are not sure why there is a change in visualization.

So let's visualize how the WSS object model of SharePoint is seen.

- The parent object in the SharePoint hierarchy is the SPFarm object.
- SPFarm will have collection of server objects i.e. the 'SPServer' objects.
- 'SPServer' objects further have 'SPDatabaseServiceInstance' object.
- 'SPDatabaseServiceInstance' has a 'SPContentDatabase' object instance.
- From the 'SPFarm' we can also browse to services on farm level. 'SPFarm' has 'SPService' collection.
- 'SPService' in turn allow us to browse through IIS application i.e. 'SPWebApplication.'
- 'SPWebApplication' has site collection which in turn has site object which can be browsed using 'SPSite' object.

Now let's understand the object hierarchy below the 'SPSite.' 'SPSite'/Site belong to site collection. In other words, one site collection can have many sites inside it. Site will have lists and list will have fields.

Below is the code snippet which takes the Farm object, browses through all its services, using the service object browses through all its web application and then using web application browses through all sites.

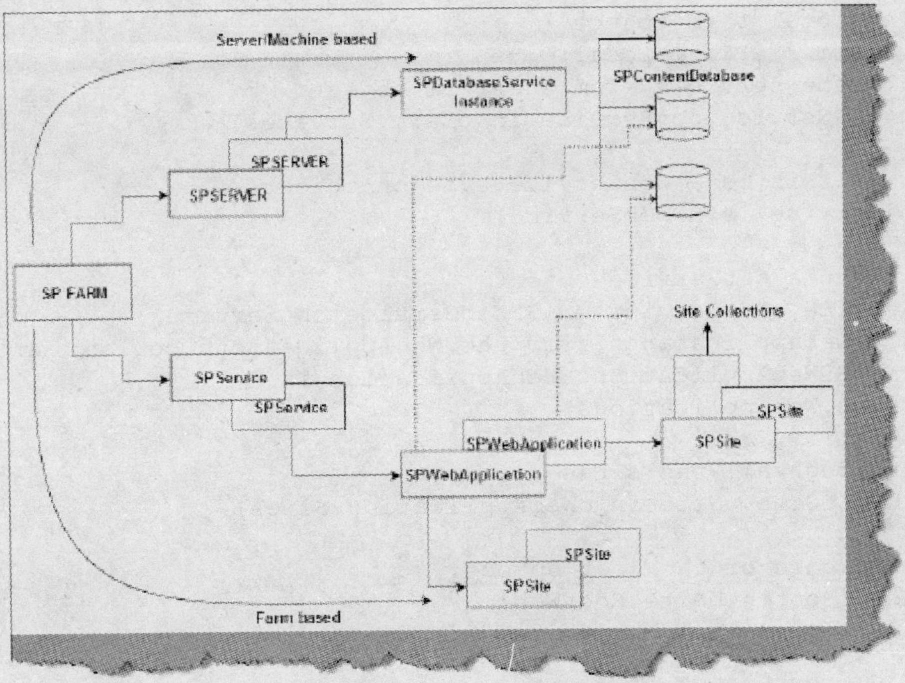
Server/Machine based
SPDatabaseService Instance
SPContentDatabase
SPSERVER
SPSERVER
SP FARM
Site Collections
SPService
SPService
SPSite
SPWebApplication
SPSite
SPWebApplication
SPSite
SPSite
Farm based

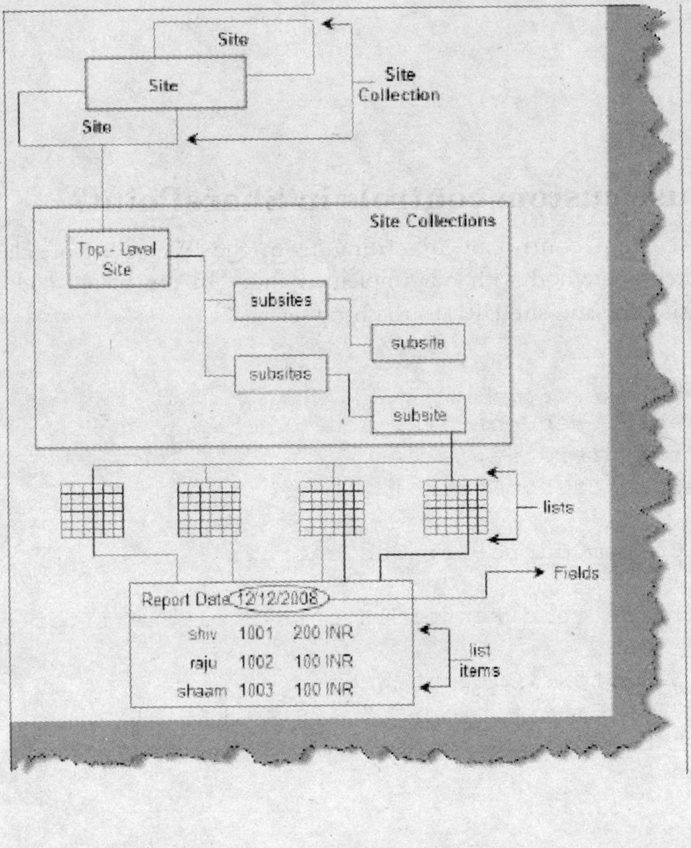
Site
Site
Site Collection
Site
Site Collections
Top - Level Site
subsites
subsite
subsites
subsite
lists
Fields
Report Date 12/12/2008
shiv 1001 200 INR
raju 1002 100 INR
shaam 1003 100 INR
list items

```
//Get The local farm object
SPFarm oFarm = SPFarm.Local;
//Get all the services from the farm object
foreach (SPService objService in oFarm.Services)
{
//Check if this is a WebService type of object
 if (objService is SPWebService)
 {
//Cast it to a WebService object
 SPWebService oWebService = (SPWebService)objService ;
//Get all Webapplications from the WebApplications collection
 foreach (SPWebApplication oWebApplication in
oWebService.WebApplications)
 {
//Loop through all the sites
 foreach (SPSite oSite in oWebApplication.Sites)
 {
//Get reference of the Root object
 SPWeb oWebRoot = oSite.RootWeb;
      //Any kind of processing

      //Do not forget to dispose
 oWeb.Dispose();
 oSite.Dispose();
 }
 }
 }
}
```

How can we use custom controls in SharePoint?

Step 1: Create the custom control by inheriting from the 'WebControl' class and override the 'RenderContents' method with our implementation. In the below code snippet, we are just writing the site title and site URL to the browser.

```
using System.Web.UI;
using System.Web.UI.WebControls;
using Microsoft.SharePoint;
namespace NameSpaceCustomControl
{
 public class CustomControl1 : WebControl
 {
 protected override void RenderContents(HtmlTextWriter output)
 {
 SPWeb site = SPContext.Current.Web;
 output.Write("The Site title is " + site.Title);
 output.Write("<br/>");
```

```
output.Write("The URL of the site is " + site.Url);
}
}
}
```

Step 2: Compile the custom control class and generate the DLL from the same. Once the compiled DLL is generated, register the same in GAC.

Step 3: Refer the custom control assembly in our ASPX page using the register attribute. Please note to specify the public key token of the GAC.

```
<%@ Register
Assembly="CustomControl,Version=1.0.0.0,Culture=neutral,PublicKeyToken=4adae03f3c0d5b8e"
Namespace="NameSpaceCustomControl" TagPrefix="CustomSitePages" %>
Specify the custom control with a proper unique ID.
<CustomSitePages:CustomControl1 ID="cc1" runat="server"/>
```

Below is the complete code of the page.

```
<%@ Page Language="C#" MasterPageFile="~masterurl/default.master"
meta:progid="SharePoint.WebPartPage.Document"%>
<%@ Register
Assembly="CustomControl,Version=1.0.0.0,Culture=neutral,PublicKeyToken=4adae03f3c0d5b8e"
Namespace="NameSpaceCustomControl" TagPrefix="CustomSitePages" %>
<asp:Content runat="server" ContentPlaceHolderID="PlaceHolderMain">
 <h3>Hi this is a Site Page</h3>
<CustomSitePages:CustomControl1 ID="cc1" runat="server"/>
</asp:Content>
```

Now if we run the page, we can see the custom control in action.

> **Note:** *You can get the custom code sample in CD in folder 'UserControlsSample.'*

How can you view a detail error in SharePoint?

SharePoint does not give error in a user-friendly manner. For instance, below figure shows it has shown 'File not found; but the root cause is something different. Developers would like to get the exact function/method name in which the error has occurred.

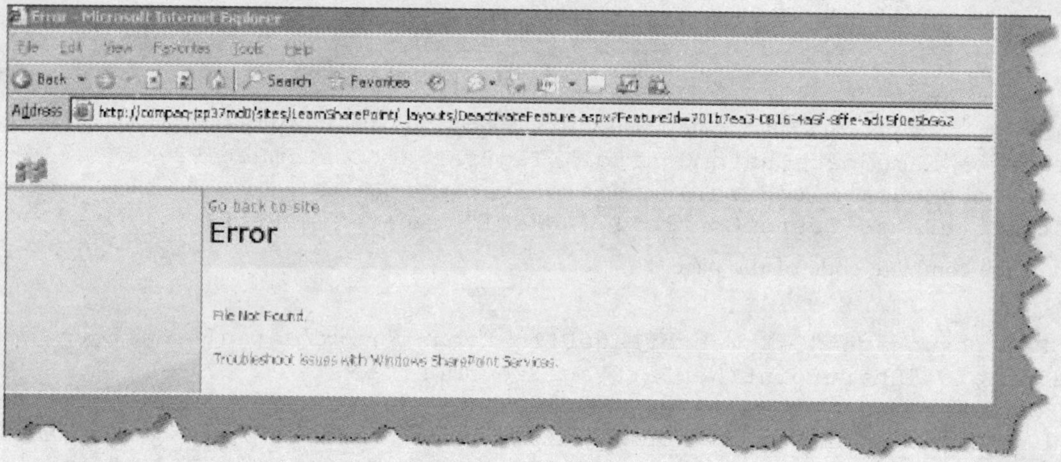

There are four steps, in other words, there are three changes we need to make to the config file and do IIS reset. So let's go through the four steps to get the actual cause of the above error.

As said previously, we need to change the 'web.config' file in three different places. We can get the 'web.config' file from 'C:\Inetpub\wwwroot\wss\VirtualDirectories\80' folder.

Step 1: Change callstack value from false to true in SafeMode attribute as shown below.

Change

```
<SafeMode MaxControls="200" CallStack="false"...>
```

to

```
<SafeMode MaxControls="200" CallStack="true"...>
```

Step2: Change 'customErrors' tag mode from 'On' to 'Off.'

Change

```
<customErrors mode="On"/>
```

to

```
<customErrors mode="Off"/>
```

Step3: Change 'Debug' from 'false' to 'true' in 'Compilation' attribute.

Change

```
<compilation batch="false" debug="false">
```

to

```
<compilation batch="true" debug="true">
```

Step 4: Restart the IIS.

We can now see a detail stack error which shows which method exactly has the issue. For instance, in this scenario the 'FeatureDeactivation' event has the error.

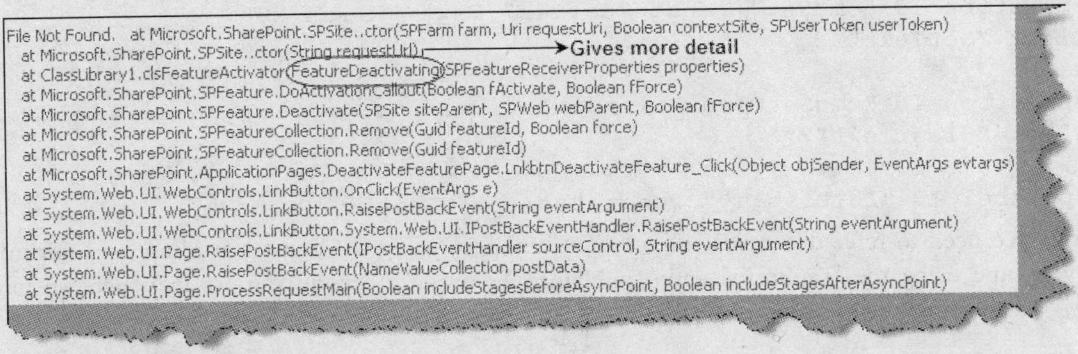

The error in 'FeatureDeactivation' event happened because of the wrong URL specified for the 'SPSite.' If we see the previous error it showed as 'File not found,' but in actual it was due to wrong URL name.

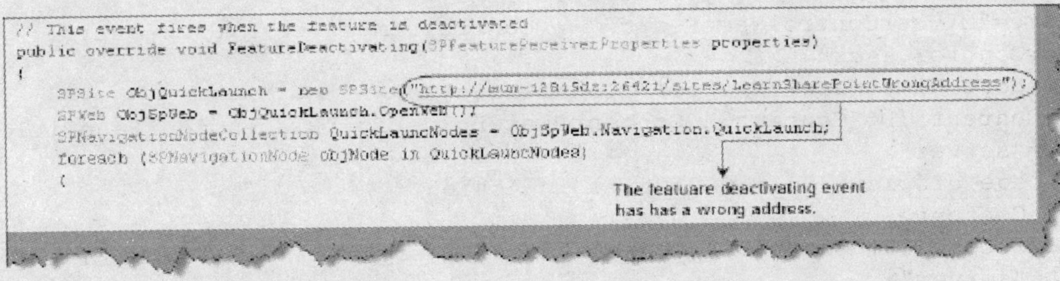

How can we display ASCX control in SharePoint pages?

Custom controls in ASP.NET provide huge level of reusability in ASP.NET. They are normally simple controls with ASCX extensions which can be reused in different ASPX pages. To load an ASCX control in SharePoint environment is a simple five-step process:

Step 1: We need to create an ASCX. So below is a simple ASCX file which has a label 'lblDisplay.' There are two functions: 'setText' and 'ClearText' - one which sets the label to value and the other clear the label. Both these methods 'setText' and 'clearText' are called by event click of two buttons 'cmdSet' and 'cmdClear,' respectively.

```
<%@ Control Language="C#" %>
<script runat="server">
protected void SetText(object sender, EventArgs e)
{
```

```
 lblDisplay.Text = "This is a user control";
}
protected void ClearText(object sender, EventArgs e)
{
 lblDisplay.Text = "";
}
</script>
<asp:Button ID="cmdSet" runat="server" Text="Click Me"
OnClick="SetText"/>
<br/>
<asp:Button ID="cmdSetClear" runat="server" Text="Click to clear text"
OnClick="ClearText"/>
<br/>
<asp:Label ID="lblDisplay" runat="server" Text=""/>
```

Step 2: We need to refer this ASCX file in an ASPX page using the register attribute and refer the same using the 'TagPrefix' and 'TagName.' Below is the code snippet in which we have highlighted the same in bold.

```
<%@ Assembly Name="Microsoft.SharePoint,Version=12.0.0.0,
Culture=neutral,PublicKeyToken=71e9bce111e9429c" %>
<%@ Page Language="C#" MasterPageFile="~/_layouts/application.master"
Inherits="Microsoft.SharePoint.WebControls.LayoutsPageBase" %>
<%@ Register TagPrefix="MyUserControlPrefix"
TagName="MyUserControlName" src="~/_controltemplates/MyUserControl/
MyUserControl.ascx" %>
<%@ Import Namespace="Microsoft.SharePoint" %>
<asp:Content ID="Content3" ContentPlaceHolderId="PlaceHolderPageTitle"
runat="server">
This page displays Custom Control in Action
</asp:Content>
<asp:Content ID="Content1" ContentPlaceHolderId="PlaceHolderMain"
runat="server">
<MyUserControlPrefix:MyUserControlName ID="id2" runat="server"/>
</asp:Content>
<asp:Content ID="Content2"
ContentPlaceHolderId="PlaceHolderPageTitleInTitleArea" runat="server">
We never knew custom control is so easy to display.
</asp:Content>
```

Below figure shows the overall view, interaction and explanation of 'MyUserControl.ascx' and 'PageUsingCustomControl.aspx.'

Step 3: We need to copy the ASCX control in the 'C:\Program Files\Common Files\Microsoft Shared\web server extensions\12\TEMPLATE\CONTROL TEMPLATES' directory. For this sample we have created a simple directory called as 'MyUserControl' and uploaded

'MyUserControl.ascx' in the same. The ASCX file has already been referred using the virtual path sign '~' with the 'MyUserControl' folder.

```
<%@ Register TagPrefix="MyUserControlPrefix" TagName="MyUserControlName" src="~/
_controltemplates/MyUserControl/MyUserControl.ascx" %>
```

Step 4: We also need to paste the ASP.NET page 'PageUsingCustomControl.aspx' in the layouts folder located at 'C:\Program Files\Common Files\Microsoft Shared\web server extensions\12\TEMPLATE\LAYOUTS.'

Step 5: This is the easiest step we need to the run the ASPX page and enjoy how the user control runs under the SharePoint environment. Below is how the user controls looks. If we click the button 'Click me' the label is set with a text 'This is a user control.' If we click on 'Click to clear text' it will just clear the values of the label.

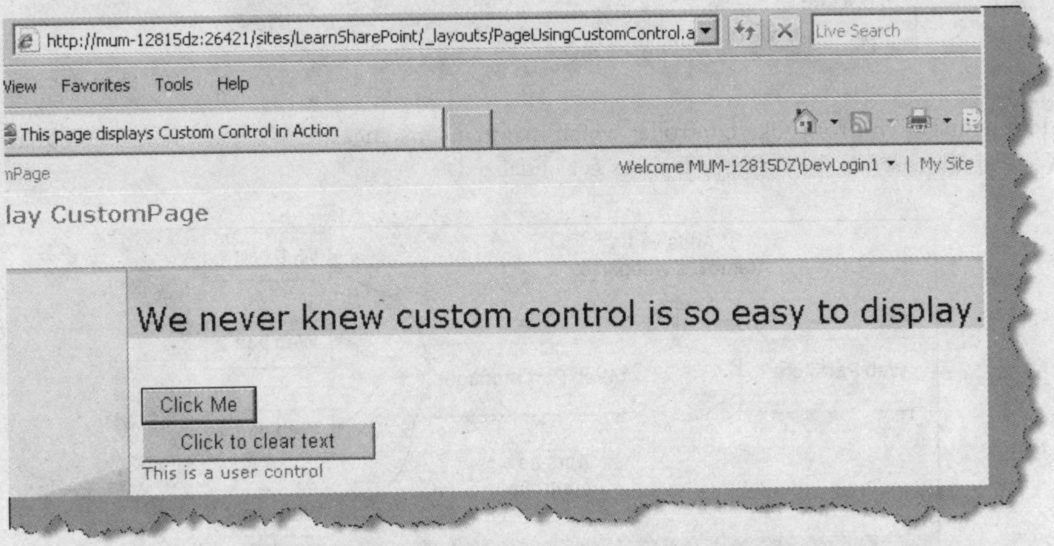

> **Note:** *If you are using behind code, you need to register the behind code in to GAC and refer the same in the ASCX. In this example, we have just used in-line code for simplicity. You can get the above sample from CD from 'UserControlsSample' folder.*

What are WebParts and in what ways does it vary in SharePoint environment?

It helps to build reusable components which can be customized and personalized according to business user. We can either make our own webpart or we can reuse the existing ones from SharePoint itself.

Following WebParts are available with WSS:

Data View Web Part: Displays data with rich design support through Microsoft SharePoint Designer.

List View Web Part: Helps us to display list content for any list in the SharePoint site.

Image Web Part: Helps us to display image files.

Content Editor Web Part: Use this to display static HTML content using a WYSIWYG editor or to link to a text file.

Members Web Part: Helps us to display members of the site.

Page Viewer Web Part: Displays web page in an Iframe.

WebPart is nothing but a simple class which inherits from System.Web.UI.WebControls.WebParts. In other words, we can say WebPart is kind of a WebControl which can be deployed in a WebPartZoneControl.

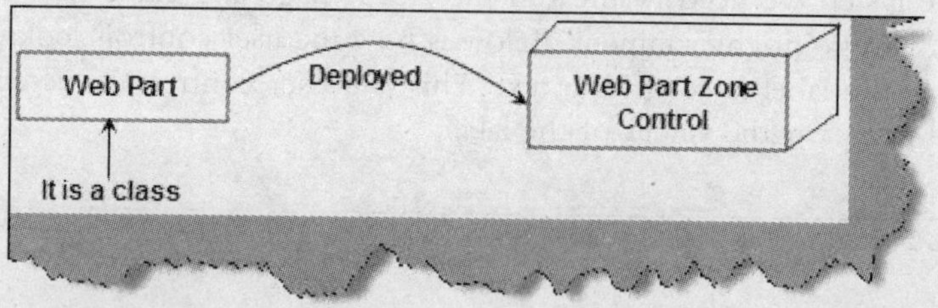

WebPart manager control is like controller which maintains instances of Webpart. It adds WebParts to the WebPartZone when the ASP.NET pages get initialized.

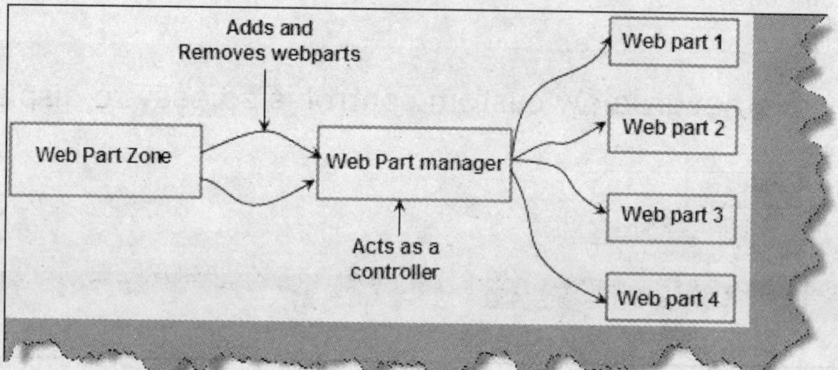

Now let's try to how 'WebParts' work in SharePoint environment. 'WebPartManager' uses the SPWebPartManager.' 'WebPartZone' interacts with the 'WebPartManager' who in-turn stores a serialized instance of the 'WebPart' in the content database. In other words, code is stored in content database for customization.

> **Note:** *The big difference is that the 'WebPart' code is stored in content database. So some of the differences as compared to normal ASP.NET is that, the code is deployed in content database and is parsed using 'SafeModeParser.'*

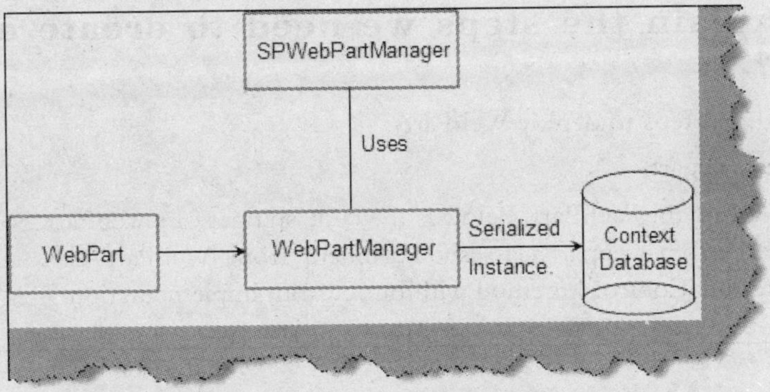

What are the different life cycle events that WebPart goes through?

A 'WebPart' control goes through various events and has a typical life cycle.

OnInit: This is the initialization event and is the first event to occur.

OnLoad: The load event.

CreateChildControls: When any child controls are added to a composite control, this event fires.

EnsureChildControls: This event makes sure that 'CreateChildControls' fires.

OnPreRender: This fires just before the render event.

Page.PreRenderComplete: When all controls have executed the 'OnPreRender' event, this event fires.

Render: Render the full control.

RenderContents: Renders the contents of the control only.

What's the difference between WebParts in WSS 2.0 and 3.0?

'WebParts' was born when WSS 2.0 was first introduced. In ASP.NET 2.0 framework, new version of 'WebPart' was built which can run without WSS. WSS 3.0 uses the ASP.NET 2.0 'WebPart' framework. So, if we are doing new development using WSS 3.0 we should use ASP.NET 2.0 'WebPart' framework. But, if we want backward compatibility, we can use 'Microsoft.SharePoint.WebPartPages.WebPart' class.

So the decision will be more based on what level of back ward compatibility we are looking for. Below sheet shows the new WebPart classes as compared to SharePoint Backward compatible class:

ASP.NET Web Parts classes	SharePoint Backward Compatibility classes
WebBrowsableAttribute	BrowsableAttribute
WebDisplayName	FriendlyName
WebDescription	Description
Personalizable	WebPartStorage
PersonalizationScope	Storage
EditorPart	ToolPart
EditorPartCollection	ToolPart[]
CreateEditorParts()	GetToolParts()
RenderContents()	RenderWebPart()
SetPersonalizationDirty()	SaveProperties

Can you explain the steps we need to create a WebPart in SharePoint?

There are overall three steps to deploy WebParts:

Step 1: Create the Webpart

The first step is to create the WebPart. Below is the code snippet of a webPart. So we need to reference the 'WebParts,' the custom webpart class should inherit from 'WebPart' class and finally we need to override the 'CreateChildControls' method with our custom implementation.

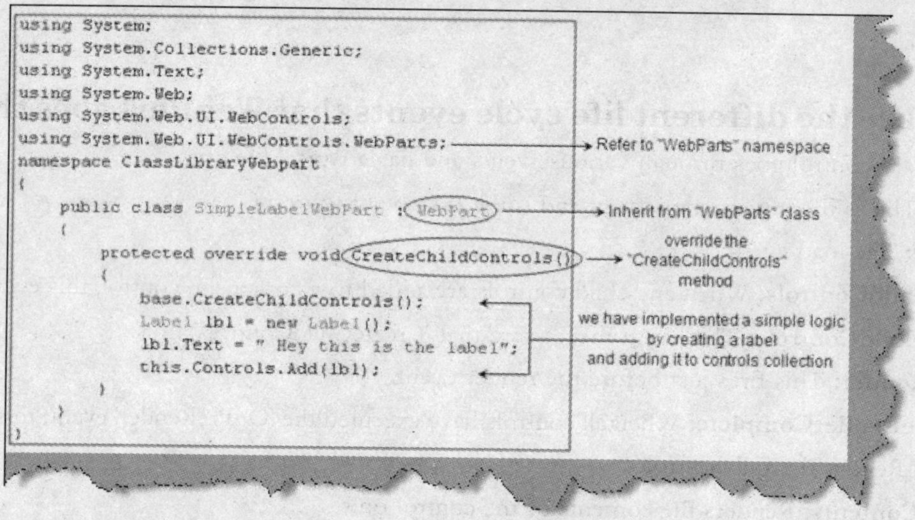

Step 2: Copy the compile DLL to the virtual directory in the BIN folder.

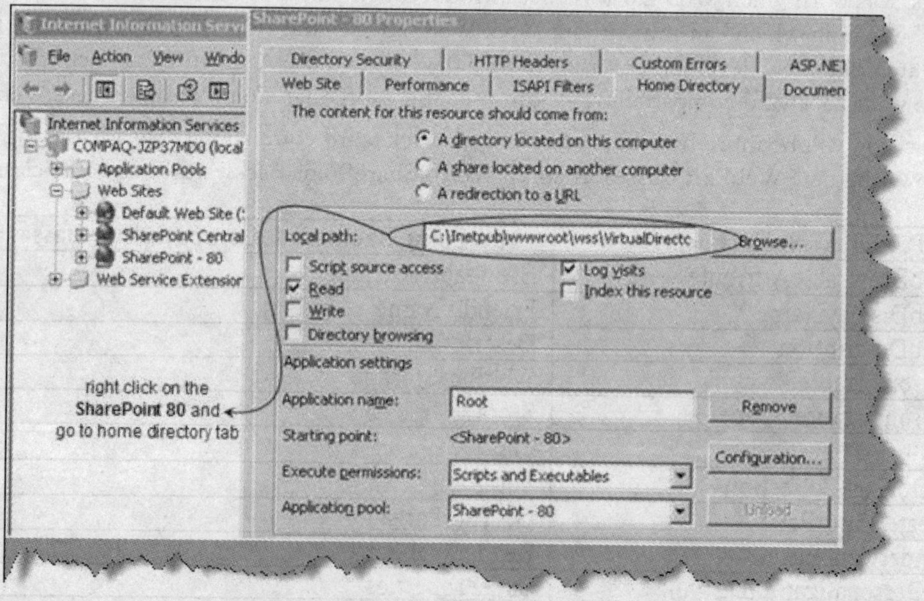

The second step is to copy the compiled DLL in the virtual directory of the SharePoint site.

We can get the virtual directory from the IIS from home directory tab in IIS. For instance, the current website is hosted on the SharePoint 80 virtual site which is actually located at 'C: \Inetpub\wwwroot\wss\VirtualDirectories\80.'

So, now let's browse to 'C: \Inetpub\wwwroot\wss\VirtualDirectories\80\bin' directory and copy the DLL in the bin folder.

Step 3: Make entry of the WebPart in to web.config file.

Now that we have copied the DLL to 'bin' folder, we need to make a 'SafeControl' entry in the 'Web.Config' file of the virtual directory.

So now let's browse to 'C:\Inetpub\wwwroot\wss\VirtualDirectories\80,' open the web.config file and add the class library name in the 'SafeControls' section of the web.config file. Below code snippet shows the same in a visual manner.

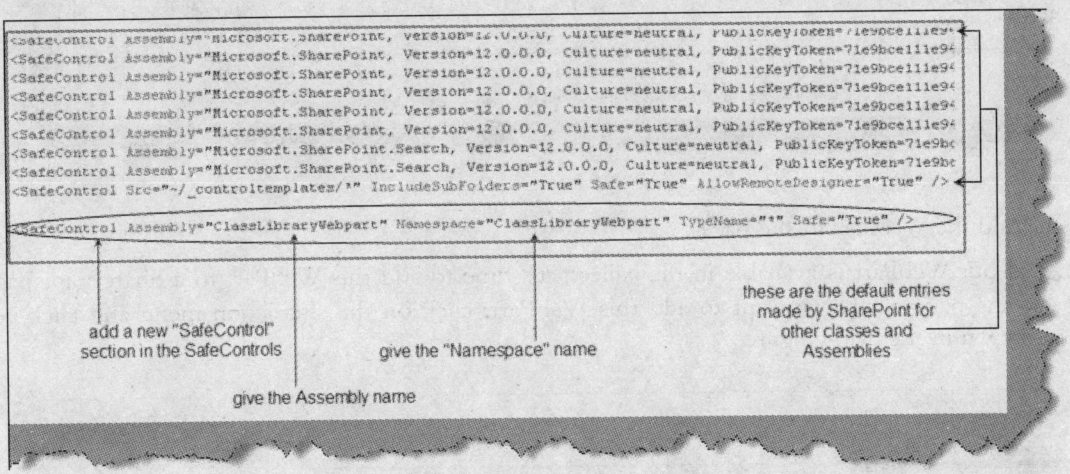

Step 3: Add it to the WebPart gallery

Now that we have added the WebPart in the 'web.config' file, its time to make it available in the web part gallery. So click on Site settings ' then click webparts ' Click new button, we should see the figure shown below.

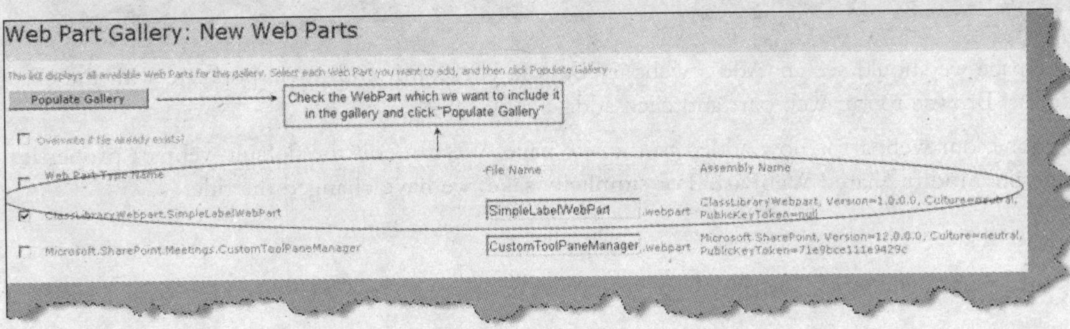

We can also see the webpart which we recently added is seen the gallery. To make it available, click the check box and click populate gallery.

We should now see our webpart (for this context it is SimpleLabelWebPart) in the WebPart gallery.

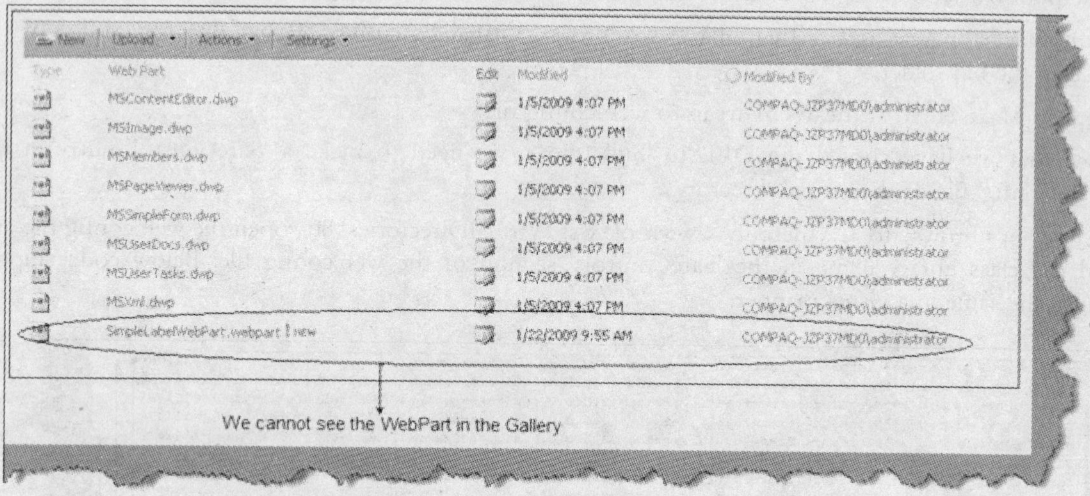

Step 4: Add the WebPart to site pages.

Now, that our WebPart is available in the gallery, it's time to add this WebPart to a SharePoint page. So go to the page where we want to add this WebPart, click on the site action menu and click edit page as shown in the below figure.

On the page we should see an 'Add a webpart' button, click on it and it will populate with the existing web parts. Browse to our web part and click add.

Once done, our webpart is now added to the site page. We can edit the default webpart properties by clicking on 'Modify Shared WebPart.' For simplicity sake, we have changed the title.

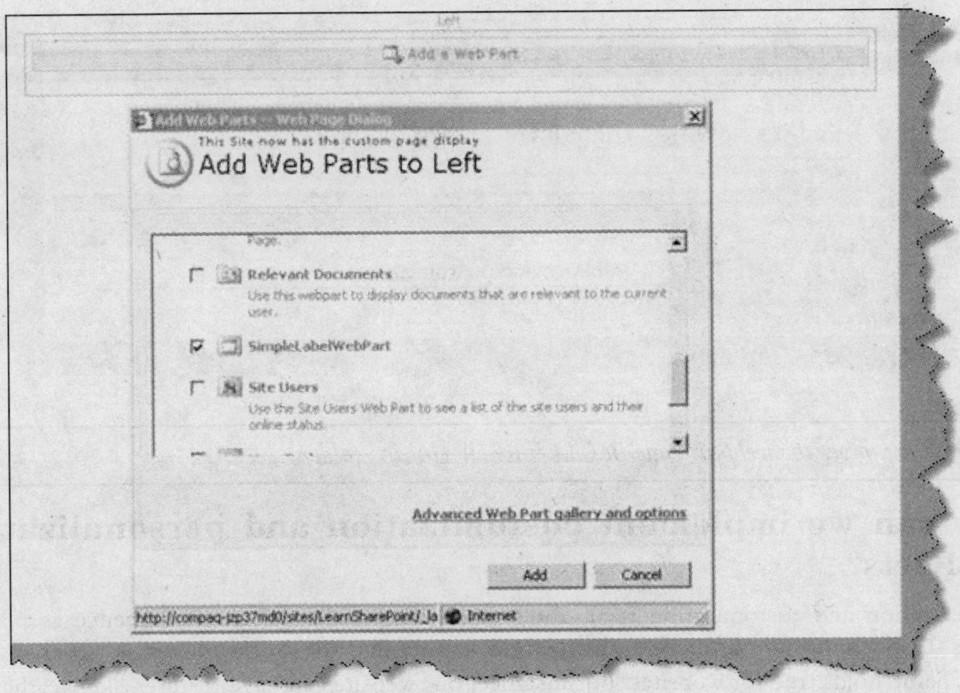

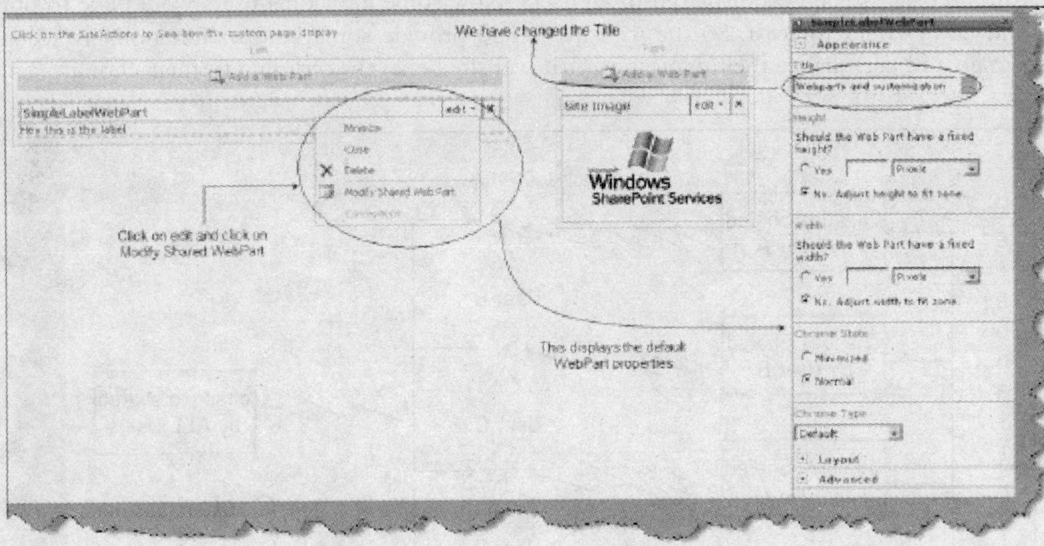

Step 5: View the WebPart

We can see the changed title display when view the page normally. So with a few lines of coding, we can see how huge customization can be achieved.

Note: You can get the webpart code in CD from 'WebPart' folder.

How can we implement customization and personalization in WebParts?

Personalization and customization is all about improving individual user experience as per personal choices. Every human is different and everybody wants that the world moves as per their individual choice. Same holds true for websites. For instance, our website can have features like weather forecast, business news and sports news. As an administrator, we have the capability to change the look and feel of the website which gets displayed to all users. Now some individual users would like to only see news and not weather forecast. So the website should provide some kind of functionality where the users can go and personalize their choices so that website behaves according to their choice.

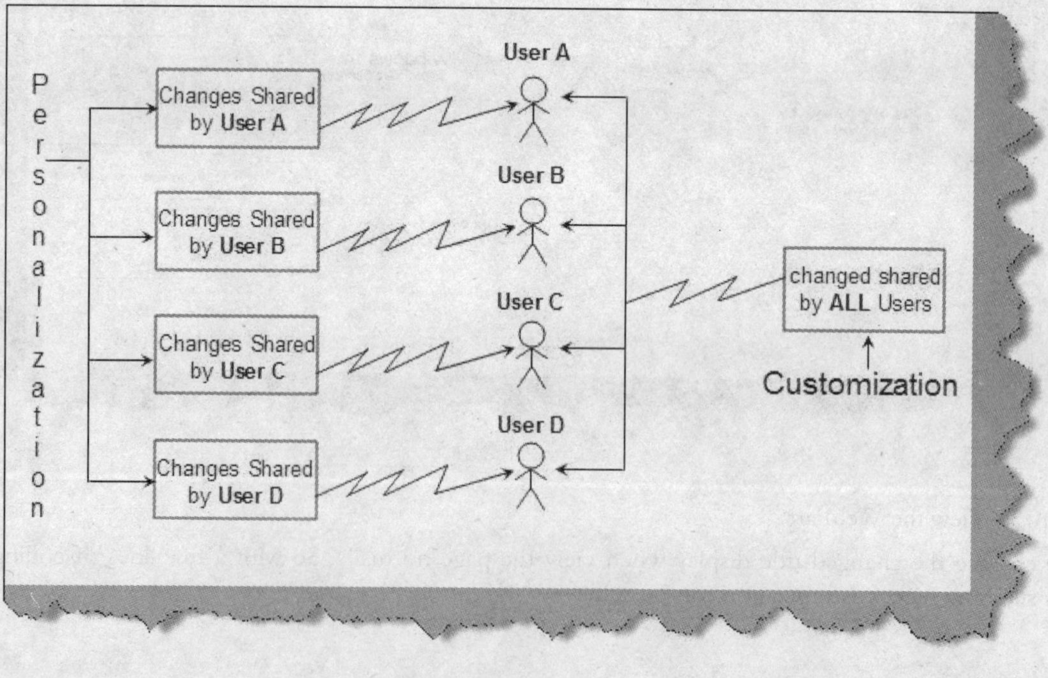

Now from the capability where the admin can change the look and feel is called a customization. This change is reflected to every viewer who comes to the site. The capability that individual users can either choose to view the news with weather forecast and not is personalization.

Just cutting it short when changes made to site are shared by all users it's called as customization. When we make changes to some feature which is only shared and seen by individual users, it is termed as personalization.

Let's try understanding personalization and customization in SharePoint using a small sample. Let's make a label whose text/data can be personalized by every user, but its font size can only be customized by admin. The font size customization activity is only limited to admin and cannot be personalized by every end user who logs into the website.

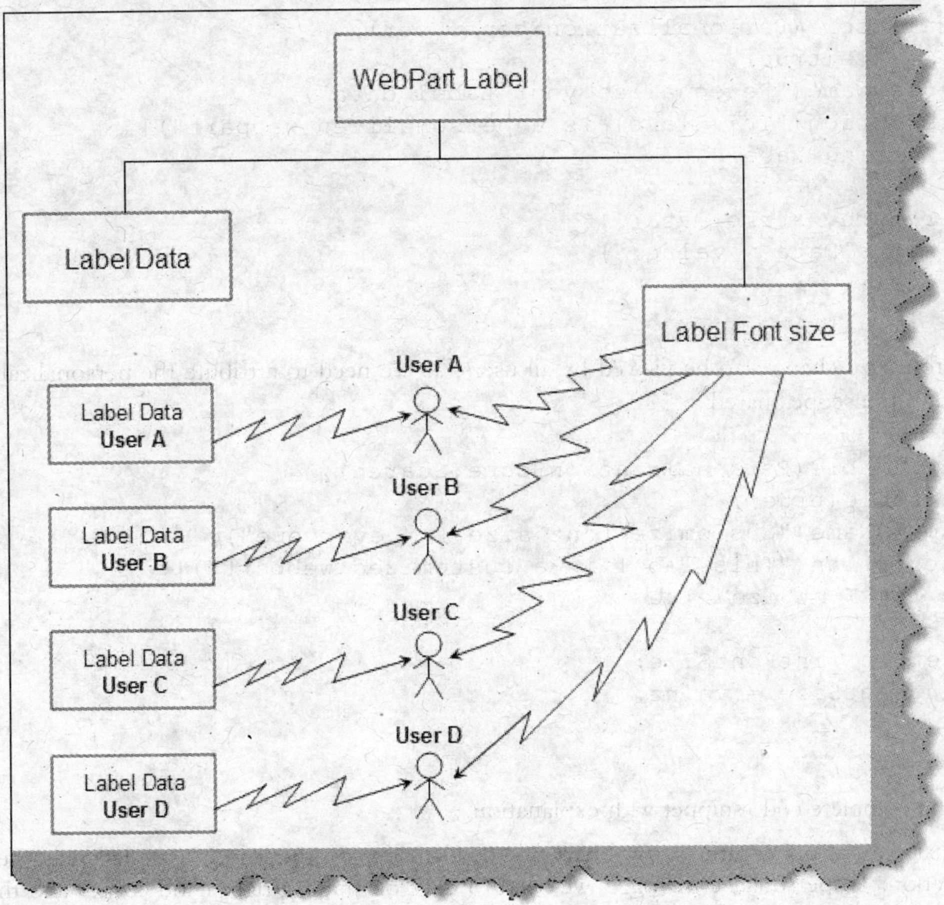

Let's create the label webpart whose label data can be personalized as per every user and the font size can only be customized by the admin.

The first thing is that we need to create a class for the webpart. Below is the code snippet of the webpart class. We have created two private properties: font size and label data.

```
public class SimpleLabelCustomization : WebPart
{
private int _intFontSize;
private string _strLblData = "";
```

Second thing we need to do is to define the personalization scope for both of these properties. We want the label data changes to be personalized as per user. So we need to attribute the personalizable to personalizationscope.user. In order to display description and display name, we specified the 'WebDisplayName' and 'WebDescription.'

```
[Personalizable(PersonalizationScope.User),
WebBrowsable(true),
WebDisplayName("Personalize your Label data"),
WebDescription("This label is a personalized webpart")]
public string LabelData
{
get { return _strLblData; }
set {_strLblData = value; }
}
```

We want font size changes to be viewed by all users, so we need to attribute the personalizable value to personalizationscope.Shared.

```
[Personalizable(PersonalizationScope.Shared),
WebBrowsable(true),
WebDisplayName("Customize font size for everyone"),
WebDescription("This label is a customized webpart")]
public int FontSizeValue
{
get{ return _intFontSize; }
set{_intFontSize = value; }
}
```

Below is the complete code snippet with explanation.

So now that we are done with our webpart, we need to deploy the same. Now let's see the fun of personalization. To personalize the page, we need to click on the top right hand corner and then click personalize page. Now if we edit the webpart we will see only the label data can be changed.

This is because we have given label data as user based personalization and font size as shared personalization.

To customize the webpart, we need to click on site action and click edit page. We can now see both the properties. The site actions menu can be restricted to administrators to have a better control on customization and personalization.

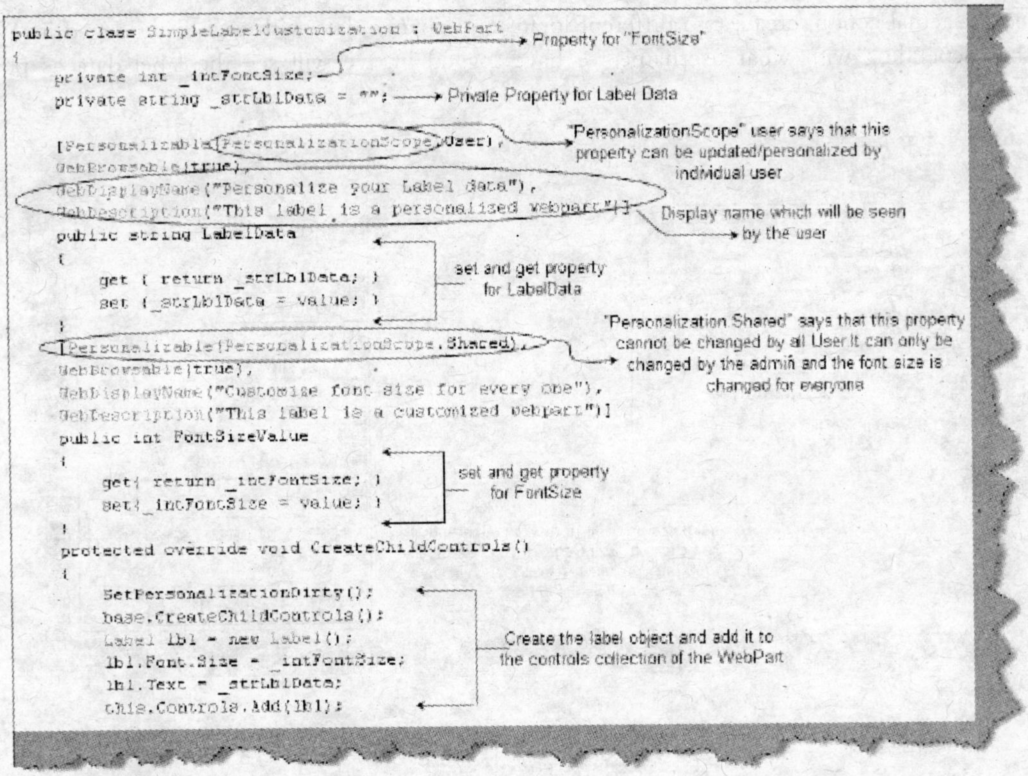
public class SimpleLabelCustomization : WebPart
{
private int _intFontSize;
private string _strLblData = "";
[Personalizable(PersonalizationScope.User),
WebBrowsable(true),
WebDisplayName("Personalize your Label data"),
WebDescription("This label is a personalized webpart")]
public string LabelData
{
get { return _strLblData; }
set { _strLblData = value; }
}
[Personalizable(PersonalizationScope.Shared),
WebBrowsable(true),
WebDisplayName("Customize font size for every one"),
WebDescription("This label is a customized webpart")]
public int FontSizeValue
{
get{ return _intFontSize; }
set{ _intFontSize = value; }
}
protected override void CreateChildControls()
{
SetPersonalizationDirty();
base.CreateChildControls();
Label lbl = new Label();
lbl.Font.Size = _intFontSize;
lbl.Text = _strLblData;
this.Controls.Add(lbl);
Property for "FontSize"
Private Property for Label Data
"PersonalizationScope" user says that this property can be updated/personalized by individual user
Display name which will be seen by the user
set and get property for LabelData
"Personalization Shared" says that this property cannot be changed by all User.It can only be changed by the admin and the font size is changed for everyone
set and get property for FontSize
Create the label object and add it to the controls collection of the WebPart

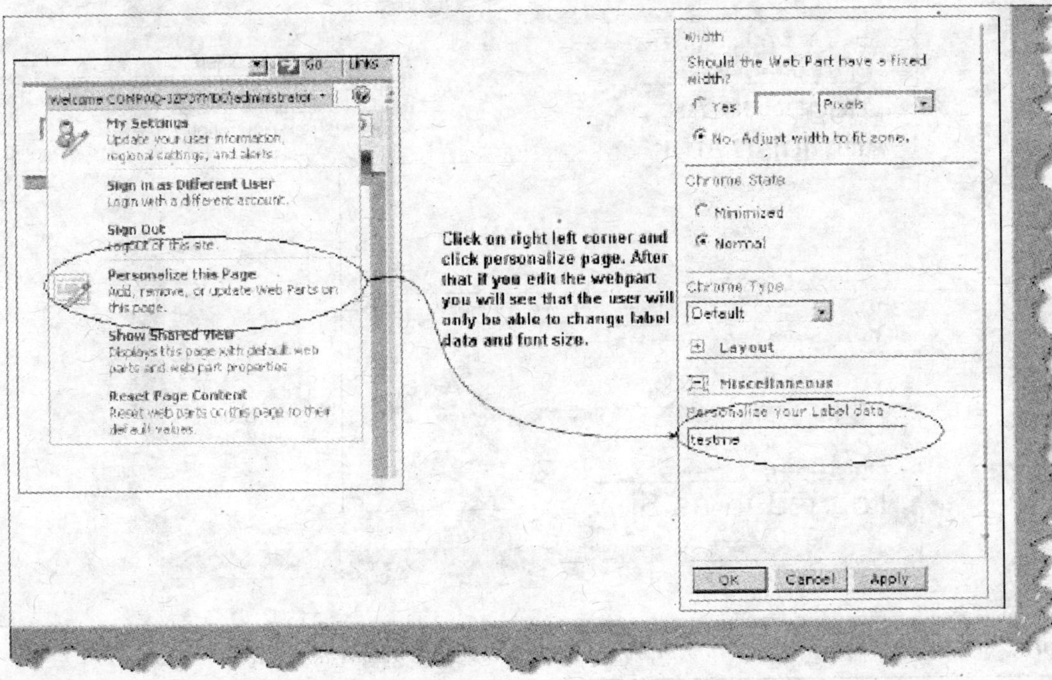
Go
Links
My Settings
Update your user information, regional settings, and alerts
Sign in as Different User
Login with a different account.
Sign Out
Logout of this site.
Personalize this Page
Add, remove, or update Web Parts on this page.
Show Shared View
Displays this page with default web parts and web part properties
Reset Page Content
Reset web parts on this page to their default values.
Click on right left corner and click personalize page. After that if you edit the webpart you will see that the user will only be able to change label data and font size.
Width
Should the Web Part have a fixed width?
Yes
Pixels
No. Adjust width to fit zone.
Chrome State
Minimized
Normal
Chrome Type
Default
Layout
Miscellaneous
Personalize your Label data
testme
OK
Cancel
Apply

To see the actual action, create two different logins and change data with each user logged in. We will see that depending with what username we have logged in, we will see the label data as per user personalization.

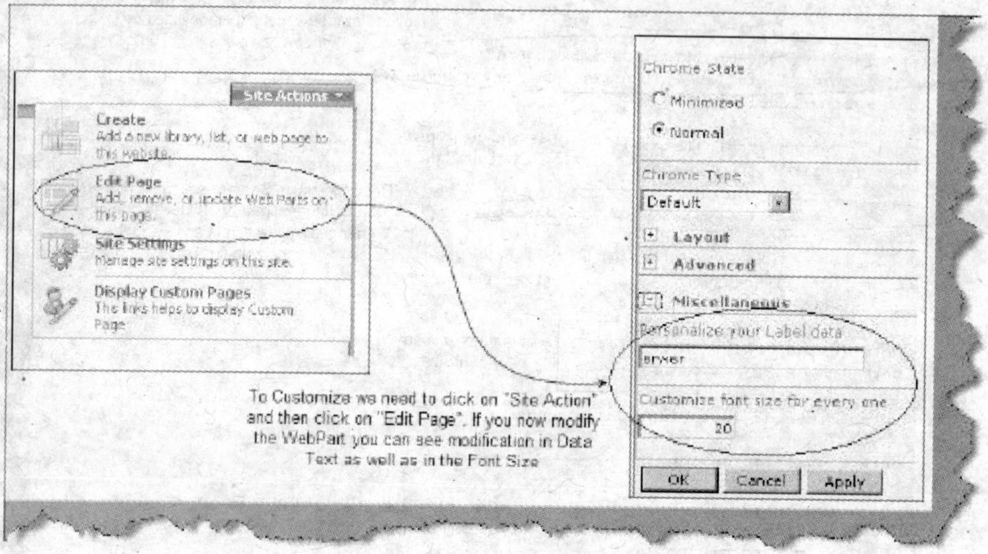

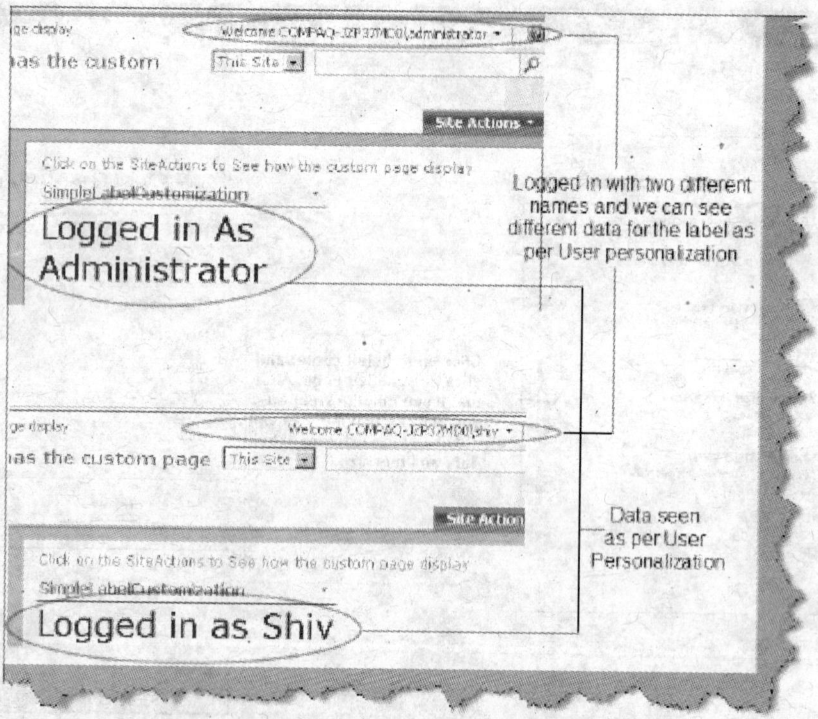

Note: *You can get the above customization code from CD in 'WebPart' folder.*

How can we create a custom editor for WebPart?

There are situations where we want to use our own custom WebPart editor rather than using the default WebPart editor.

> **Note:** *In case you do not know how to deploy a WebPart, we advise you to read the answer for question "Can you explain the steps we need to create a WebPart in SharePoint"?*

To make our own custom web part editor is a four-step procedure.

Step 1: So the first thing is to create the WebPart. We need to make a slight change i.e. 'WebBrowsable (false)" so that it does not use the default 'WebPart' editor. Below is the code snippet of the same font size 'WebPart' which has 'WebBrowsable' value as false.

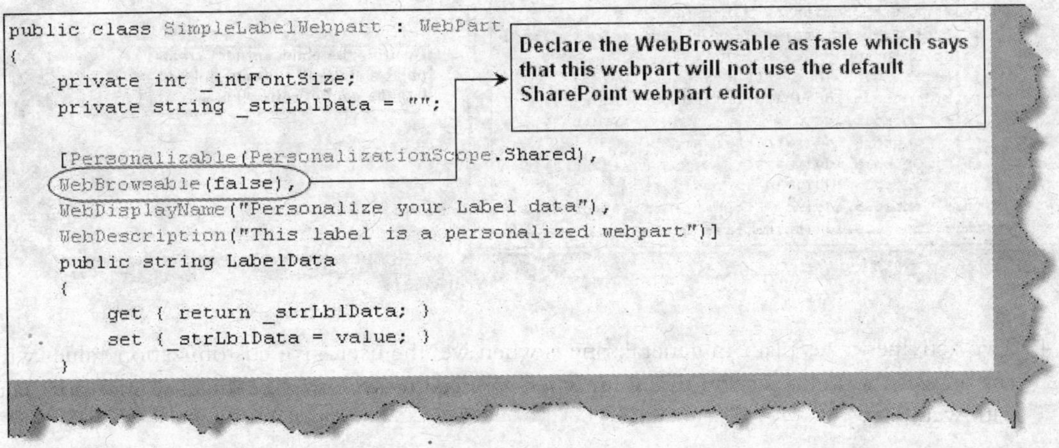

Step 2: The other thing which we need to do in the WebPart is to override the 'CreateEditorParts' method and add our custom webpart editor. We will be seeing in the next step how we can create the web part editor. For this example we have created 'SimpleWebPartEditor.'

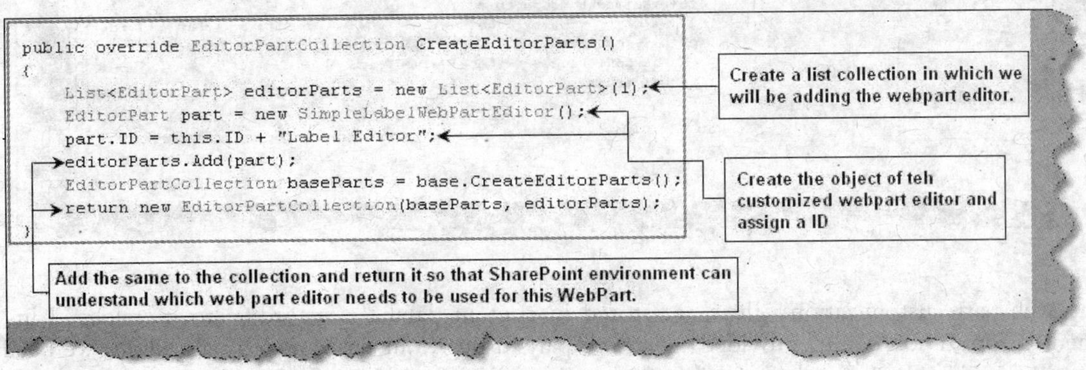

Step 3: In order to create our custom web part editor, the first step we need to do is inherit from 'EditorPart' class. Currently we have created a custom web part editor class called as

'SimpleLabelWebPart.' In this custom class we have create two labels and two text boxes. The two textboxes will take font size and label value while the labels will display description for those text boxes. In other words, we have defined our UI which take inputs which can customize our web part.

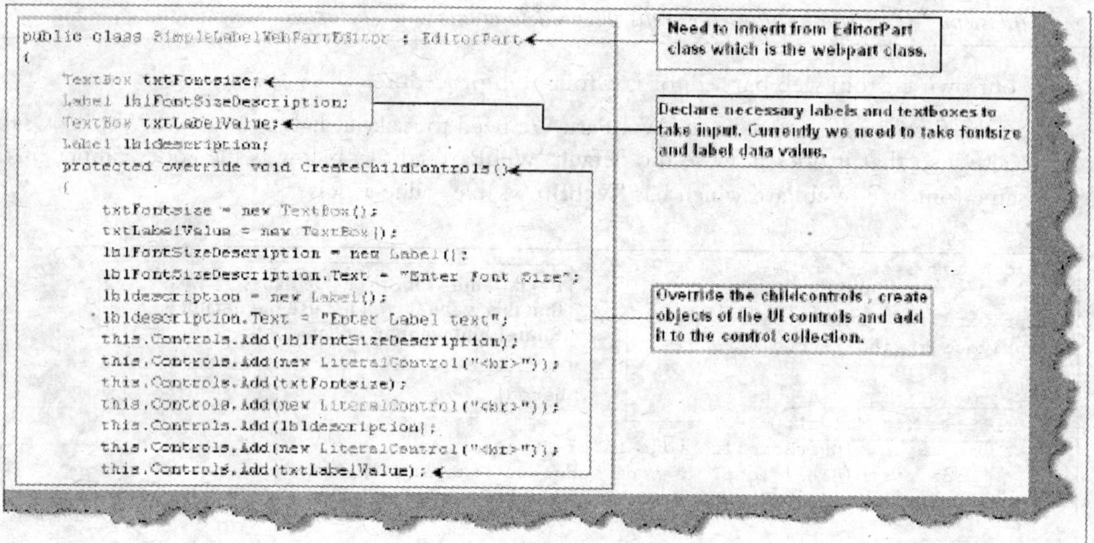

Step 4: Two activities takes place in general: one is when we, the user, give customization values which customizes the web part and the other when we need to synchronize the customization values with web part.

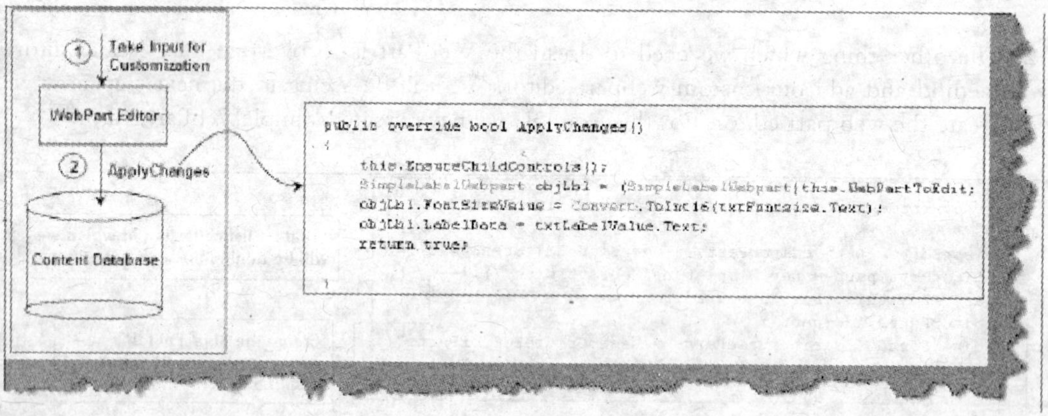

The web part customization values are stored in content database according to user logged in. So when customization data is provided for a web part through our custom web part editor, we need to override the 'ApplyChanges' method and push the customization data to the web part object. So in other words, the data is pushed from the web part editor to the content database on per user basis.

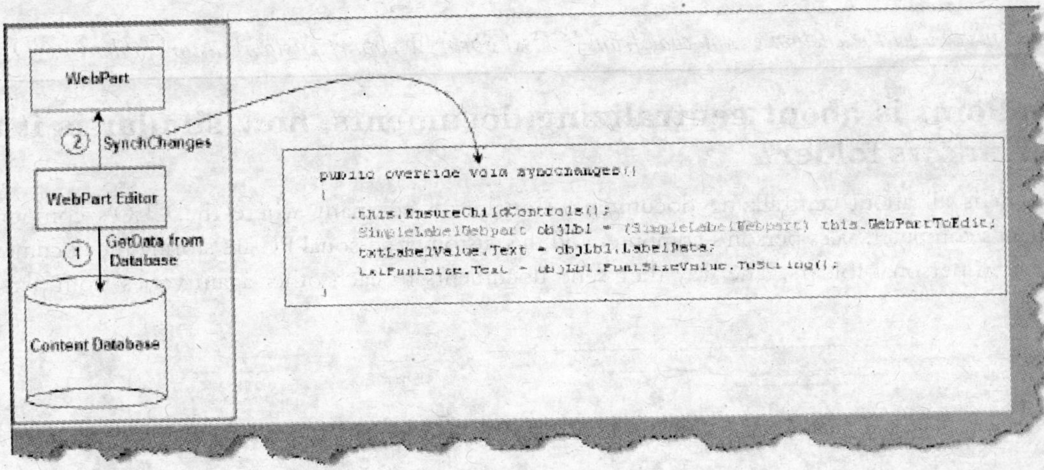

Now comes the second aspect where we need to synch the web part data from content database with the web part itself. For this, we need to override the 'syncchanges' method and push the data from the web part object in to the web part editor user interface.

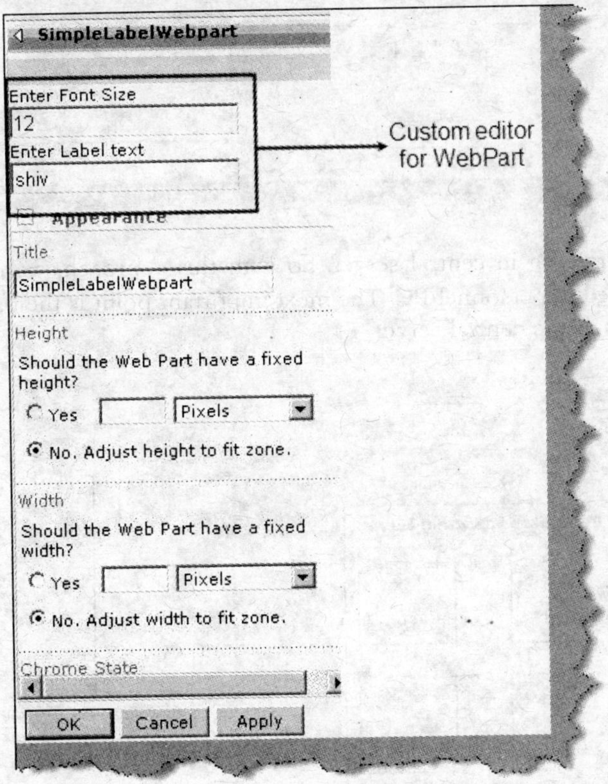

Ok, now if we edit our web part we can see how the custom editor looks like.

> ***Note:*** *You can get the custom editor code from 'ClassLibraryWebpartCustomEditor' folder in CD.*

SharePoint is about centralizing documents, how similar is it to the Windows folder?

SharePoint is all about centralizing documents. Consider a company where the CEO's computer, accountant's computer, sales person's computer and the customer personal PC are storing the documents in their own personal folders. The way they send documents to each other again varies from person to person.

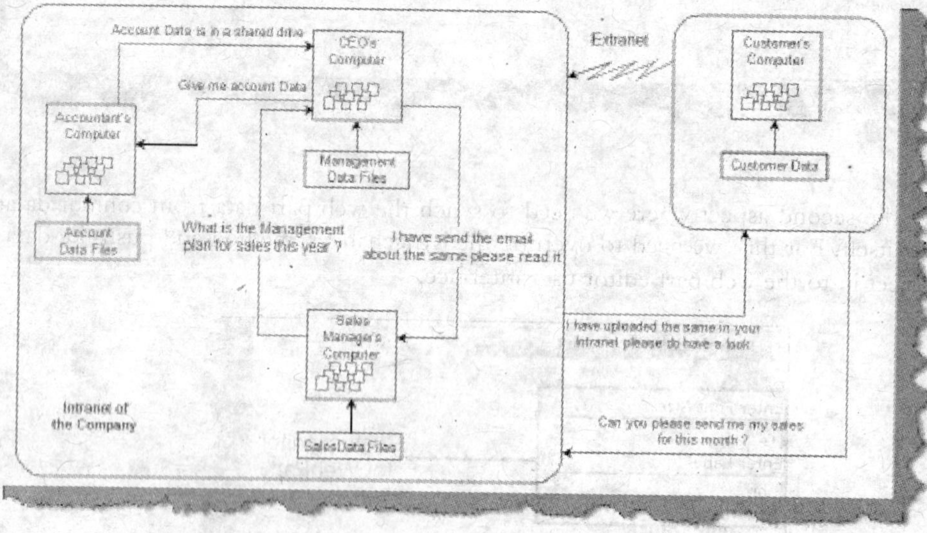

SharePoint centralized everything in central server. So with this approach, we do not have different copies of document scattered in personnel PC. The most important point is the backups and versioning can now be managed through the central server.

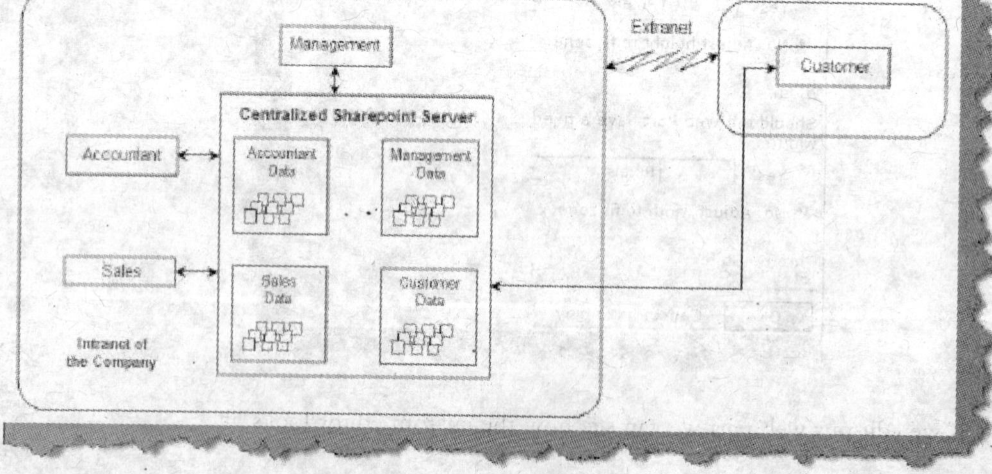

Consider the below figure which shows a simple folder with 'courses' as the top folder which has later has 'networking' and 'programming' folder. The 'programming' folder has 'dotnet' and 'java' folder, which has a word document 'SharePointFoBeginners.doc.'

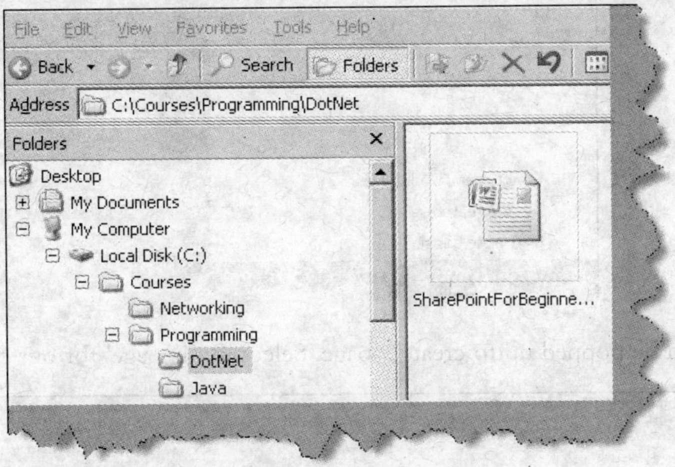

Below is a just a zoomed picture of the folder structure we see above.

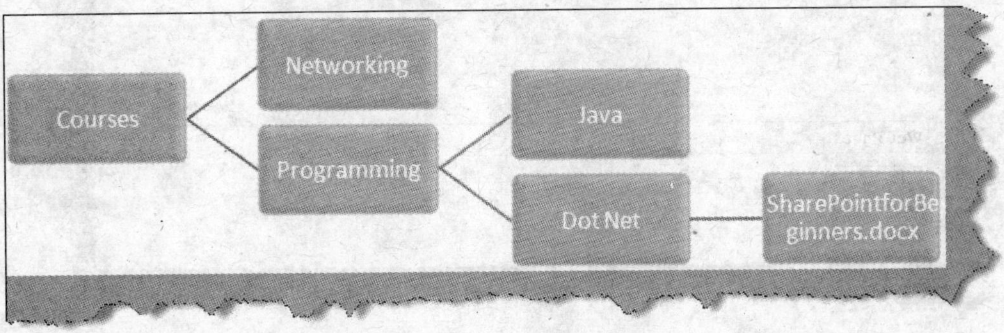

So if we want to implement the same in SharePoint, following steps should be followed:

Step 1: Click on the right side 'Site actions' menu and click on 'Site Settings.'

Step 2: We will see a lot of option, click on 'Site libraries and lists' and then click on 'Create Content.'

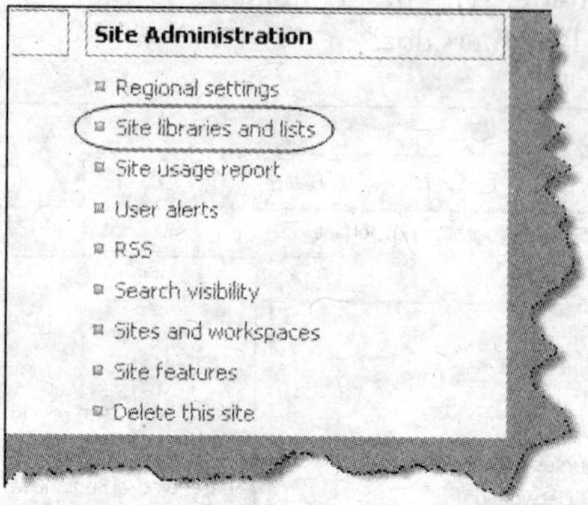

Step 3: We will then be popped up to create a page. Select 'Basic page' for our current situation.

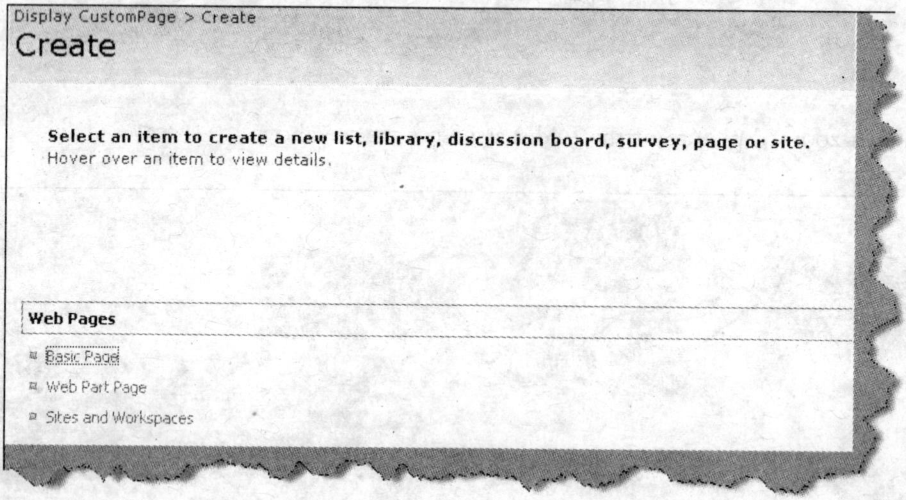

Step 4: Give a page name and click on 'Create a new document library.' The document library helps us to provide the necessary folder structure and document centralization.

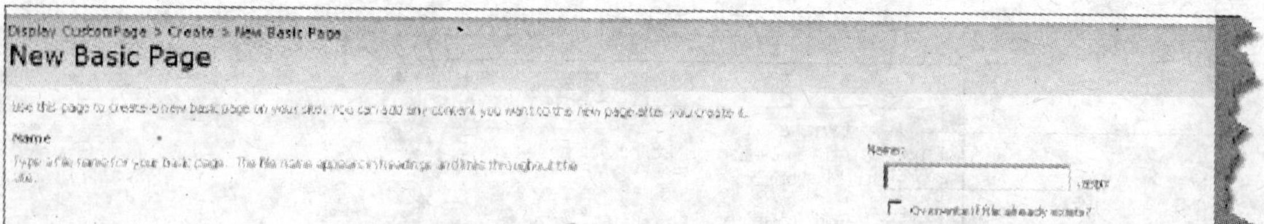

Step 5: We need to specify a name for the document library. We will specify the name as 'Courses' because that forms the folder name for the top folder.

Step 6: Once we click on create, we will see the courses directory at the right hand side of the quick launch menu.

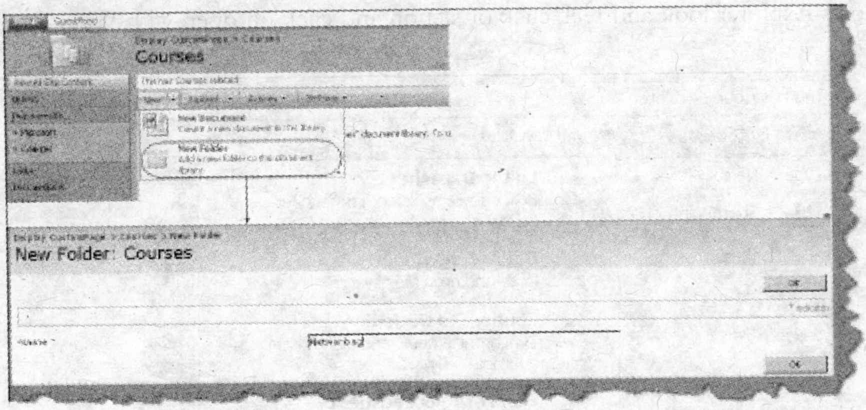

Step 7: So we have repeated step 6 and created our folder hierarchy. Now we can upload document using the upload document as shown in the figure below.

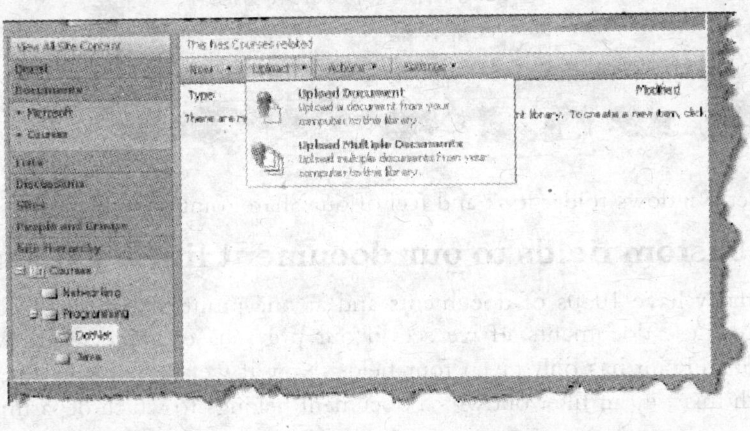

Once document is uploaded, we can see the document with folder structure as shown below. Below folder structure represents exactly our Windows folder structure.

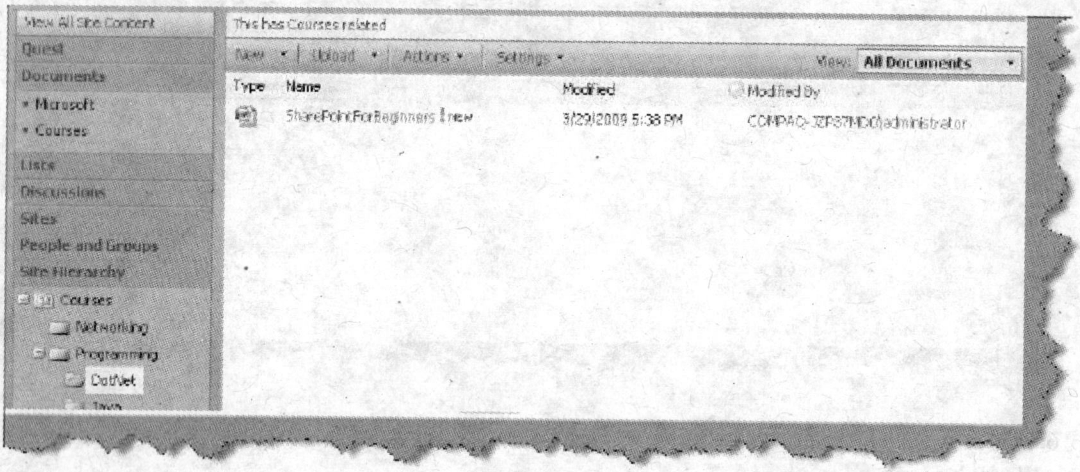

To get a Windows Explorer look and feel, click on action and click on open with Windows Explorer.

We can see the exact Windows folder look and feel of our SharePoint documents.

Can we add custom fields to our document library documents?

Organizations normally have 1000s of documents and at one point of time, it becomes difficult to search and organize these documents. If we see in our previous example where we had created a document library, SharePoint has only given four fields. Now if we want to add a new field called as department and with this we can filter out which document belongs to which department.

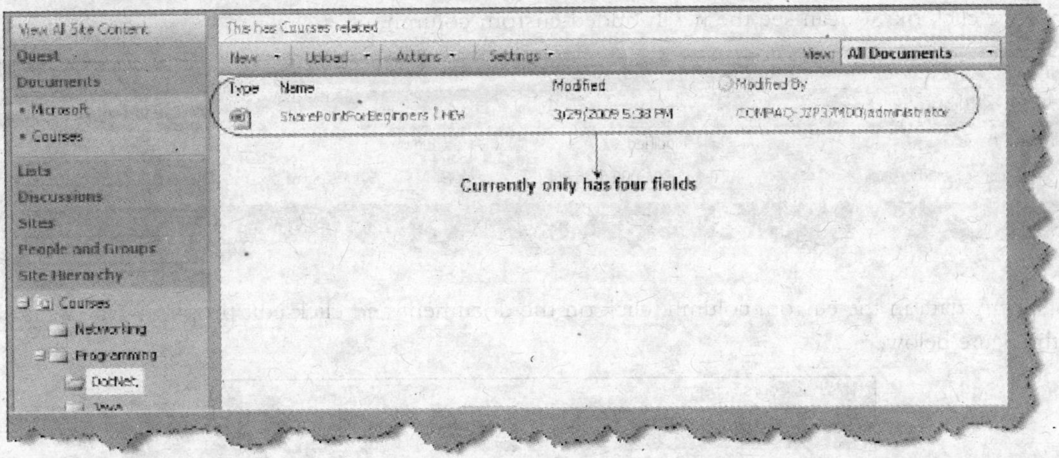

To add a custom column, click on settings and click on create column as shown in the below figure.

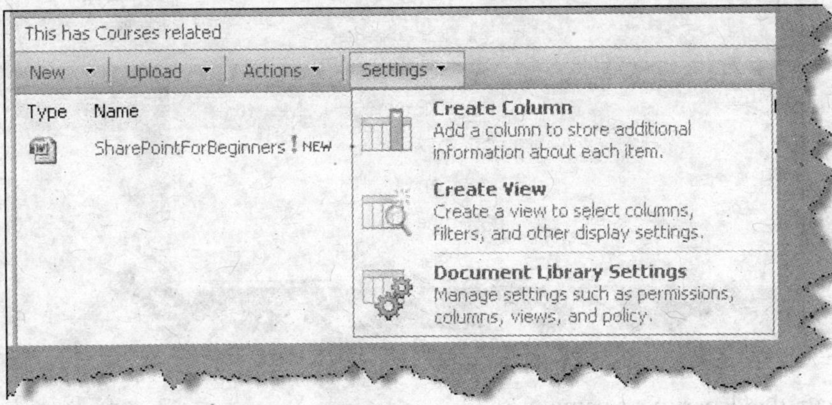

We will then be popped to specify a name for the custom column. For the current scenario, we have named it as 'DepartMent.'

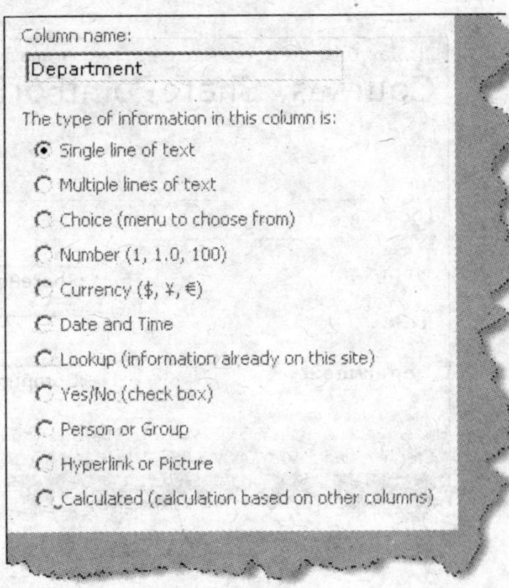

Once we click ok, we can see the newly added custom column.

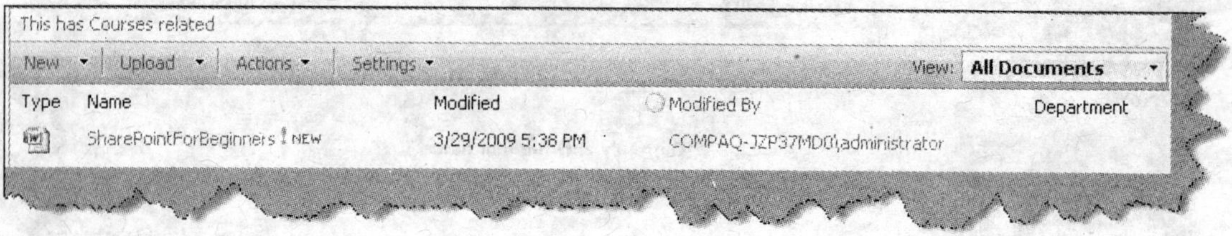

To specify data in the custom column, click on the document and click edit properties menu as shown in the figure below.

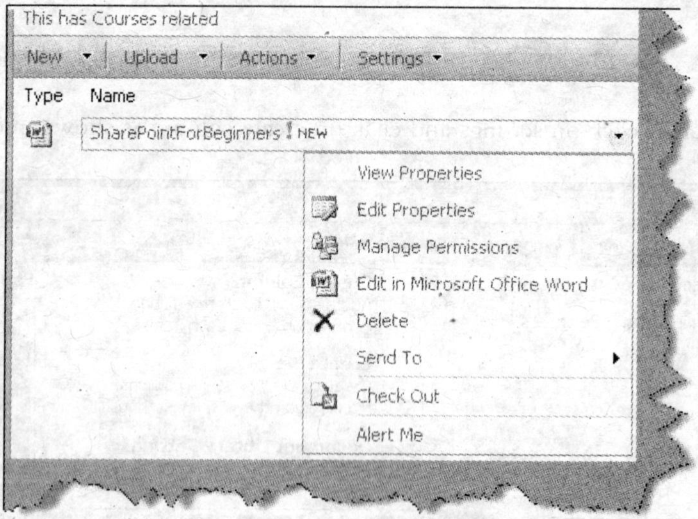

We can now specify the department name.

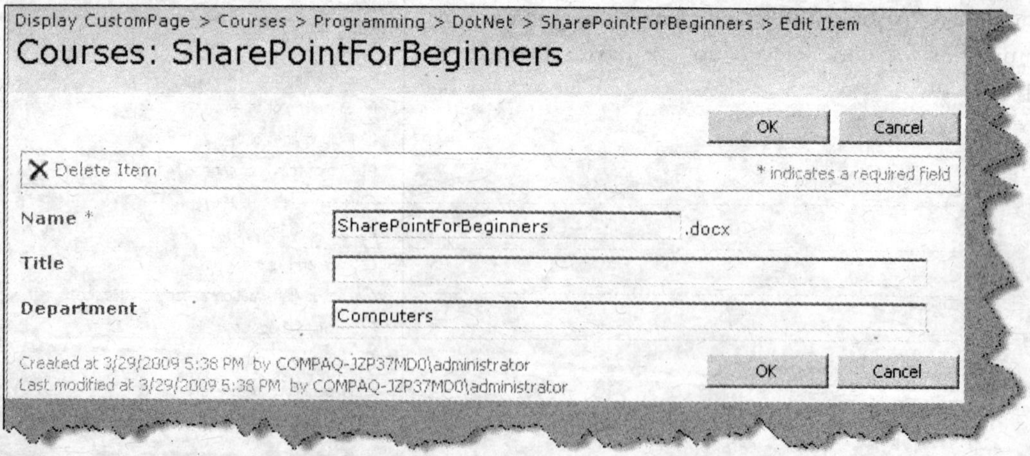

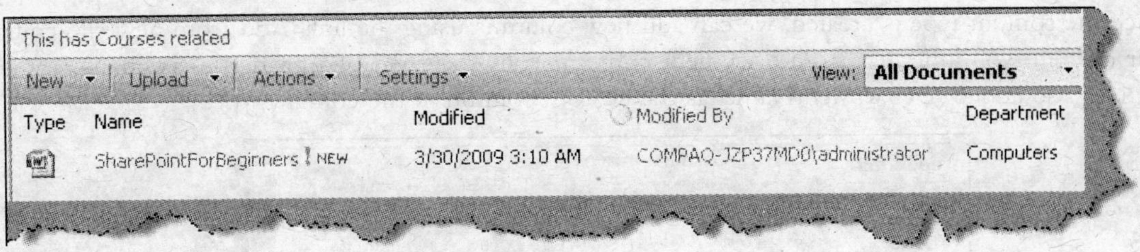

We can now use the custom column for search and applying filters.

What are content types in SharePoint?

Content types are extensions to custom types. Content types bring in central control and consistency on custom data type. For instance, we can add custom type as 'Department' while someone can add the custom field as 'Dept.' In other words, this can bring in inconsistency and we will not be able to query and filter data in a consistent manner or we can define a content type and then apply this content type across documents. In other words, we can really drive organization level policies using content types.

To create a content type, click on site action - site settings - from galleries section, click site content types and we will see a list of existing content types.

To create a new content type, click create hyperlink from the same screen which is showing list of content types.

We will be thrown up a screen where we need to specify the name of our content type, the parent content type and group for the same.

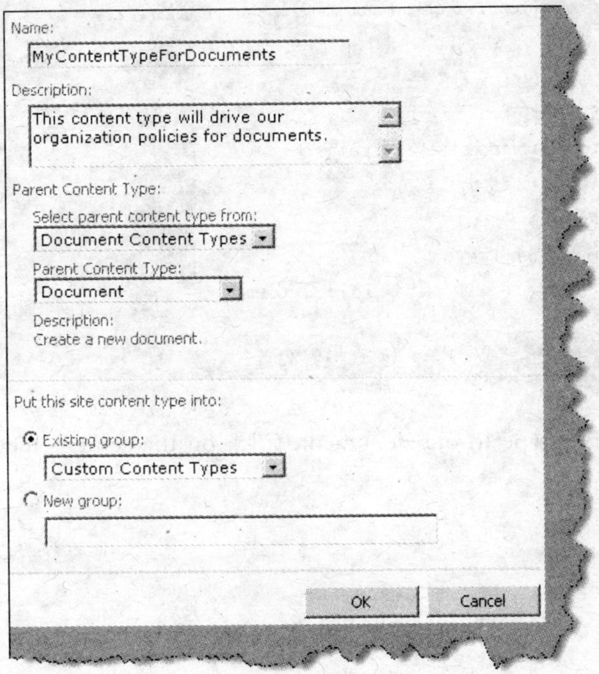

Once the content type is created, we can add new columns using the link 'Add from new site column.' Our custom type inherited from document content types so it had two properties i.e. name and title. We had also added 'DepartMentName' as the custom column in the content type.

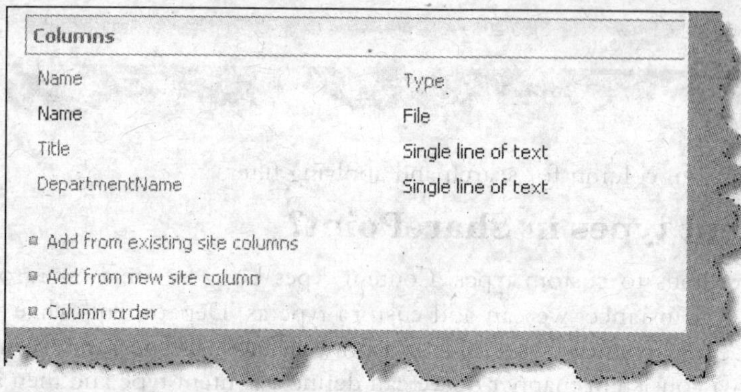

We can add new columns using the 'Add from new site column.' We had added the 'departmentname' custom field for the current instance. Below figure shows different options and data type for custom columns which are added.

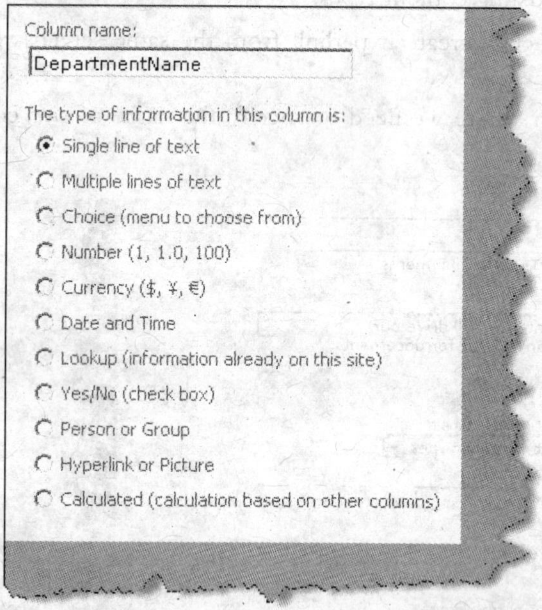

We can now apply this content type to our document. Click on the settings menu and then click on 'Document library settings.'

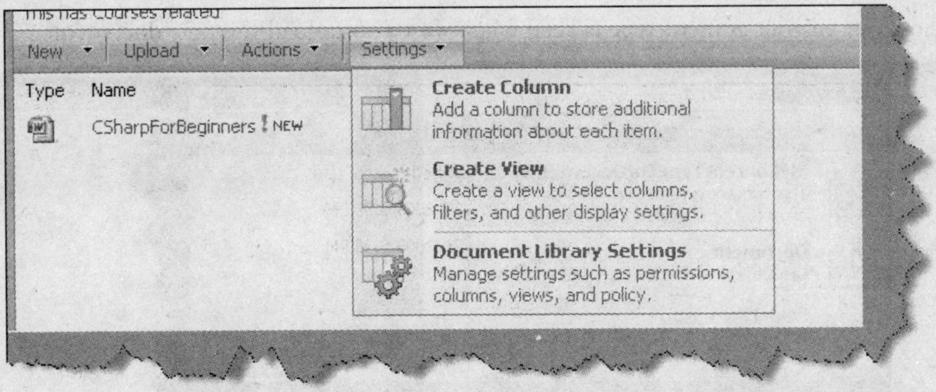

We will be popped up with the details of the content type. Click on 'Add from existing site content types' and select the custom content type we have just created i.e. 'MyContentTypeForDocuments.'

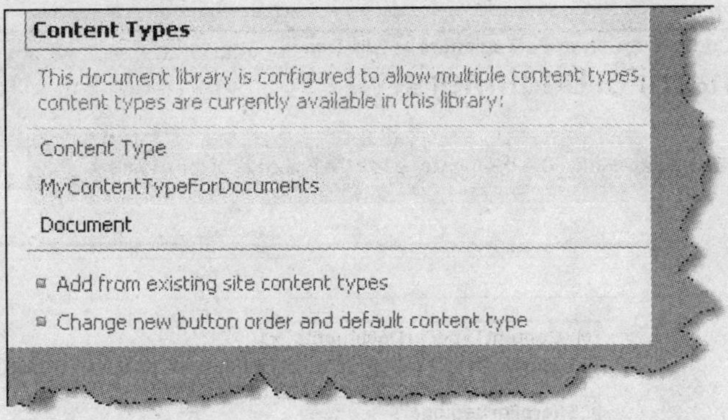

We can now select the content type for our document library.

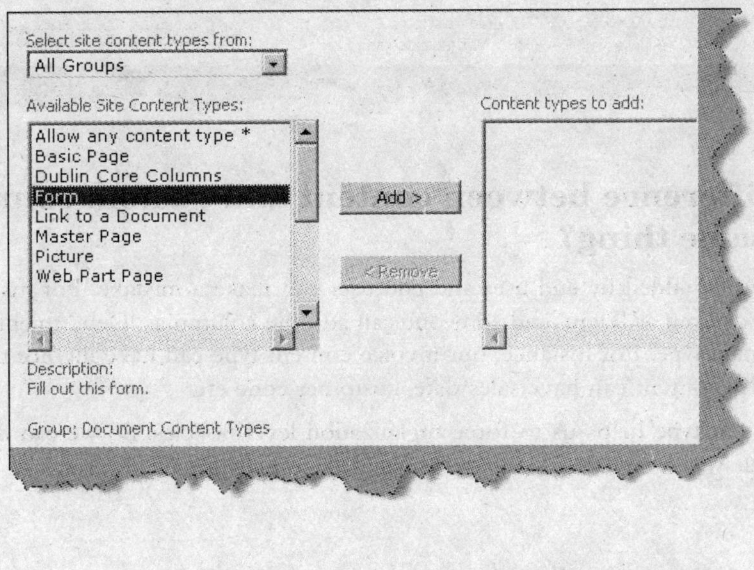

We can see how our custom content type is seen when we try to upload the new document.

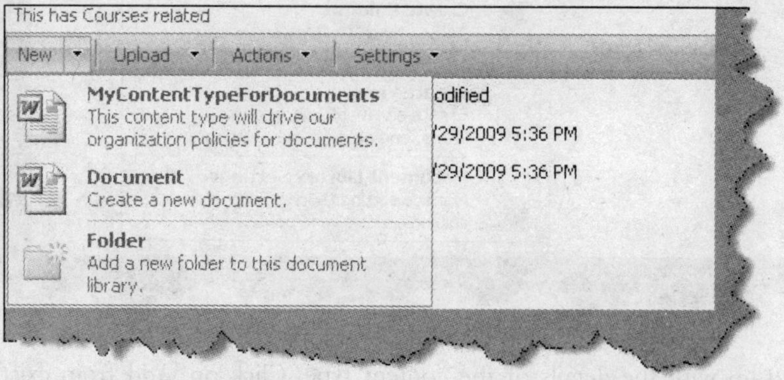

If we edit the properties, we can see the 'departmentname' custom column in our content type.

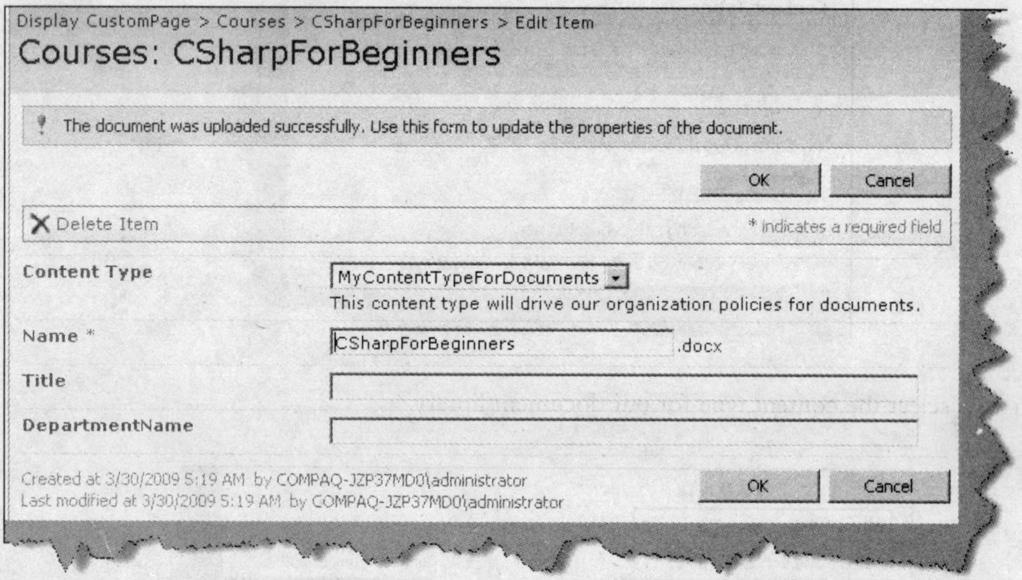

What's the difference between content and custom columns or do they do the same thing?

Custom columns can be added by end user and end user can make a mistake. For instance, someone can add the custom column as 'Dept' and someone can add the column as 'Departmentname.' Content define a document data type. For instance, our invoice content type can have invoice number, invoice amount etc. Our sales content can have sales date, customer code etc.

In other words content type helps us to force organization level policies. So we can define a content type at the site level. When any user wants to create a document library, he can use the appropriate content type. Let's say the organization wants to implement a policy saying that every document should have department name and version number. So the SharePoint administrator can create a content type called as 'CompanyContentType' and all document libraries can use this content type.

So we can use custom columns where the column is very much specific to that document library and will not be repeated and we can use the custom column. If we want to implement document level policy and fields across organization, we can use content types.

Can you elaborate more on List and Content Types in SharePoint?

SharePoint is all about data and collaboration of the data between different types of users. When we talk about data, it varies from user to user and different types of meta-data. For instance, below are four kinds of users: project manager, accountant, security personnel and HR.

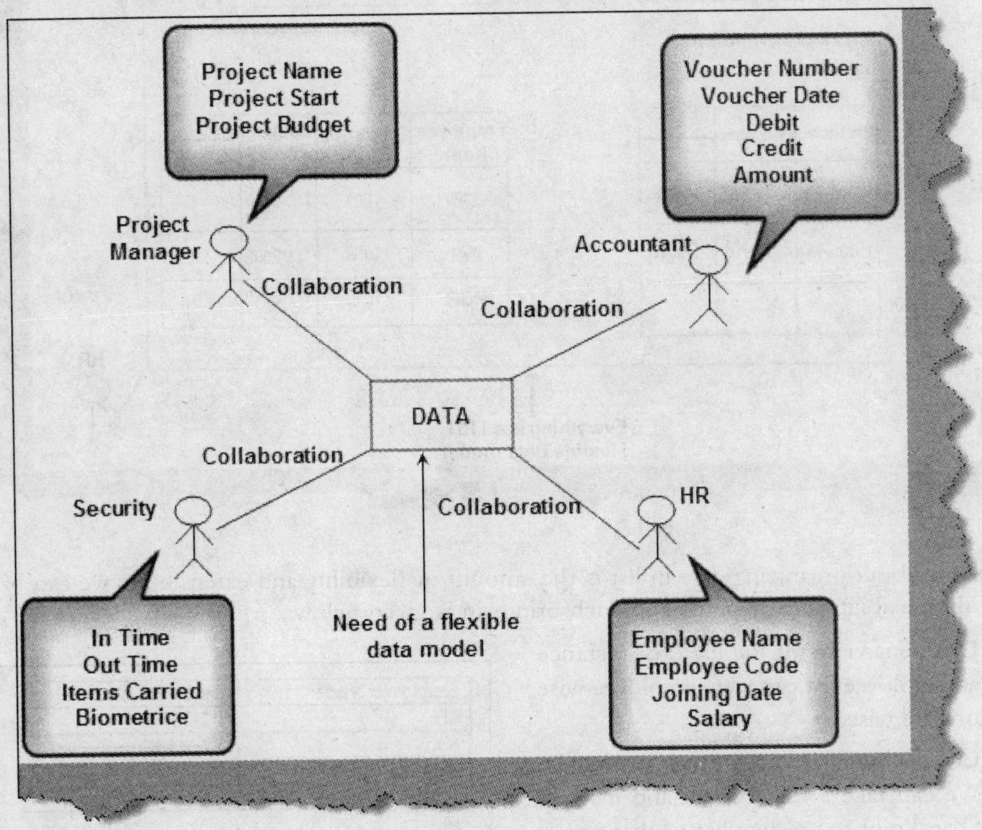

All these four users have different kind of data formats. For instance, the accountant needs to save data with different data types and fields like voucher number (20 character string), voucher date (MM/DD/YYYY), debit (Boolean true), credit (Boolean false) and amount (Double). The security needs in-time, out-time, items carried and biometrics data.

In order to bring a flexible collaborative data model which can be further extended, SharePoint brought in something called as List and Content Types. Data was visualized in terms of List data as shown below. With this approach, we can add more fields and content type on a need basis.

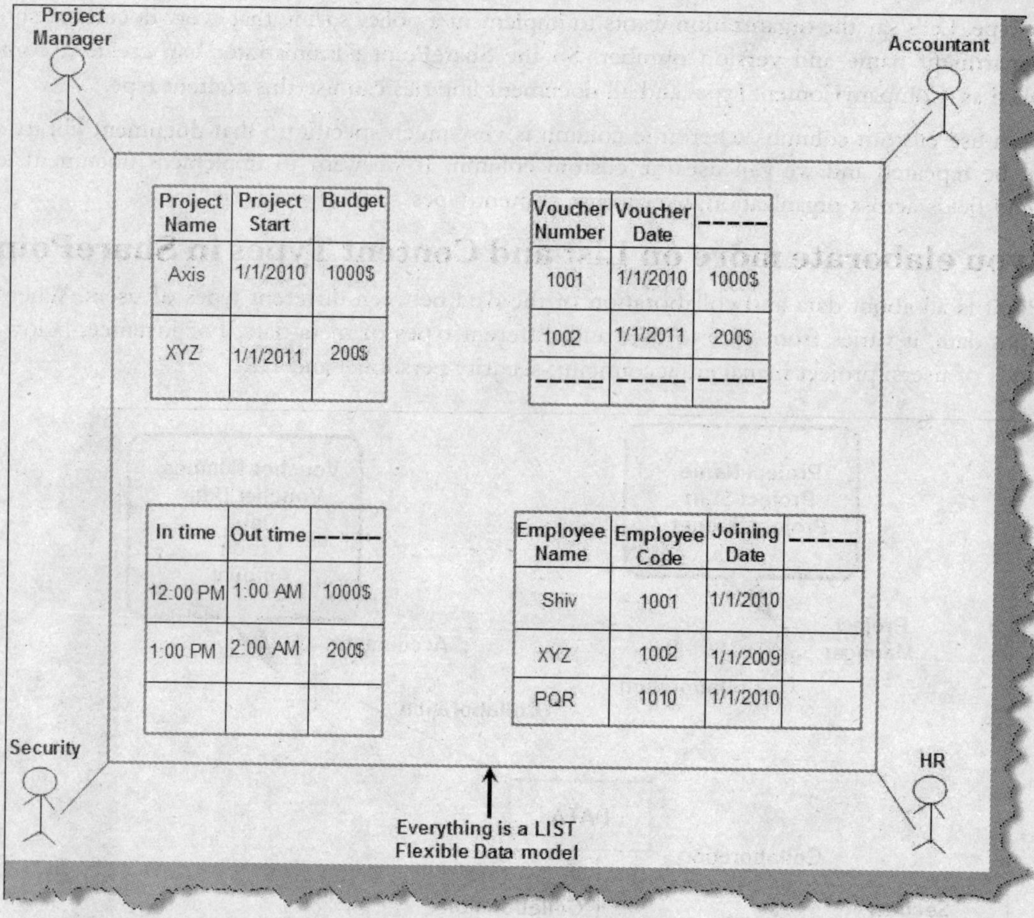

The best part about organizing data in list is the amount of flexibility and extensibility we can bring in. Some of the flexibility a list type of approach brings in is given below:

1. Different views of the list: For instance an employee list can view employee wise or date wise.
2. Create content from external list storage: We can take a Excel sheet and instruct SharePoint to create a list of that type.

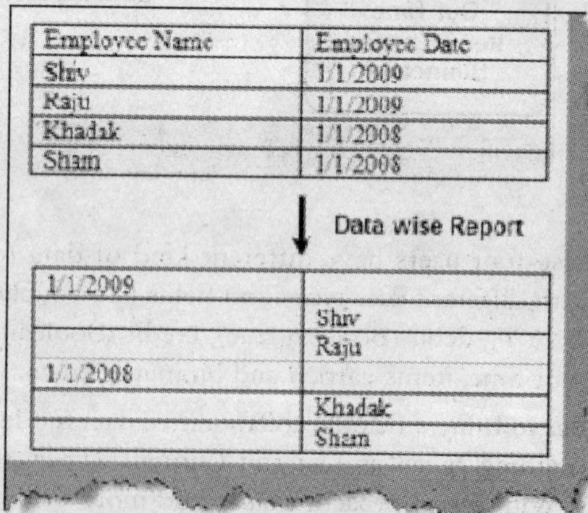

Which are the various readymade list types that SharePoint provides currently?

There are approximately thirteen different readymade list types, below mentioned are some of the most used ones.:

1. **Document library:** Used for collaborating on documents with support for versioning, check-in, check-out and workflow. It includes support for deep integration with Microsoft Office.
2 **Form library:** Used to store XML documents and forms for use with Microsoft Office InfoPath.
3. **Wiki page library:** Used for collaborative Web pages based on wiki pages, which are dynamically generated and collaboratively edited Web pages.
4. **Picture library:** A specialized document library enhanced for use with pictures. Includes support for slide shows, thumbnails, and simple editing through Microsoft Office Picture Manager.
5. **Announcements:** Used for simple sharing of timely news with support for expiration.
6. **Contacts:** A list for tracking people and contact information, with support for integration into Microsoft Office Outlook and other WSS-compatible contacts applications.
7. **Discussions:** A simple list for threaded discussions with support for approval and managing discussion threads.
8. **Links:** A list for managing hyperlinks.
9. **Calendar:** A list for tracking upcoming events and deadlines. Includes support for integration and synchronization with Office Outlook.
10. **Tasks:** A list of activity-based items that can integrate with workflow.
11. **Project tasks:** An enhanced tasks list with support for Gannt chart rendering and integration with Microsoft Office Project.
12. **Issue tracking:** A list for tracking issues and resolution, with support for prioritization.
13. **Custom list :** An empty list definition for extending with custom columns, or created using Microsoft Office Excel spreadsheets.

What is Windows Workflow Foundation?

WWF is a programming model for building workflow-enabled applications on Windows. System. Workflow namespace has all the necessary modules to develop any type of workflow.

What is a Workflow?

A Workflow is a set of activities, which is stored as model and they depict a process. Below figure depicts clearly the difference between Workflow and Activity. Every task is an activity and group of activity depicts a complete workflow. Workflow is run by the Workflow runtime engine.

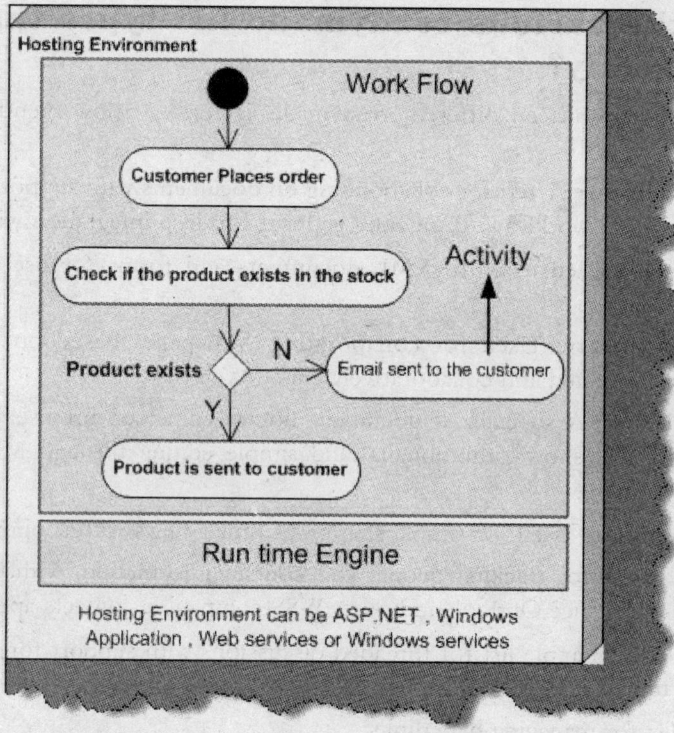

Workflow Foundation Architecture

Workflow model can be written in pure .NET code, pure XAML or Mix of XAML and .NET Code. A workflow model is compiled and can execute under Windows, ASP.NET, Web services or Windows services application.

What are different types of Workflow in Windows Workflow foundation?

There are two basics type of workflow Sequential Workflow and State machines workflow.

A sequential workflow has clear start and finish boundaries. Workflow controls execution in Sequential workflow. In sequential execution, one task is executed after other. Sequential workflow is more rigid in format and execution path has a determistic in nature.

A State machine workflow is more dynamic in nature. Workflow has states and the state waits for events to help it move to next state. In State machine execution path is undetermestic nature.

Below figure shows visual conceptualization of fundamentals. We can see in Sequential workflow the execution path is very determent. Shiv performs the entire task sequentially and these tasks are very determent. Now have a look at the second workflow. Every state goes to other state when it receives some external events. For instance when Shiv is seeing star trek there is an event of flashing news which triggers him to see the flashing news.

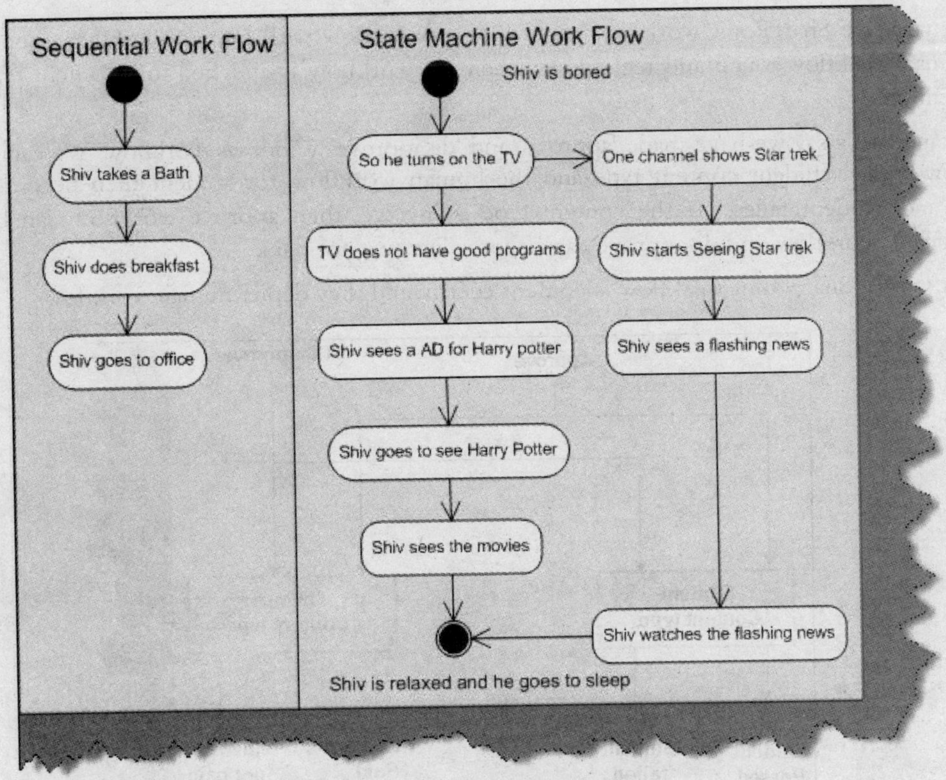

Sequential and State machine workflow

Is SharePoint workflow same as Windows workflow?

The first basic important point to note is thay SharePoint workflow and Windows are not different entities. The base for SharePoint workflow is window workflow. In other words, SharePoint workflow sits on the top of Windows workflow and adds the human workflow flavor.

The below figure reflects the broader definition of SharePoint workflow. It takes the core Windows workflow from .NET framework and then applies content-centric workflow on it. Content centric workflows are nothing but simple Windows workflow attached to list, documents and custom contents.

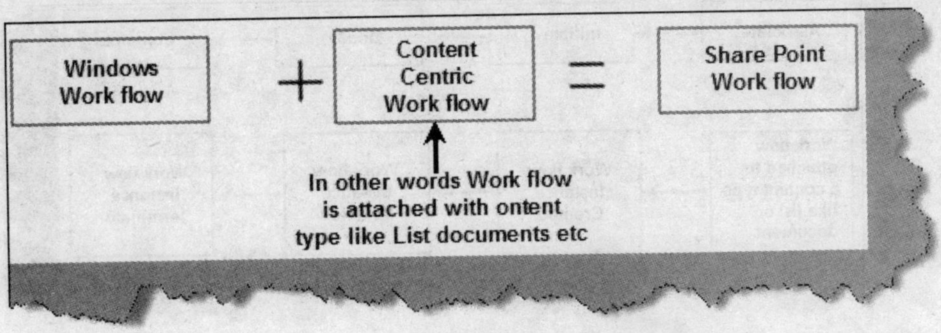

Figure: Content type workflow

We can visualize SharePoint workflows as Windows workflow with human workflow touch and feel. The human workflow touch and feel comes when the workflow is attached to a content type like list, document etc.

For instance, let's say we have made 'approve' and 'disapprove' Windows workflow. We can attach this workflow with a student content type and the human workflow for student then becomes 'student passed' and 'student failed.' If the content type is invoice, then approve workflow can become an 'invoice paid' workflow and disapprove can become 'invoice not paid.'

In other words, SharePoint workflow is content-centric and they depict human workflow.

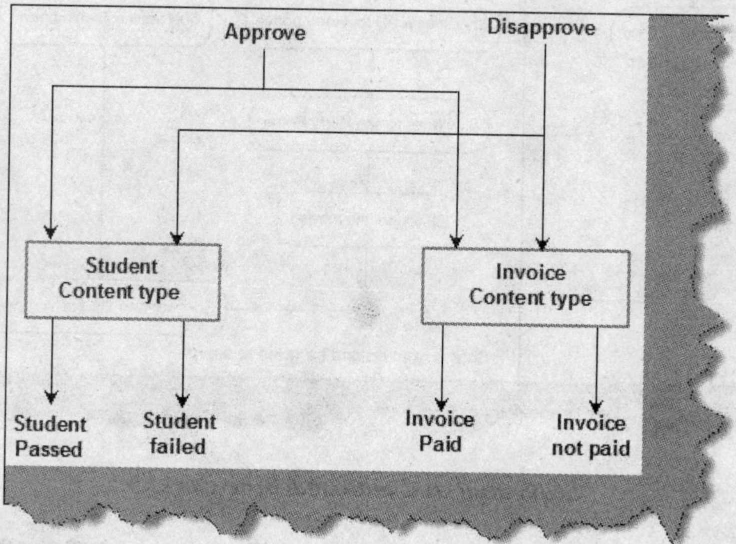

Figure: Approve and Disapprove

What are the different stages of SharePoint workflow life cycle?

SharePoint workflow cycle is very much unique to SharePoint environment. SharePoint workflows are always connected in context with SharePoint content like list or a document.

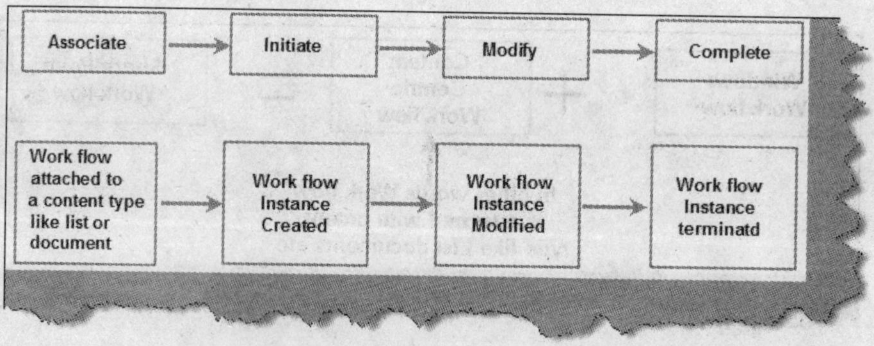

Four different stages in SharePoint workflow

There are four stages in the SharePoint workflow cycle: associate, initiate, modify and complete.

Associate: As said workflows in SharePoint are always talked in context with a content type. So the first step is to associate a workflow with a content type like list or a document.

Initiate: The second step is to initiate the workflow instance. Workflows are nothing but classes finally, so a workflow instance needs to be created to start the workflow in action.

Modify: Later the workflow instance is modified as per the workflow stages.

Complete: Finally the workflow object is terminated.

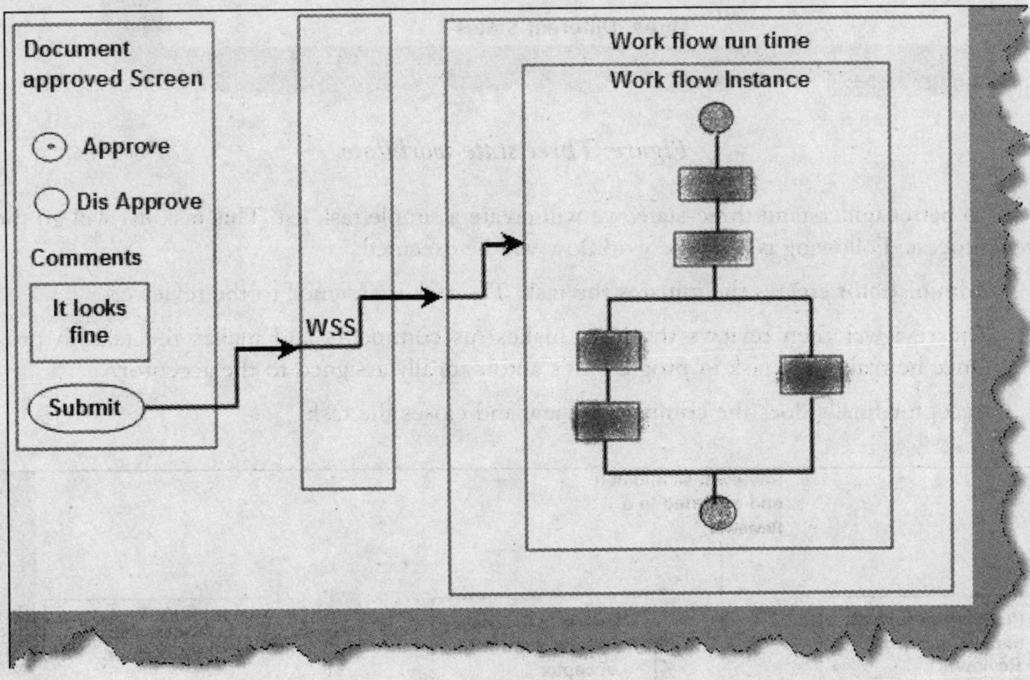

Figure ;- Screen and SharePoint workflow

The web forms of SharePoint interact with WSS which in turn then interacts with the Windows workflow runtime. The Windows workflow runtime passes details to the appropriate workflow instance depending on the data passed by WSS. The SharePoint workflow instance then runs the workflow logic and takes appropriate action accordingly.

What is a three-state workflow in SharePoint?

Three-state workflow helps organization to track workflows, which has three states and two transitions. It's designed to track status of list item, task etc. With each transition between states, the workflow assigns the task to some person and sends an email alert about the task.

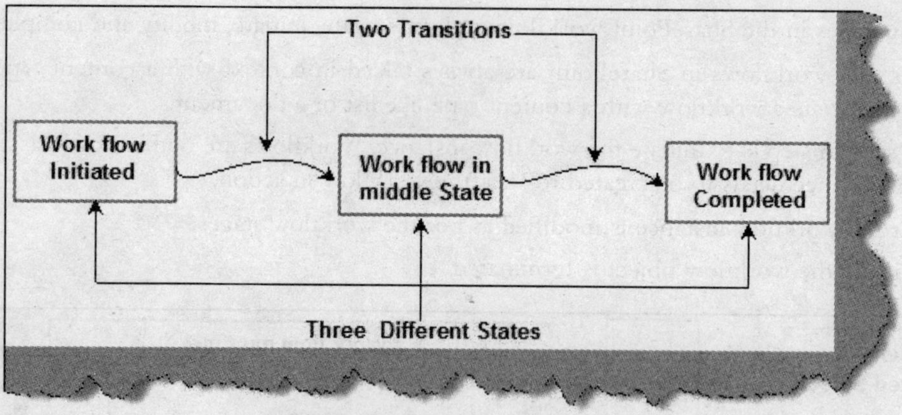

Figure: Three state workflow

In order to better understand three-state, we will create a simple task list. This task list will go through a review process. Following is how the workflow will be executed:

- Administrator creates the initiates the task. The task is assigned to the reviewer.
- The reviewer then reviews the task, makes his comments and makes the task in progress. Once he makes the task in progress, it's automatically assigned to the acceptor.
- Acceptor finally does the complete review and closes the task

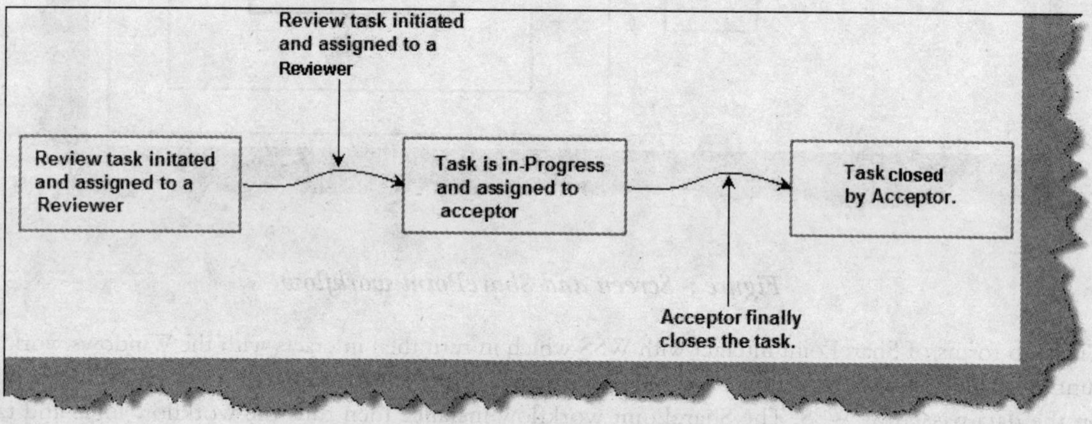

Figure: Three-state example

The first thing is to add two users in our computer domain: one is the reviewer who will review and the other is the acceptor who will close the task initiative.

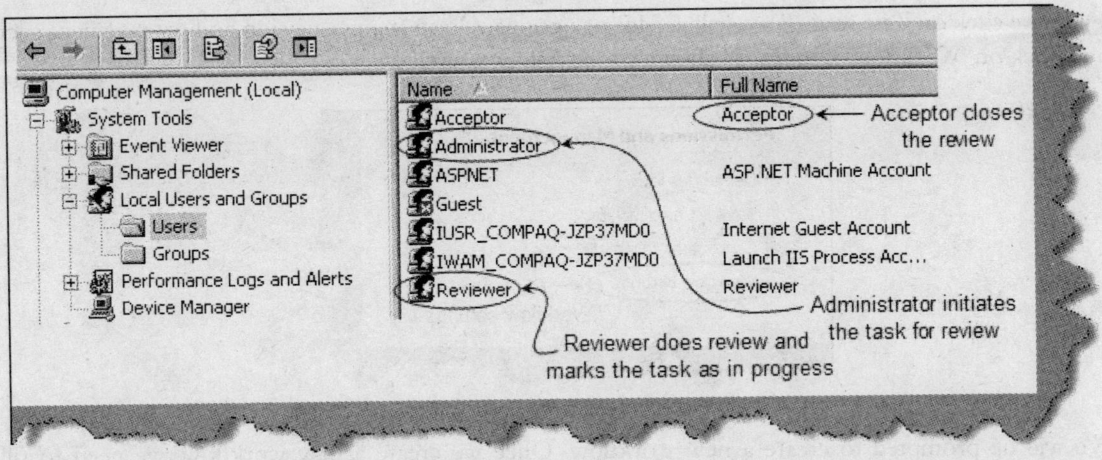

To see the workflow, go to Site actions ' Site settings ' Workflows. We will see the 'Three-state' workflow as shown in the below figure.

Let's first create a team site, so click on Site actions ' Site libraries and lists ' create a new content ' Sites and workspaces and give some nice name like 'My team site.'

Now click on 'My team site,' click on tasks and then click on list settings as shown in the below figure.

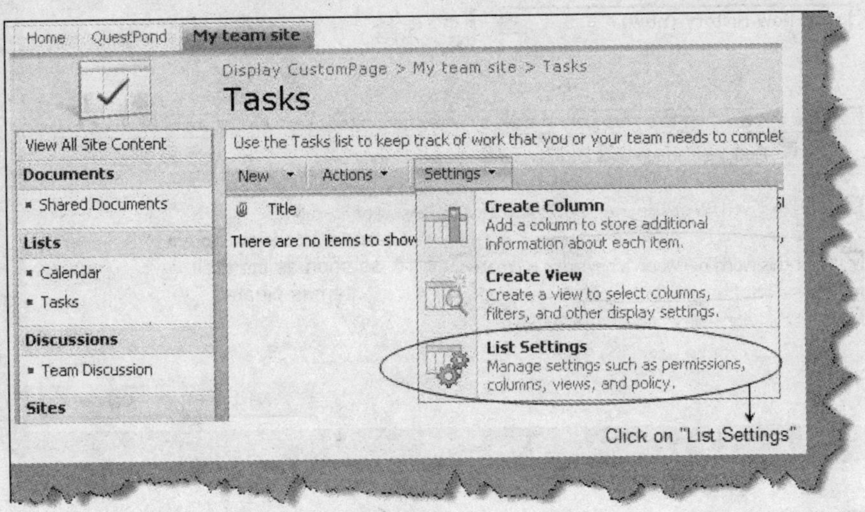

Once we click on 'List setting' we will see lot of options. Go to the permission and management section and click on 'Workflow Settings' as shown in the below figure.

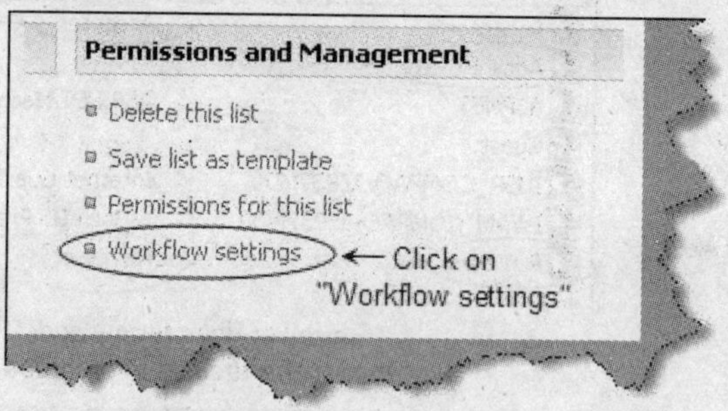

We will be prompted to create a new workflow. Once we create a new workflow, we need to fill in details of the workflow as shown in the below figure. Give a nice name to the workflow, for the current sample, we have given the name as 'My workflow.' We have specified saying that create workflow as soon as the item is created.

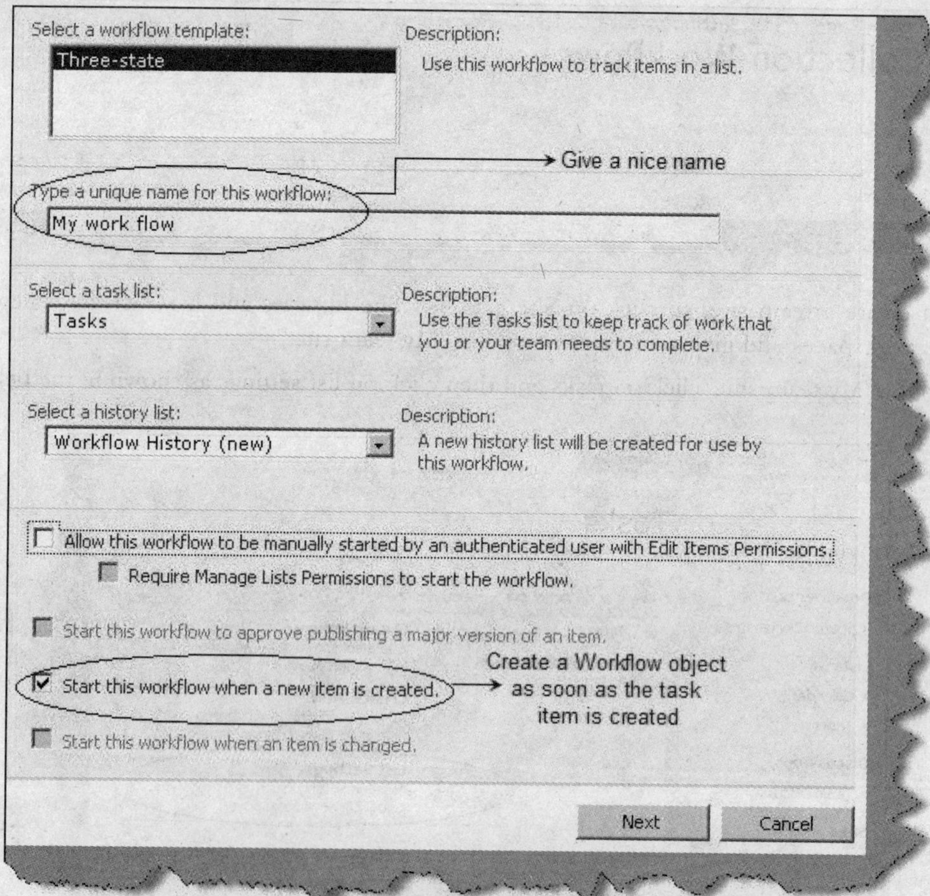

A workflow will have three states: an initial state, middle state and final state. These states will be decided on the choice field of the task list. So when the status is having value 'Not Started,' then the workflow is in the initial state. When the status is with value 'In progress' then the workflow is in middle state. When the status is completed that means the workflow object will be terminated and the workflow will be marked as closed.

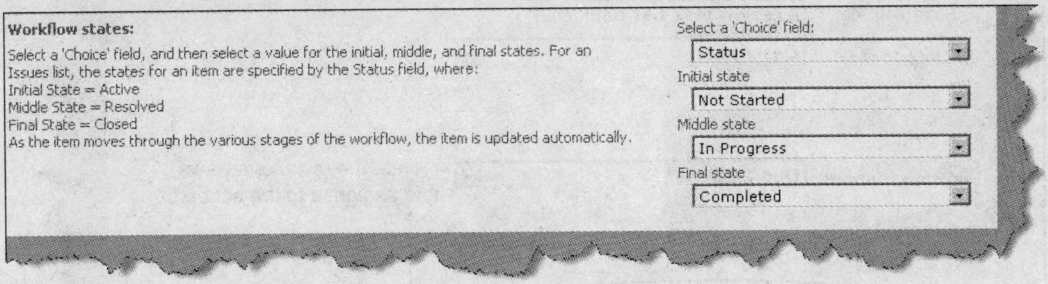

Now the second step is to tell the three-state workflow what needs to be done on every workflow state. So let's fill what should happen when the workflow is initiated. When the workflow is initiated, it will be allocated to the user 'reviewer.' We can see the values visually in the below figure.

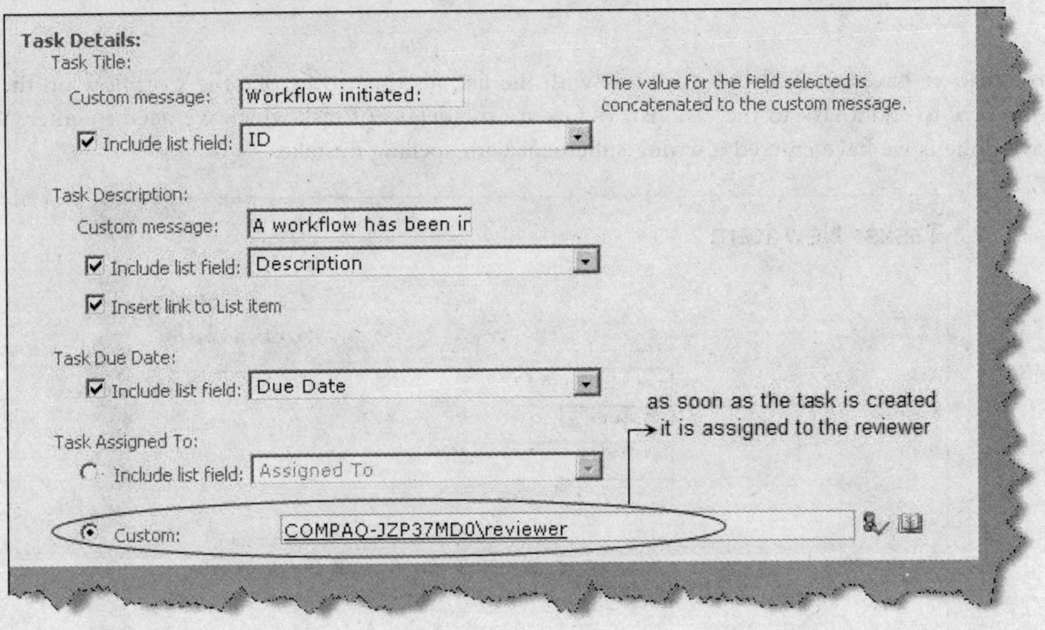

When the reviewer reviews the document, it's assigned to an acceptor. So when the workflow is in the in progress state, it's assigned to the acceptor for final closure.

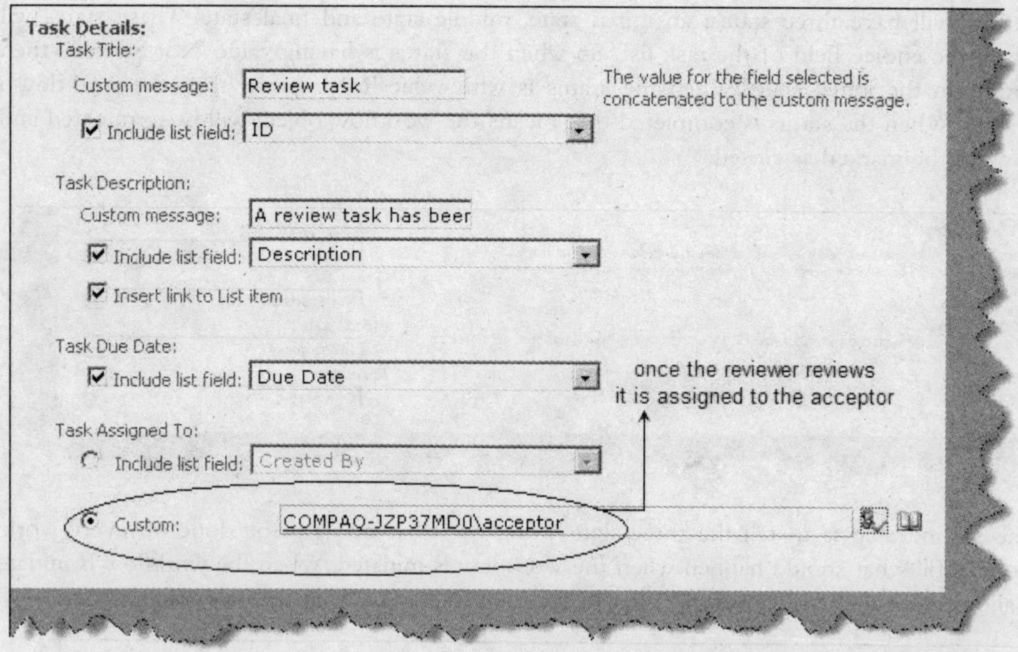

So now that we have attached the workflow with the list, it's time to invoke the workflow on the list. Click on new to add a task to the task list. Below are the details of task which we need to enter. What we have done is we have entered a wrong statement with spelling mistakes.

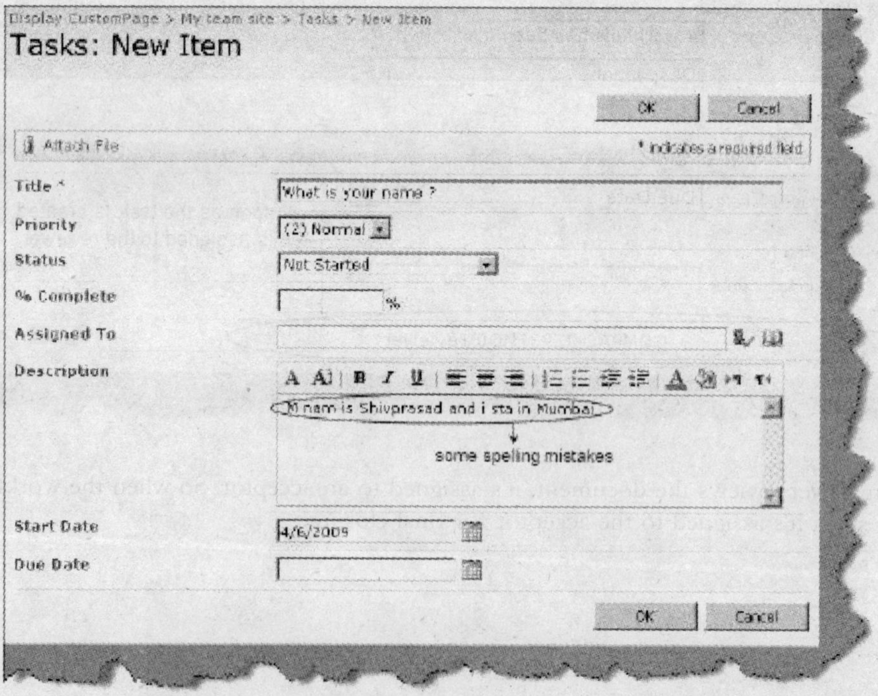

Now as soon as we click ok, we will see that the task is assigned to a reviewer.

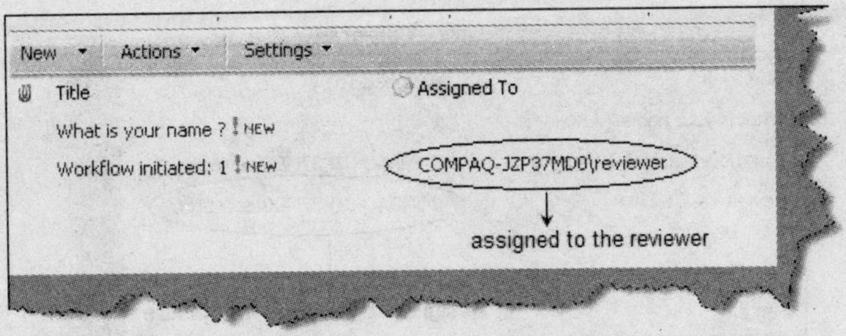

Now login as reviewer and click on 'What is your name'?

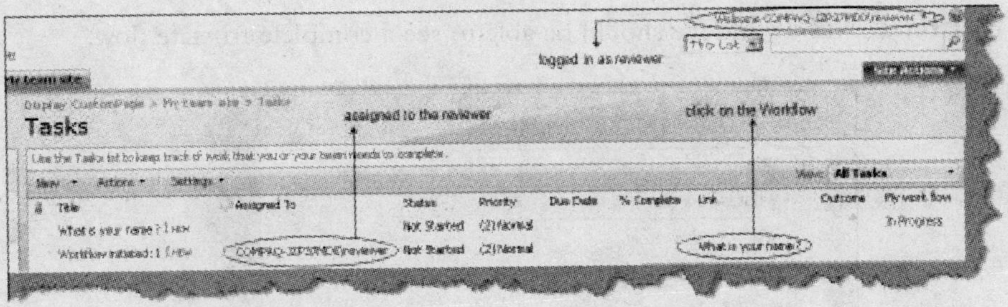

Now as reviewer, we will correct the sentence and mark the task as 'In progress.'

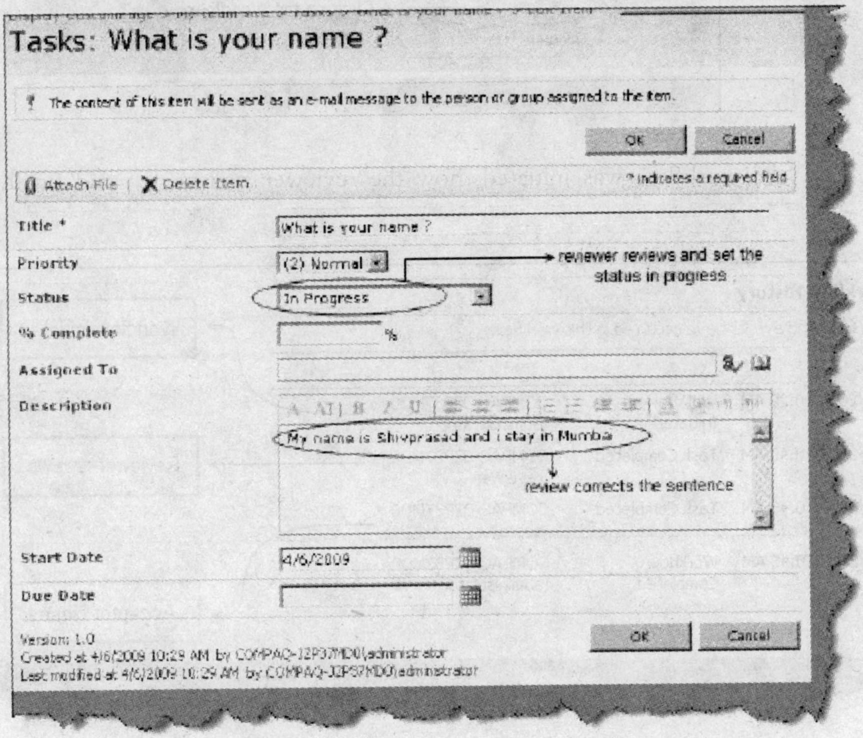

As soon as we mark the task as in progress, it's assigned to the acceptor. Now login as an acceptor and mark the task as complete.

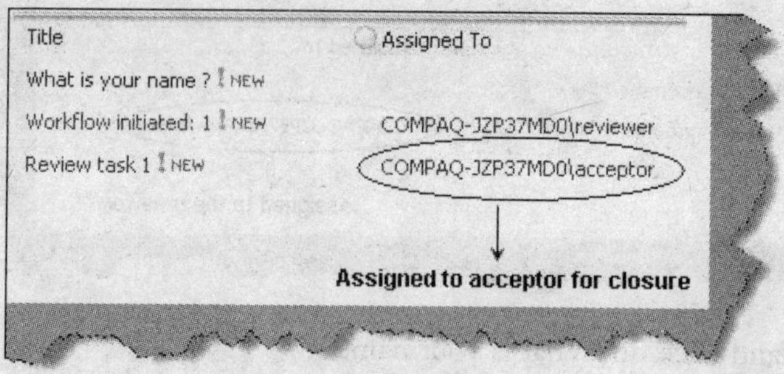

Once done, click on workflows and we should be able to see a complete tri-state flow.

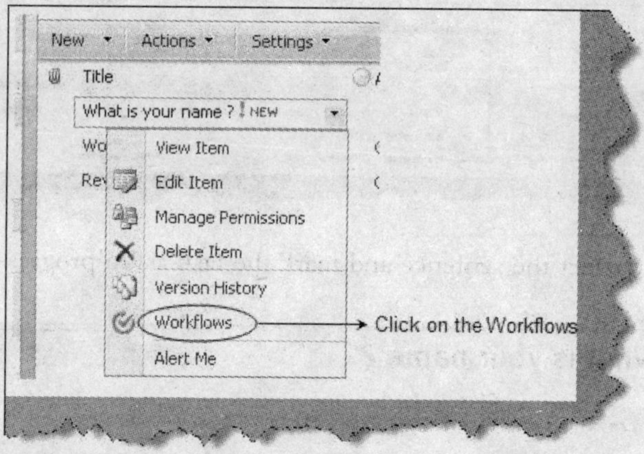

We can see how the workflow was initiated, how the reviewer reviewed it and finally the acceptor closed it.

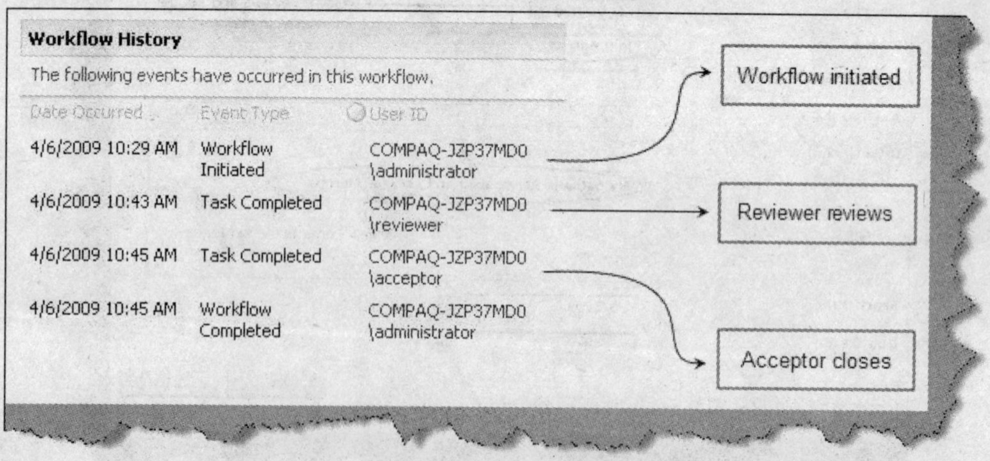

Does SharePoint only have three-state workflow?

If we install WSS, then we will only see one workflow that is three-state workflow. But with MOSS, we will see 4 more workflows which cover almost all the scenarios we will ever need for a workflow.

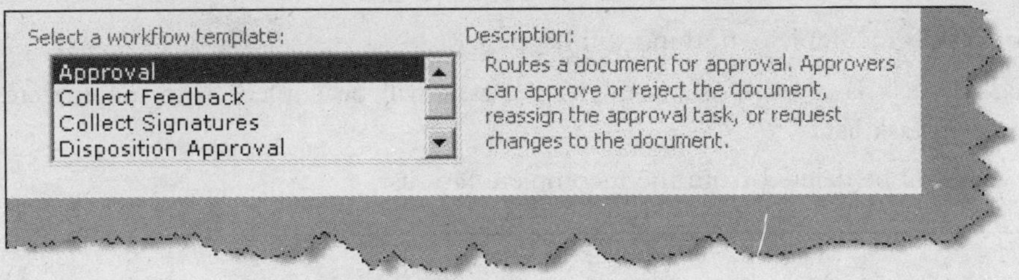

Workflow name	Description
Approval	Routes a document for approval. Approvers can approve or reject the document, reassign the approval task, or request changes to the document.
Collect feedback	Routes a document for review. Reviewers can provide feedback, which is compiled and sent to the document owner when the workflow has completed.
Collect signatures	Gathers signatures needed to complete a Microsoft Office document. This workflow can be started only from within an Office client.
Disposition workflow	Manages document expiration and retention by allowing participants to decide whether to retain or delete expired documents.

How can we create SharePoint workflow using SharePoint designer?

SharePoint designer helps us to create workflows and attach the workflows to a content type like list, document etc. In other words, SharePoint designer creates workflows and publishes the workflow on the SharePoint server site.

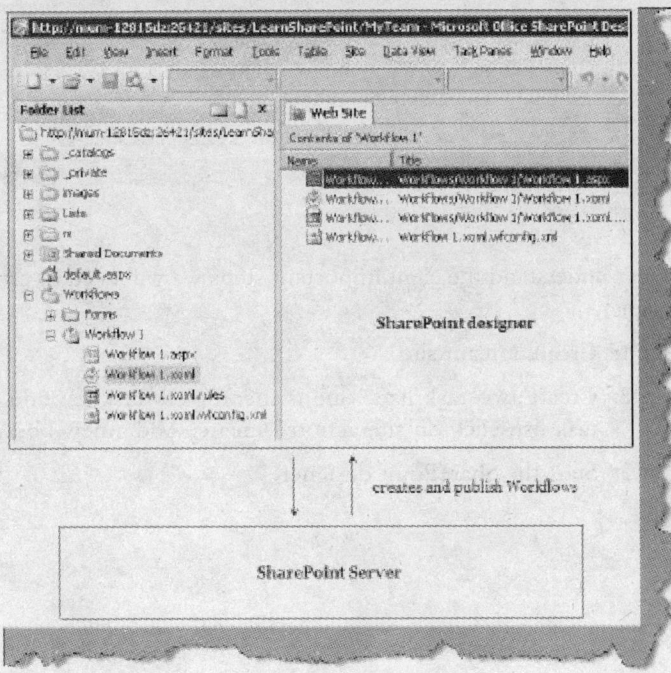

To understand it better, we will build a simple workflow of completed and incomplete tasks. We will create two lists one is the incomplete tasks and the other the completed tasks. The workflow will flow something like this:

- User will create a task and enter the status of the task.
- If the task is incomplete, nothing will happen.
- Once the task is marked as complete, the task will be copied from incomplete task list to completed task list.
- The task will be deleted from the incomplete task list.

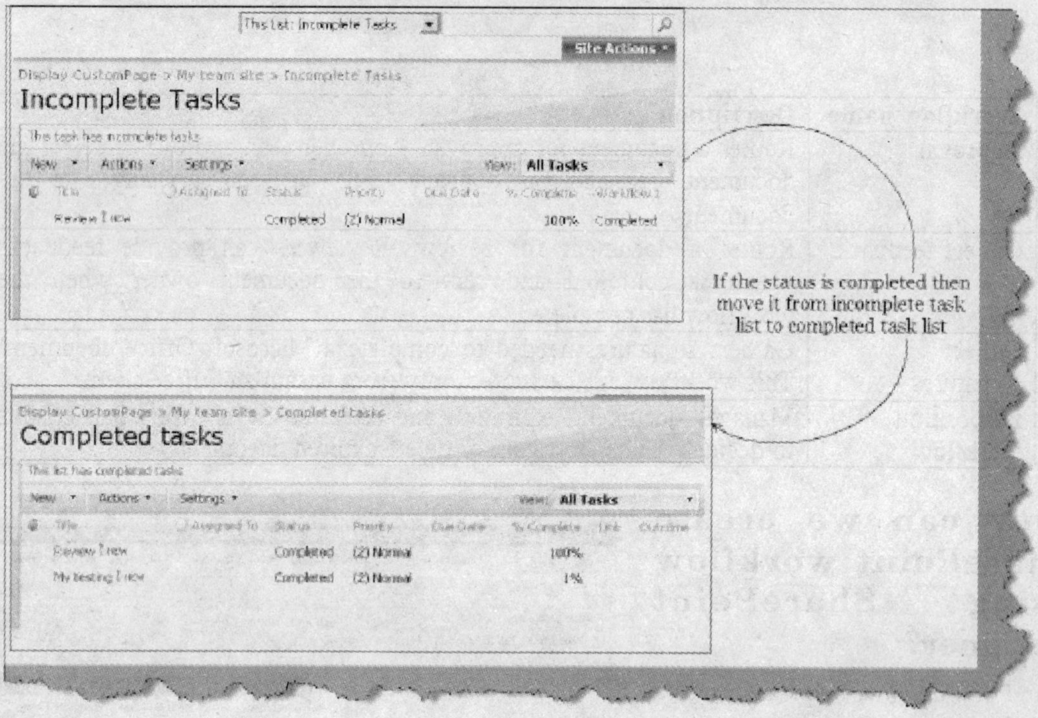

So let's understand the eight important steps we will need to create the above workflow using SharePoint designer:

Step 1: Create a team site.

Step 2: Create two task lists: one is incomplete task list and the other completed task list. To create task list, click on site action ' Create: Add a new library list ' create a task.

Step 3: Start the SharePoint designer.

Step 4: Open the site in our SharePoint designer using click on file 'open site.

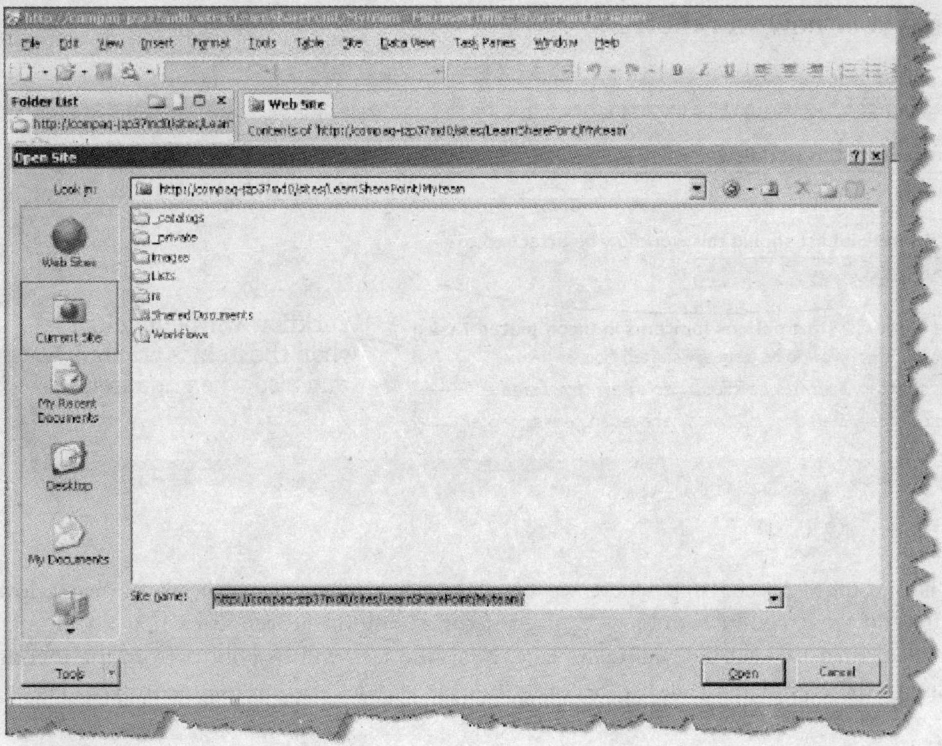

Step 5: Go to workflows by clicking on file ' new ' SharePoint content and click ok as shown in the below figure.

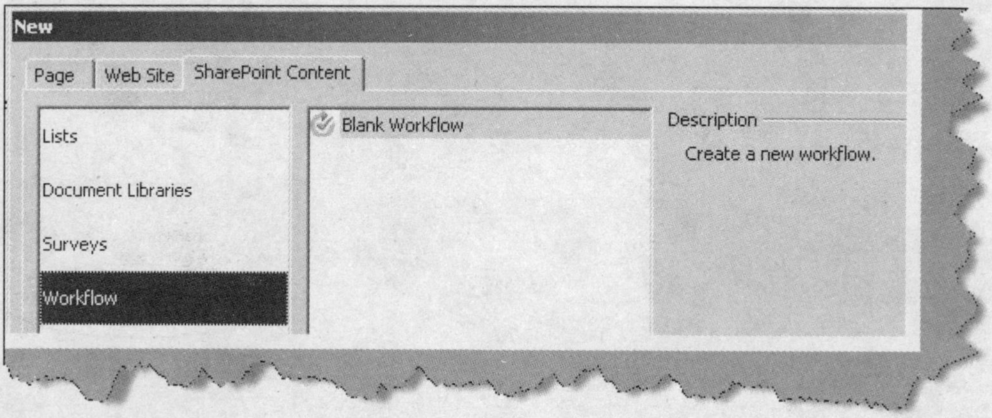

Step 6: This is an important step. In this step, we define two important things: first is this workflow will be attached to which list. Currently we have attached the workflow to incomplete tasks list. Second, we need to define the events on which the workflow should be activated. For the current scenario, we have considered two events: one when the item is created and the second when the item is updated.

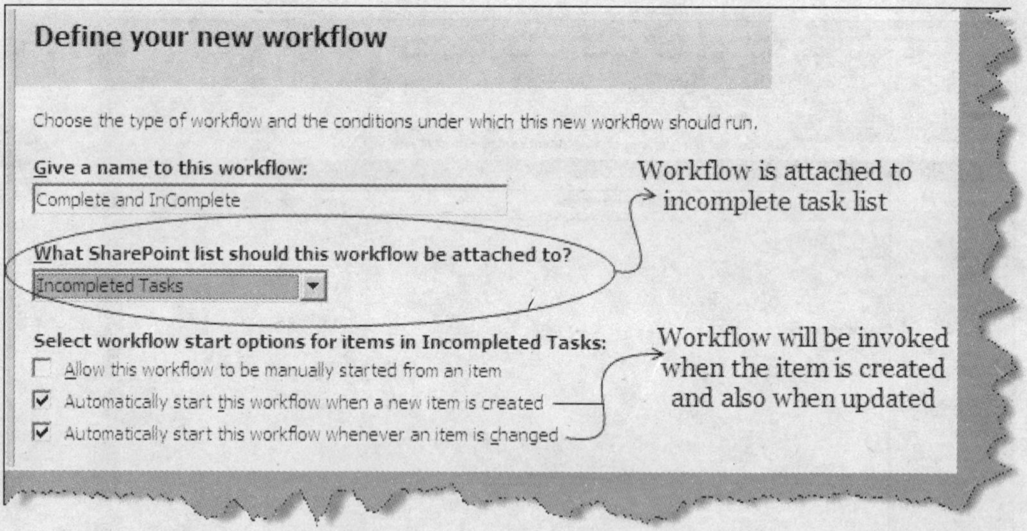

Step 7: This is one more crucial step where we need to define on what condition the workflow will execute and what action should take place if the condition is true. So when a task status is completed, then two actions will take place. First, the task will be copied from the incomplete task list to the completed task list. Second, the task is deleted from the incomplete task list.

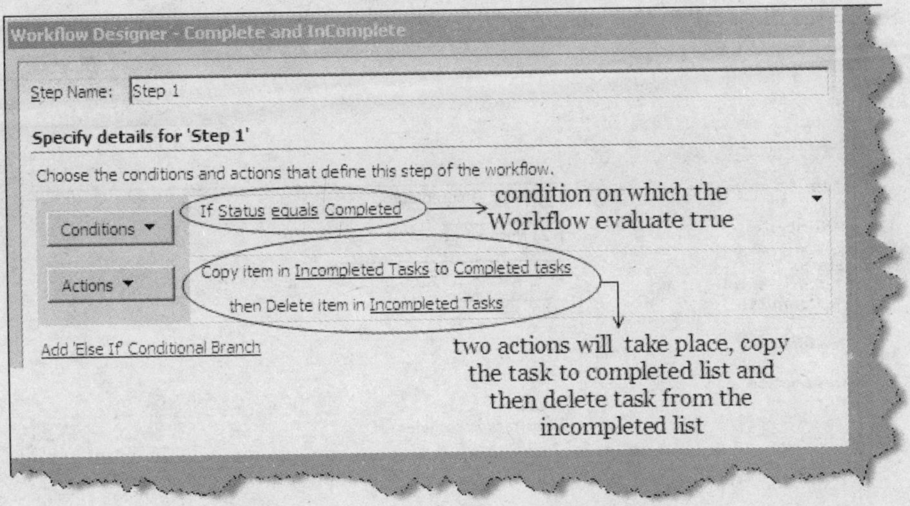

Once we click finish, we can see the workflow created in the SharePoint designer. This workflow is also published to the SharePoint server.

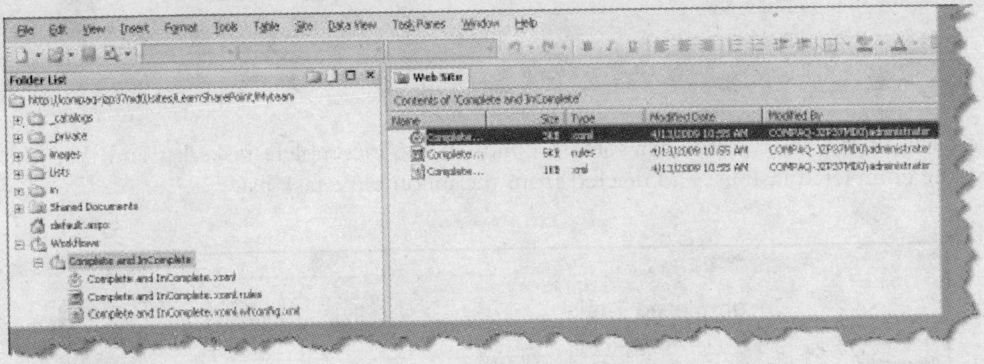

We can see if the workflow is associated with the incomplete task list. Go to incomplete tasks ' Settings ' List settings ' Workflow settings, we can see the workflow is attached to the incomplete task list.

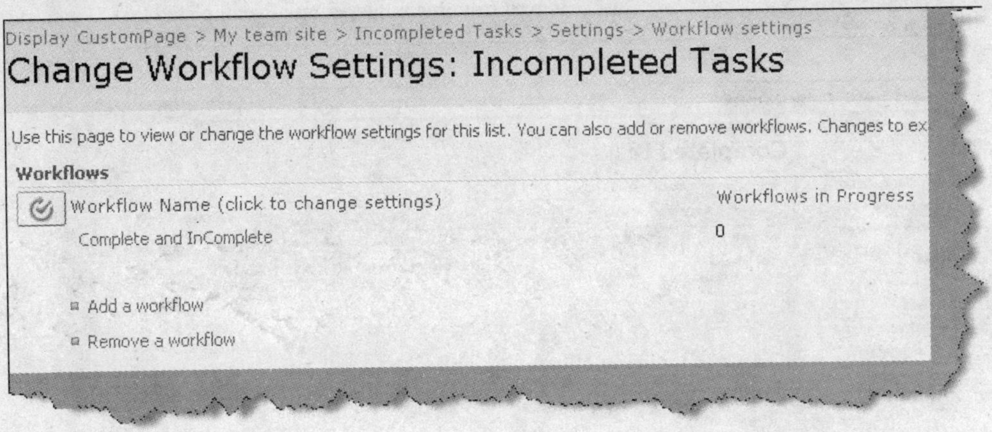

Step 8: To see the workflow in action, go to incomplete task list and create a task with status completed.

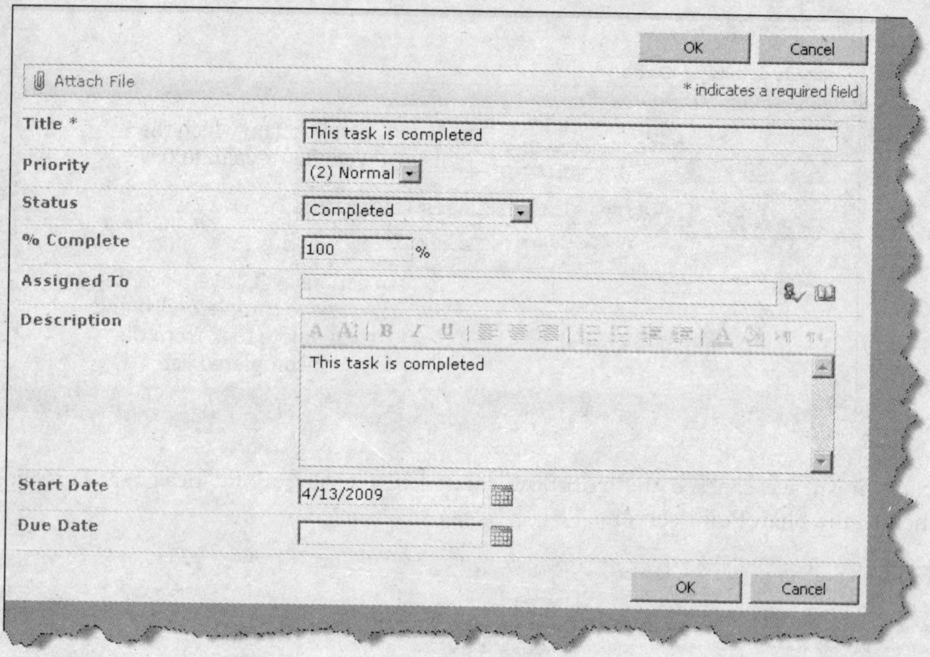

Once we click ok, we see the task for some seconds in the incomplete tasks list and then the task is copied to the completed task list and deleted from the incomplete task list.

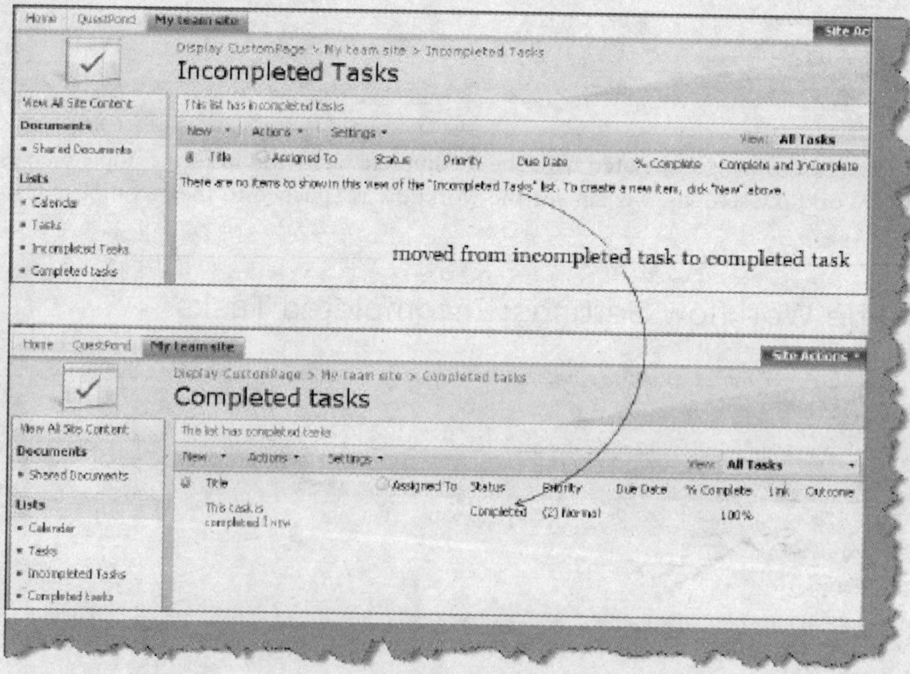

What is Infopath?

Infopath was introduced in 2003 as a part of office system. Infopath helps us to design forms which can serve as user inputs to save and retrieve data.

In what format is the Infopath form design saved?

Infopath works completely on XML technology. The form design layout is saved as XSD schema internally. We can also generate views using Infopath. When the views are generated, it uses XSLT to render the views. The data entered in Infopath is saved in XML format. In other words, Infopath is completely XML centric.

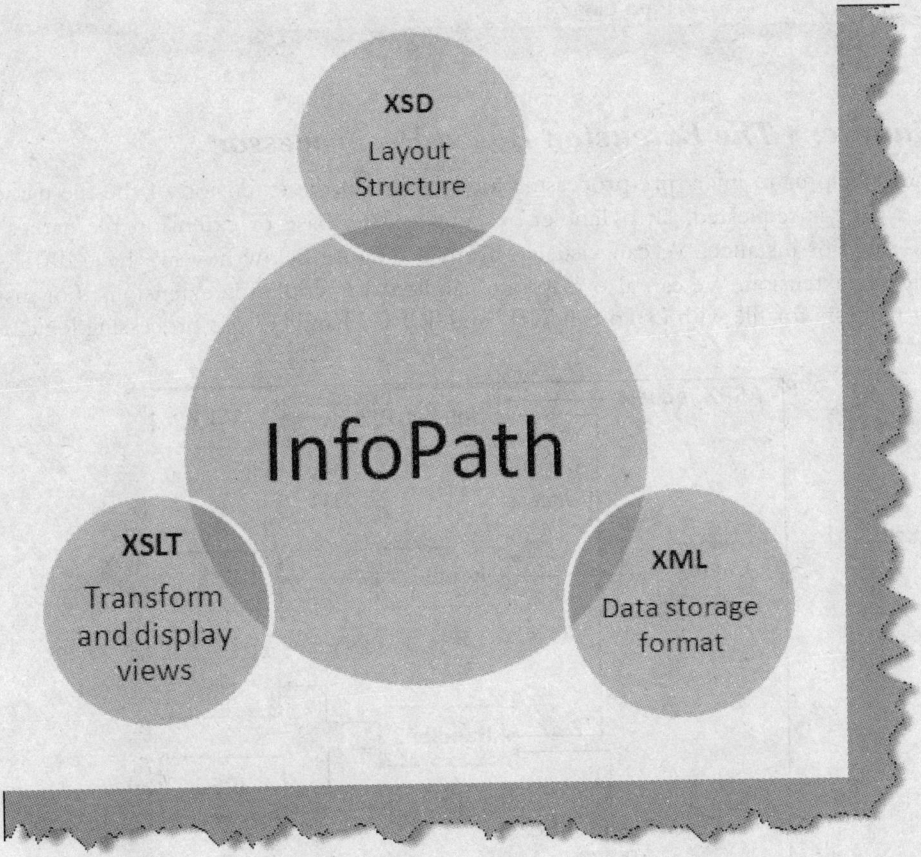

Reference

HttpModule and HttpHandler

Many times, we need to inject some kind of logic before the page is requested. Some of the commonly used pre-processing logics are stat counters, URL rewriting, authentication/authorization and many more. We can do this in the code behind but then that can lead to lot of complication and tangled code. The code behind will not solve the purpose because in some implementations like authorization, we want the logic to execute before it reaches the resource. ASP.NET provides two ways of injecting logic in the request pipeline HttpHandlers and HttpModules.

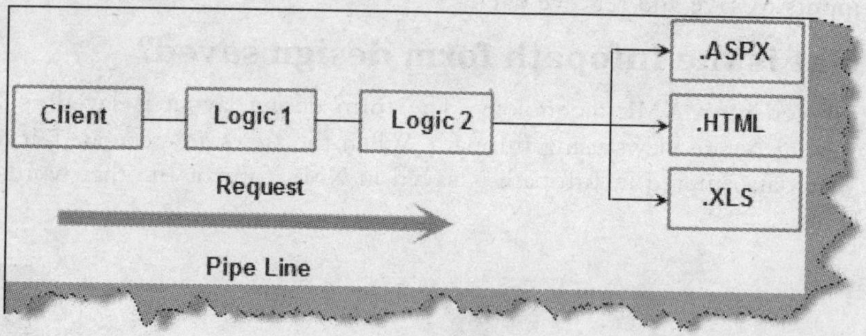

HttpHandler - The Extension Based Preprocessor

HttpHandler help us to inject pre-processing logic based on the extension of the file name requested. So when a page is requested, HttpHandler executes on the base of extension file names and on the base of verbs. For instance, we can visualize from the figure below how we have different handlers mapped to file extension. We can also map one handler to multiple file extensions. For instance, when any client requests for file with extension 'GIF' and 'JPEG,' handler3 pre-processing logic executes.

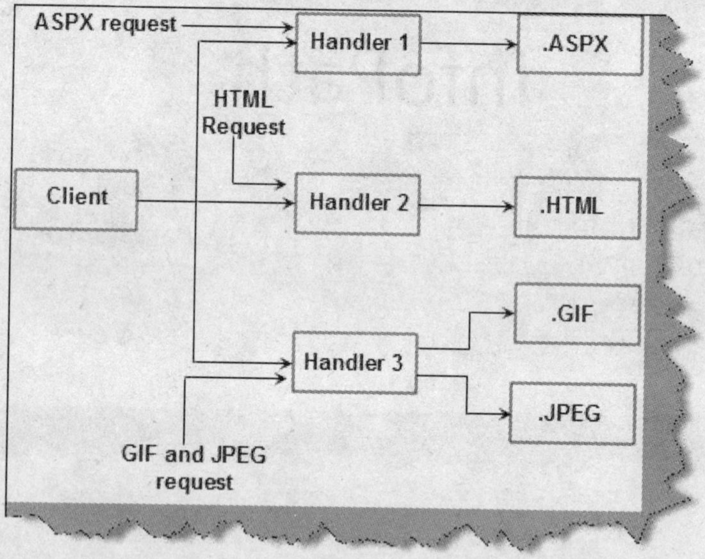

HttpModule - The Event Based Preprocessor

HttpModule is an event based methodology to inject pre-processing logic before any resource is requested. When any client sends a request for a resource, the request pipeline emits a lot of events as shown in the figure below:

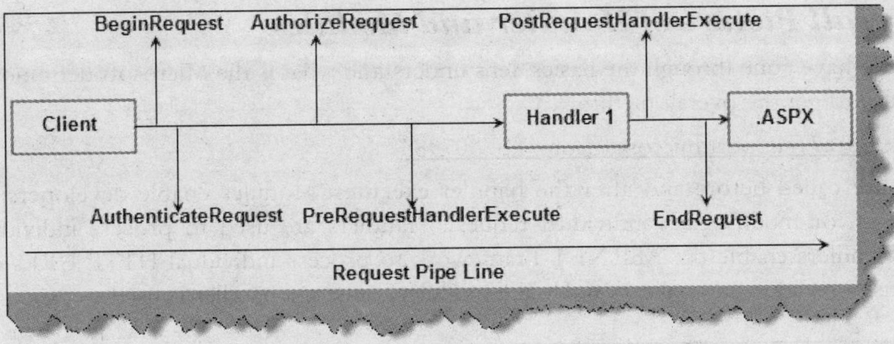

Below is a detailed explanation of the events. The below details are taken from Microsoft website link http://support.microsoft.com/kb/307985

- BeginRequest: Request has been started. If we need to do something at the beginning of a request (for example, display advertisement banners at the top of each page), synchronize this event.
- AuthenticateRequest: If we want to plug in our own custom authentication scheme (for example, look up a user against a database to validate the password), build a module that synchronizes this event and authenticates the user in a way that we want to.
- AuthorizeRequest: This event is used internally to implement authorization mechanisms (for example, to store our access control lists (ACLs) in a database rather than in the file system). Although we can override this event, there are not many good reasons to do so.
- PreRequestHandlerExecute: This event occurs before the HTTP handler is executed.
- PostRequestHandlerExecute: This event occurs after the HTTP handler is executed.
- EndRequest: Request has been completed. We may want to build a debugging module that gathers information throughout the request and then writes the information to the page.

We can register these events with the HttpModules. So when the request pipe line executes depending on the event registered, the logic from the modules is processed.

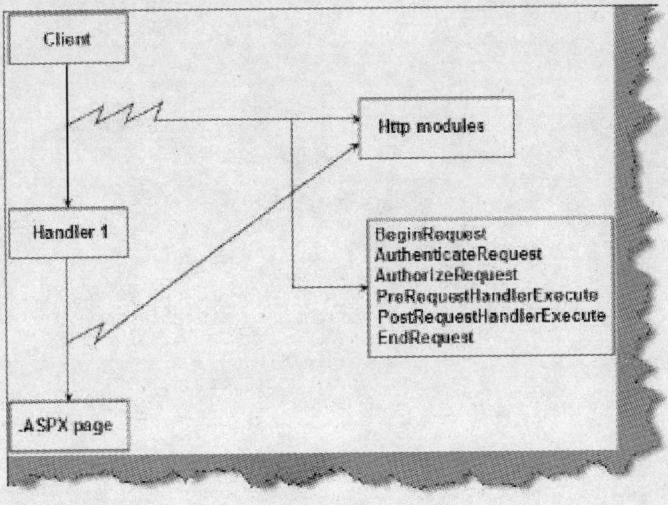

The Overall Picture of Handler and Modules

Now that we have gone through the basics, let's understand what is the Microsoft definition for handler and modules to get the overall picture.

Reference: http://support.microsoft.com/kb/307985

"Modules are called before and after the handler executes. Modules enable developers to intercept, participate in, or modify each individual request. Handlers are used to process individual endpoint requests. Handlers enable the ASP.NET Framework to process individual HTTP URLs or groups of URL extensions within an application. Unlike modules, only one handler is used to process a request."

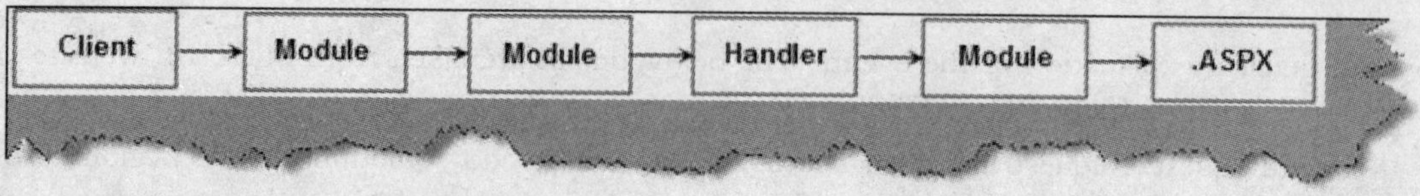

.NET Interview Questions

Basic .NET Framework

What is an IL?

What is a CLR?

What is CTS?

What is a CLS (Common Language Specification)?

What is a Managed Code?

What is a Assembly?

What are the different types of Assembly?

What is NameSpace?

What is Difference between NameSpace and Assembly?

If you want to view an Assembly how do you go about it?

What is Manifest?

Where is version information stored of an assembly?

Is versioning applicable to private assemblies?

What is GAC?

What is the concept of strong names?

How to add and remove an assembly from GAC?

What is Delay signing?

What is garbage collection?

Can we force garbage collector to run?

What is reflection?

What are different types of JIT?

What are Value types and Reference types?

What is concept of Boxing and Unboxing?

What is the difference between VB.NET and C#?

What is the difference between System exceptions and Application exceptions?

What is CODE Access security?

What is a satellite assembly?

How to prevent my .NET DLL to be decompiled?

What is the difference between Convert.toString and.toString () method?

What is Native Image Generator (Ngen.exe)?

If we have two version of same assembly in GAC how do we make a choice?

What is CodeDom?

.NET Interoperability

How can we use COM Components in .NET?

We have developed the COM wrapper do we have to still register the COM?

How can we use .NET components in COM?

How can we make Windows API calls in .NET?

When we use Windows API in .NET is it managed or unmanaged code?

What is COM?

What is Reference counting in COM?

Can you describe IUKNOWN interface in short?

Can you explain what DCOM is?

How do we create DCOM object in VB6?

How to implement DTC in .NET?

How many types of Transactions are there in COM + .NET?

How do you do object pooling in .NET?

What are types of compatibility in VB6?

What is equivalent for regsvr32 exe in .NET?

Threading

What is Multi-tasking?

What is Multi-threading?

What is a Thread?

Did VB6 support multi-threading?

Can we have multiple threads in one App domain?

Which namespace has threading?

What does Address Of operator do in background?

How can you reference current thread of the method?

What is Thread.Sleep () in threading?

How can we make a thread sleep for infinite period?

What is Suspend and Resume in Threading?

What the way to stop a long running thread?

How do I debug thread?

What is Thread.Join () in threading?

What are Daemon threads and how can a thread be created as Daemon?

How is shared data managed in threading?

Can we use events with threading?

How can we know a state of a thread?

What is use of Interlocked class?

What is a monitor object?

What are wait handles?

What is ManualResetEvent and AutoResetEvent?

What is Reader Writer Locks?

How can you avoid deadlock in threading?

What is the difference between thread and process?

Remoting and Webservices

What is an application domain?

What is .NET Remoting?

Which class does the remote object has to inherit?

What are two different types of remote object creation mode in .NET?

Describe in detail Basic of SAO architecture of Remoting?

What are the situations you will use singleton architecture in remoting?

What is fundamental of published or precreated objects in Remoting?

What are the ways in which client can create object on server in CAO model?

Are CAO stateful in nature?

To create objects in CAO with 'new' keyword what should be done?

Is it a good design practice to distribute the implementation to Remoting Client?

What are LeaseTime, SponsorshipTime, RenewonCallTime and LeaseManagerPollTime?

Which config file has all the supported channels/protocol?

How can you specify remoting parameters using Config files?

Can Non-Default constructors be used with Single Call SAO?

How can we call methods in remoting asynchronously?

What is Asynchronous One-Way Calls?

What is marshalling and what are different kinds of marshalling?

What is ObjRef object in remoting?

What is a Web Service?

What is UDDI?

What is DISCO?

What is WSDL?

What the different phase/steps of acquiring a proxy object in Web service?

What the different phase/steps of acquiring a proxy object in Web service?

What is file extension of Web services?

Which attribute is used in order that the method can be used as WebService?

What are the steps to create a web service and consume it?

Do webservice have state?

Caching Concepts

What is an application object?

What is the difference between Cache object and application object?

How can get access to cache object?

What are dependencies in cache and types of dependencies?

Can you show a simple code showing file dependency in cache?

What is Cache Callback in Cache?

What is scavenging?

What are different types of caching using cache object of ASP.NET?

How can you cache different version of same page using ASP.NET cache object?

How will implement Page Fragment Caching?

Can you compare ASP.NET sessions with classic ASP?

Which are the various modes of storing ASP.NET session?

Is Session_End event supported in all session modes?

What are the steps to configure StateServer Mode?

What are the steps to configure SQLServer mode?

Where do you specify session state mode in ASP.NET?

What are the other ways you can maintain state?

What are benefits and Limitation of using Hidden fields?

What is ViewState?

Does the performance for viewstate vary according to User controls?

What are benefits and Limitation of using Viewstate for state management?

How can you use Hidden frames to cache client data?

What are benefits and limitations of using Hidden frames?

What are benefits and limitations of using Cookies?

What is Query String and what are benefits and limitations of using Query Strings?

What is Absolute and Sliding expiration?

What is cross page posting?

How do we access viewstate value of this page in the next page?

Can we post and access view state in another application?

What is SQL Cache Dependency in ASP.NET 2.0?

How do we enable SQL Cache Dependency in ASP.NET 2.0?

What is Post Cache substitution?

Why do we need methods to be static for Post Cache substitution?

OOPS

What is Object Oriented Programming?

What is a Class?

What is an Object?

What is the relation between Classes and Objects?

What are different properties provided by Object-oriented systems?

How can we achieve inheritance in VB.NET?

What are abstract classes?

What is a Interface?

What is difference between abstract classes and interfaces?

What is a delegate?

What are Events?

Do events have return type?

Can events have access modifiers?

Can we have shared events?

What is shadowing?

What is the difference between Shadowing and Overriding?

What is the difference between delegate and events?

If we inherit a class do the private variables also get inherited?

What is the different accessibility levels defined in .NET?

Can you prevent a class from overriding?

What is the use of "Must inherit" keyword in VB.NET?

Do interface have accessibility modifier?

What are similarities between Class and structure?

What is the difference between Class and structure's?

What does virtual keyword mean?

What are shared (VB.NET)/Static(C#) variables?

What is Dispose method in .NET?

What is the use of "Overrides" and "Overridable" keywords?

Where are all .NET Collection classes located?

What is ArrayList?

What is a HashTable?

What are queues and stacks?

What is ENUM?

What is nested Classes?

What is Operator overloading in .NET?

For the below code which constructor will fire first?

What is the significance of Finalize method in .NET?

How can we suppress a finalize method?

What is the use of DISPOSE method?

How do I force the Dispose method to be called automatically, as clients can forget to call Dispose method?

In what instances you will declare a constructor to be private?

Can we have different access modifiers on get/set methods of a property?

If we write a goto or a return statement in try and catch block will the finally block execute?

What is Indexer?

Can we have static indexer in C#?

Can two catch blocks be executed?

What is the difference between System.String and System.StringBuilder classes?

ASP.NET

What is the sequence in which ASP.NET events are processed?

In which event are the controls fully loaded?

How can we identify that the Page is Post Back?

How does ASP.NET maintain state in between subsequent request?

What is event bubbling?

How do we assign page specific attributes?

How do we ensure viewstate is not tampered?

What is the use of @ Register directives?

What is the use of Smart Navigation property?

What is AppSetting Section in "Web.Config" file?

Where is View State information stored?

What is the use of @ Output Cache directive in ASP.NET?

How can we create custom controls in ASP.NET?

How many types of validation controls are provided by ASP.NET?

Can you explain "AutoPostBack"?

How can you enable automatic paging in Data Grid?

What is the use of "GLOBAL.ASAX" file?

What is the difference between "Web.config" and "Machine.Config"?

What is a SESSION and APPLICATION object?

What is the difference between 'Server.Transfer' and 'response. Redirect'?

What is the difference between Authentication and authorization?

What is impersonation in ASP.NET?

Can you explain in brief how the ASP.NET authentication process works?

What are the various ways of authentication techniques in ASP.NET?

How does authorization work in ASP.NET?

What is difference between Data grid, Datalist, and repeater?

From performance point of view, how do they rate?

What is the method to customize columns in Data Grid?

How can we format data inside Data Grid?

How to decide on the design consideration to take a Data grid, data list, or repeater?

Difference between ASP and ASP.NET?

What are major events in GLOBAL.ASAX file?

What order they are triggered?

Do session use cookies?

How can we force all the validation control to run?

How can we check if all the validation control are valid and proper?

If client side validation is enabled in your Web page, does that mean server side code is not run?

Which JavaScript file is referenced for validating the validators at the client side?

How to disable client side script in validators?

How can I show the entire validation error message in a message box on the client side?

You find that one of your validations is very complicated and does not fit in any of the validators, what will you do?

What exactly happens when ASPX page is requested from a browser?

How can we kill a user session?

How do you upload a file in ASP.NET?

How do I send email message from ASP.NET?

What are different IIS isolation levels?

ASP used STA threading model, what is the threading model used for ASP.NET?

What is the use of <%@ page aspcompat=true %> attribute?

Explain the differences between Server-side and Client-side code?

Can you explain Forms authentication in detail?

How do I sign out in forms authentication?

If cookies are not enabled at browser end does form Authentication work?

How to use a checkbox in a data grid?

What are the steps to create a Windows service in VB.NET?

What is the difference between "Web farms" and "Web garden"?

How do we configure "Web Garden"?

What is the main difference between Grid layout and Flow Layout?

What's the difference between trace and debug in ASP.NET?

How do you enable tracing in on an ASP.NET page?

Which namespace is needed to implement debug and trace?

Can you explain the concept of trace listener?

What are trace switches?

.NET Architecture

What are design patterns?

What is the difference between Factory and Abstract Factory Patterns?

What is MVC pattern?

How can we implement singleton pattern in .NET?

How do you implement prototype pattern in .NET?

What are the situations you will use a Web Service and Remoting in projects?

Can you give a practical implementation of FAÇADE patterns?

How can we implement observer pattern in .NET?

What is three-tier architecture?

Have you ever worked with Microsoft Application Blocks, if yes then which?

What is Service Oriented architecture?

What are different ways you can pass data between tiers?

What is Windows DNA architecture?

What is aspect oriented programming?

ADO.NET

What is the namespace in which .NET has the data functionality class?

Can you give an overview of ADO.NET architecture?

What are the two fundamental objects in ADO.NET?

What is difference between dataset and data reader?

What are major difference between classic ADO and ADO.NET?

What is the use of connection object?

What is the use of command objects?

What is the use of data adapter?

What are basic methods of Data adapter?

What is Dataset object?

What are the various objects in Dataset?

How can we connect to Microsoft Access, FoxPro, and Oracle etc?

How do we connect to SQL SERVER, which namespace do we use?

How do we use stored procedure in ADO.NET and how do we provide parameters to the stored procedures?

How can we force the connection object to close after my data reader is closed?

I want to force the data reader to return only schema of the data store rather than data?

How can we fine-tune the command object when we are expecting a single row?

Which is the best place to store connection string in .NET projects?

What are the steps involved to fill a dataset?

What are the various methods provided by the dataset object to generate XML?

How can we save all data from dataset?

How can we check that some changes have been made to dataset since it was loaded?

How can we add/remove row is in "Data Table" object of "Dataset"?

What is basic use of "Data View"?

What is the difference between "Dataset" and "Data Reader"?

How can we load multiple tables in a Dataset?

How can we add relation between tables in a Dataset?

What is the use of Command Builder?

What's difference between "Optimistic" and "Pessimistic" locking?

How many ways are there to implement locking in ADO.NET?

How can we perform transactions in .NET?

What is difference between Dataset?

Can you explain the difference between an ADO.NET Dataset and an ADO Record set?

Explain in detail the fundamental of connection pooling?

What is Maximum Pool Size in ADO.NET Connection String?

How to enable and disable connection pooling?

What extra features does ADO.Net 2.0 have?

SQL SERVER

What is normalization? What are different types of normalization?

What is denormalization?

What is a candidate key?

What are the different types of joins? What is the difference between them?

What are indexes? What is the difference between clustered and nonclustered indexes?

How can you increase SQL performance?

What is the use of OLAP?

What is a measure in OLAP?

What are dimensions in OLAP?

What are levels in dimensions?

What are fact tables and dimension tables in OLAP?

What is DTS?

What is fill factor?

What is RAID and how does it work?

What is the difference between DELETE TABLE and TRUNCATE TABLE commands?

If locking is not implemented, what issues can occur?

What are different transaction levels in SQL SERVER?

What are the different locks in SQL SERVER?

Can we suggest locking hints to SQL SERVER?

What is LOCK escalation?

What are the different ways of moving data between databases in SQL Server?

What are advantages of SQL 2000 over SQl 7.0?

What is the difference between a HAVING CLAUSE and a WHERE CLAUSE?

What is the difference between UNION and UNION ALL SQL syntax?

How can you raise custom errors from stored procedure?

What is ACID fundamental? What are transactions in SQL SERVER?

What is DBCC?

What is the purpose of Replication?

What are the different types of replication supported by SQL SERVER?

What is BCP utility in SQL SERVER?

What are the different types of triggers in SQl SERVER?

If we have multiple AFTER Triggers on table how can we define the sequence of the triggers?

What is SQL injection?

What is the difference between Stored Procedure (SP) and User Defined Function (UDF)?

UML

What is UML?

How many types of diagrams are there in UML?

What are advantages of using UML?

What is the sequence of UML diagrams in project?

Give a small brief explanation of all Elements in activity diagrams?

Explain Different elements of a collaboration diagram?

Explain all parts of a deployment diagram?

Describe the various components in sequence diagrams?

What are the elements in State Chart diagrams?

Describe different elements in Static Chart diagrams?

Explain the different elements of a Use Case?

Project Management

What is project management?

Is spending in IT projects constant through out the project?

Who is a stakeholder?

Can you explain project life cycle?

Are risk constant through out the project?

Can you explain different software development life cycles?

What is triple constraint triangle in project management?

What is a project baseline?

What is effort variance?

How is normally a project management plan document organized?

How do you estimate a project?

What is CAR (Causal Analysis and Resolution)?

What is DAR (Decision Analysis and Resolution)?

What is a fish bone diagram?

What is Pareto principle?

How do you handle change request?

What is internal change request?

What is difference between SITP and UTP in testing?

Which software have you used for project management?

What are the metrics followed in project management?

People in your project do not peform, what will you do?

What is black box testing and White box testing?

What is the difference between Unit testing, Assembly testing and Regression testing?

What is V model in testing?

How do you start a project?

How did you do resource allocations?

How will you do code reviews?

What is CMMI?

What are the five levels in CMMI?

What is continuous and staged representation?

What is SIX sigma?

What are DMAIC and DMADV?

What are the various roles in Six Sigma implementation?

What are function points?

What are the different types of elementary process in FPA?

What are the different elements in Functions points?

Can you explain in GSC and VAF in function points?

What are unadjusted function points and how is it calculated?

Can you explain steps in function points?

What is the FP per day in your current company?

Do you know Use Case points?

What is COCOMO I, COCOMOII and COCOMOIII?

What is SMC approach of estimation?

How do you estimate maintenance project and change requests?

XML

What is XML?

What is the version information in XML?

What is ROOT element in XML?

If XML does not have closing tag will it work?

Is XML case sensitive?

What is the difference between XML and HTML?

Is XML meant to replace HTML?

Can you explain why your project needed XML?

What is DTD (Document Type Definition)?

What is well formed XML?

What is a valid XML?

What is CDATA section in XML?

What is CSS?

What is XSL?

What is element and attributes in XML?

Which are the namespaces in.NET used for XML?

What are the standard ways of parsing XML document?

In what scenarios will you use a DOM parser and SAX parser?

How was XML handled during COM times?

What is the main difference between MSML and .NET Framework XML classes?

What are the core functionalities in XML.NET framework? Can you explain in detail those functionalities?

What is XSLT?

Define XPATH?

What is the concept of XPOINTER?

What is an XMLReader Class?

What is XMLTextReader?

How do we access attributes using "XmlReader"?

Explain simple Walk through of XmlReader?

What does XmlValidatingReader class do?

Localization/Globalization

What is Unicode & Why was it introduced?

Does .NET support UNICODE and how do you know it supports?

What is the difference between localization and globalization?

What architecture decisions you should consider while planning for international software's?

How do we get the current culture of the environment in Windows and ASP.NET?

Which are the important namespaces during localization and globalization?

What are resource files and how do we generate resource files?

Can resource file be in any other format other than resx extensions?

How is resource files actually used in project?

How can we use Culture Auto in project?

What are satellite assemblies?

How do we generate Satellite assemblies?

What is AL.EXE and RESGEN.EXE?

What is the use of resource manager class?

What precautions do we need to take while deploying satellite assemblies?

Can we get a strongly typed resource class rather than using resource manager?

Can you explain the fundamentals of "GetGlobalResourceObject" and "GetLocalResourceObject" functions?

Can we sign a satellite assembly?

Can you explain collation sequence in sql server?

How do we define collation sequence for database and tables?

Can we change the order in a select query with a specified collation sequence?

Can you list best practices for globalization and localization?

Why is the culture set to the current thread?

Windows Communication Foundation

What are the important principles of SOA (Service oriented Architecture)?

What are ends, contract, address, and bindings?

Which specifications does WCF follow?

What are the main components of WCF?

Explain how Ends, Contract, Address, and Bindings are done in WCF?

What is a service class?

What is a service contract, operation contract and Data Contract?

What are the various ways of hosting a WCF service?

How do we host a WCF service in IIS?

What are the advantages of hosting WCF Services in IIS as compared to self-hosting?

What are the major differences between services and Web services?

What is the difference WCF and Web services?

What are different bindings supported by WCF?

Which are the various programming approaches for WCF?

What is one-way operation?

Can you explain duplex contracts in WCF?

How can we host a service on two different protocols on a single server?

How can we use MSMQ bindings in WCF?

Can you explain transactions in WCF?

What different transaction isolation levels provided in WCF?

Can we do transactions using MSMQ?

Can we have two-way communications in MSMQ?

What are Volatile queues?

What are Dead letter queues?

What is a poison message?

Windows Presentation Framework

What is WPF?

What is XAML?

What are dependency properties?

Are XAML file compiled or built on runtime?

Can you explain how we can separate code and XAML?

How can we access XAML objects in behind code?

What kind of documents are supported in WPF?

Windows workflow foundation

What is Windows Workflow Foundation?

What is a Workflow?

What are different types of Workflow in Windows Workflow foundation?

When should we use a sequential workflow and when should we use state machines?

How do we create workflows using designer?

How do we specify conditions in Workflow?

How do you handle exceptions in workflow?

What is the use of XOML files.

How can we pass parameters to workflow?

ATLAS-AJAX

What problem does Ajax solve?

What is Ajax?

What is the fundamental behind Ajax?

What is JSON?

How do we use XMLHttpRequest object in JavaScript?

How do we do asynchronous processing using Ajax?

What are the various states in XMLHttpRequest and how do we check the same?

How can we get response text?

How can we send request to the server using the XMLHttpRequest component?

How do we pass parameters to the server?

How can we create a class in JavaScript using Atlas?

How do we do inheritance-using Atlas?

How do we define interfaces using Atlas?

How do we reference HTML controls using Atlas?

Can you explain Scriptmanager control in Ajax?

Can you explain Enablepartialrendering and UpdatePanel control in Ajax?

Can you explain the concept of triggers in 'UpdatePanel' control?

Can you explain the 'UpdateProgress' component?

How can you do validations in Ajax?

How do we do exception handling in Ajax?

How do we consume web service in Atlas?

How can we consume data directly in web services?

Reports

How do we access crystal reports in .NET?

What are the various components in crystal reports?

What basic steps are needed to display a simple report in crystal?

Can crystal reports be published as a web service?

How do we invoke the crystal report web service?

How do we add formulas using crystal reports?

How do we pass parameters to crystal reports?

How do we export from crystal reports?

How do we print to printer using crystal?

How do we generate cross tab reports?

How can we do grouping in crystal?

Can you explain three-pass reporting which crystal report uses?

Can you explain reporting services architecture?

We have two IIS application 'Reports' and 'Reportserver' what do they do?

Can you explain Report definition language (RDL) file in reporting services?

What is the basic process of making a report in reporting services?

How can we consume reports in ASP.NET?

Can you explain the difference between private and shared data sources?

How does report caching in reporting services work?

What are the major differences between Crystal and SQL reporting services?

ASP.NET 2.0

What improvements are provided in ASP.NET 2.0?

How does ASP.NET 2.0 eliminate tedious coding?

How do we encrypt web.config files in ASP.NET 2.0?

With the above technique can you encrypt everything in the web.config file?

In .NET 1.X how was the encryption implemented for config files?

Can you explain membership and role providers in ASP.NET 2.0?

What kind of security web controls are introduced in ASP.NET 2.0?

Can you explain master pages concept in ASP.NET?

What is the concept of Web parts?

What are the different components of the web part framework?

What are partial classes in ASP.NET?

Can you explain generics in .NET?

Can you explain the concept of generic collection?

How to

How do you send a email using ASP.NET?

How did you deployment and setup in ASP.NET?

.NET 3.5

Define LINQ?

We already have common data access model what is special about LINQ?

How can you make entity classes from the table itself?

How can we transform LINQ to objects?

How to transform LINQ to ADO.NET?

How to transform LINQ to SQL?

How to transform LINQ to XML?

How to transform LINQ to entities?

Can you explain Delegate Instantiation?

Can you explain Anonymous methods?

What is Yield in LINQ?

Can you explain Lambda Expressions?

What are Instance methods and Extension methods?

What are Anonymous types?

Revision of Simple Query syntax for LINQ?

What is silver light?

SQL Server Interview questions

Database Concepts

What is database or database management systems (DBMS)?

What's difference between DBMS and RDBMS?

What are CODD rules?

Is access database a RDBMS?

What's the main difference between ACCESS and SQL SERVER?

What's the difference between MSDE and SQL SERVER 2000?

What is SQL SERVER Express 2005 Edition?

What is SQL Server 2000 Workload Governor?

What's the difference between SQL SERVER 2000 and 2005?

What are E-R diagrams?

How many types of relationship exist in database designing?

What is normalization? What are different type of normalization?

What is denormalization?

Can you explain Fourth Normal Form?

Can you explain Fifth Normal Form?

What's the difference between Fourth and Fifth normal form?

Have you heard about sixth normal form?

What is Extent and Page?

What are the different sections in Page?

What are page splits?

In which files does actually SQL Server store data?

What is Collation in SQL Server?

Can we have a different collation for database and table?

SQL

Revisiting basic syntax of SQL?

What are "GRANT" and "REVOKE' statements?

What is Cascade and Restrict in DROP table SQL?

How to import table using "INSERT" statement?

What is a DDL, DML and DCL concept in RDBMS world?

What are different types of joins in SQL?

What is "CROSS JOIN"?

You want to select the first record in a given set of rows?

How do you sort in SQL?

How do you select unique rows using SQL?

Can you name some aggregate function is SQL Server?

What is the default "SORT" order for a SQL?

What is a self-join?

What's the difference between DELETE and TRUNCATE?

Select addresses which are between '1/1/2004' and '1/4/2004'?

What are Wildcard operators in SQL Server?

What's the difference between "UNION" and "UNION ALL"?

What are cursors and what are the situations you will use them?

What are the steps to create a cursor?

What are the different Cursor Types?

What are "Global" and "Local" cursors?

What is "Group by" clause?

What is ROLLUP?

What is CUBE?

What is the difference between "HAVING" and "WHERE" clause?

What is "COMPUTE" clause in SQL?

What is "WITH TIES" clause in SQL?

What does "SET ROWCOUNT" syntax achieves?

What is a Sub-Query?

What is "Correlated Subqueries"?

What is "ALL" and "ANY" operator?

What is a "CASE" statement in SQL?

What does COLLATE Keyword in SQL signify?

What is CTE (Common Table Expression)?

Why should you use CTE rather than simple views?

What is TRY/CATCH block in T-SQL?

What is PIVOT feature in SQL Server?

What is UNPIVOT?

What are RANKING functions?

What is ROW_NUMBER()?

What is RANK()?

What is DENSE_RANK()?

What is NTILE()?

What is SQl injection?

.NET Integration

What are steps to load a .NET code in SQL SERVER 2005?

How can we drop an assembly from SQL SERVER?

Are changes made to assembly updated automatically in database?

Why do we need to drop assembly for updating changes?

How to see assemblies loaded in SQL Server?

I want to see which files are linked with which assemblies?

Does .NET CLR and SQL SERVER run in different process?

Does .NET controls SQL SERVER or is it vice-versa?

Is SQLCLR configured by default?

How to configure CLR for SQL SERVER?

Is .NET feature loaded by default in SQL Server?

How does SQL Server control .NET run-time?

What's a "SAND BOX" in SQL Server 2005?

What is an application domain?

How are .NET Appdomain allocated in SQL SERVER 2005?

What is Syntax for creating a new assembly in SQL Server 2005?

Do Assemblies loaded in database need actual .NET DLL?

You have a assembly which is dependent on other assemblies, will SQL Server load the dependent assemblies?

Does SQL Server handle unmanaged resources?

What is Multi-tasking?

What is Multi-threading?

What is a Thread?

Can we have multiple threads in one App domain?

What is Non-preemptive threading?

What is pre-emptive threading?

Can you explain threading model in SQL Server?

How does .NET and SQL Server thread work?

How is exception in SQLCLR code handled?

Are all .NET libraries allowed in SQL Server?

What is "Hostprotectionattribute" in SQL Server 2005?

How many types of permission level are there for an assembly?

In order that an assembly gets loaded in SQL Server what type of checks are done?

Can you name system tables for .NET assemblies?

Are two version of same assembly allowed in SQL Server?

How are changes made in assembly replicated?

Is it a good practice to drop a assembly for changes?

In one of the projects following steps where done, will it work?

What does Alter assembly with unchecked data signify?

How do I drop an assembly?

Can we create SQLCLR using .NET framework 1.0?

While creating .NET UDF what checks should be done?

How do you define a function from the .NET assembly?

Can you compare between T-SQL and SQLCLR?

With respect to .NET is SQL SERVER case sensitive?

Does case sensitive rule apply for VB.NET?

Can nested classes be accessed in T-SQL?

Can we have SQLCLR procedure input as array?

Can object datatype be used in SQLCLR?

How's precision handled for decimal datatypes in .NET?

How do we define INPUT and OUTPUT parameters in SQLCLR?

Is it good to use .NET datatypes in SQLCLR?

How to move values from SQL to .NET datatypes?

What is System.Data.SqlServer?

What is SQLContext?

Can you explain essential steps to deploy SQLCLR?

How do create function in SQL Server using .NET?

How do we create trigger using .NET?

How to create User Define Functions using .NET?

How to create aggregates using .NET?

What is Asynchronous support in ADO.NET?

What is MARS support in ADO.NET?

What is SQLbulkcopy object in ADO.NET?

How to select range of rows using ADO.NET?

What are different types of triggers in SQl SERVER 2000?

If we have multiple AFTER Triggers on table how can we define the sequence of the triggers?

How can you raise custom errors from stored procedure?

ADO.NET

Which are namespaces for ADO.NET?

Can you give a overview of ADO.NET architecture?

What are the two fundamental objects in ADO.NET?

What is difference between dataset and datareader?

What are major difference between classic ADO and ADO.NET?

What is the use of connection object?

What are the methods provided by the command object?

What is the use of "Dataadapter"?

What are basic methods of "Dataadapter"?

What is Dataset object?

What are the various objects in Dataset?

How can we connect to Microsoft Access, FoxPro, Oracle etc?

What's the namespace to connect to SQL Server?

How do we use stored procedure in ADO.NET?

How can we force the connection object to close?

I want to force the datareader to return only schema?

Can we optimize command object when there is only one row?

Which is the best place to store connectionstring?

What are steps involved to fill a dataset?

What are the methods provided by the dataset for XML?

How can we save all data from dataset?

How can we check for changes made to dataset?

How can we add/remove row's in "DataTable" object of "DataSet"?

What's basic use of "DataView"?

What's difference between "DataSet" and "DataReader"?

How can we load multiple tables in a DataSet?

How can we add relation's between table in a DataSet?

What's the use of CommandBuilder?

What's difference between "Optimistic" and "Pessimistic" locking?

How many way's are there to implement locking in ADO.NET?

How can we perform transactions in .NET?

What's difference between Dataset. clone and Dataset. copy?

What's the difference between Dataset and ADO Recordset?

Notification Services

What are notification services?

What are basic components of Notification services?

Can you explain architecture of Notification Services?

Which are the two XML files needed for notification services?

What is Nscontrols command?

What are the situations you will use "Notification" Services?

Service Broker

What do we need Queues?

What is "Asynchronous" communication?

What is SQL Server Service broker?

What are the essential components of SQL Server Service broker?

What is the main purpose of having Conversation Group?

How to implement Service Broker?

How do we encrypt data between Dialogs?

XML Integration

What is XML?

What is the version information in XML?

What is ROOT element in XML?

If XML does not have closing tag will it work?

Is XML case sensitive?

What's the difference between XML and HTML?

Is XML meant to replace HTML?

Can you explain why your project needed XML?

What is DTD (Document Type definition)?

What is well formed XML?

What is a valid XML?

What is CDATA section in XML?

What is CSS?

What is XSL?

What is Element and attributes in XML?

Can we define a column as XML?

How do we specify the XML data type as typed or untyped?

How can we create the XSD schema?

How do I insert in to a table which has XSD schema attached to it?

What is maximum size for XML datatype?

What is Xquery?

What are XML indexes?

What are secondary XML indexes?

What is FOR XML in SQL Server?

Can I use FOR XML to generate SCHEMA of a table and how?

What is the OPENXML statement in SQL Server?

I have huge XML file which we want to load in database?

How to call stored procedure using HTTP SOAP?

What is XMLA?

Data Warehousing/Data Mining

What is "Data Warehousing"?

What are Data Marts?

What are Fact tables and Dimension Tables?

What is Snow Flake Schema design in database?

What is ETL process in Data warehousing?

How can we do ETL process in SQL Server?

What is "Data mining"?

Compare "Data mining" and "Data Warehousing"?

What is BCP?

How can we import and export using BCP utility?

During BCP we need to change the field position or eliminate some fields how can we achieve this?

What is Bulk Insert?

What is DTS?

Can you brief about the Data warehouse project you worked on?

What is an OLTP (Online Transaction Processing) System?

What is an OLAP (On-line Analytical processing) system?

What is Conceptual, Logical and Physical model?

What is Data purging?

What is Analysis Services?

What are CUBES?

What are the primary ways to store data in OLAP?

What is META DATA information in Data warehousing projects?

What is multi-dimensional analysis?

What is MDX?

How did you plan your Data ware house project?

What are different deliverables according to phases?

Can you explain how analysis service works?

What are the different problems that "Data mining" can solve?

What are different stages of "Data mining"?

What is Discrete and Continuous data in Data mining world?

What is MODEL is Data mining world?

How are models actually derived?

What is a Decision Tree Algorithm?

Can decision tree be implemented using SQL?

What is Naïve Bayes Algorithm?

Explain clustering algorithm?

Explain in detail Neural Networks?

What is Back propagation in Neural Networks?

What is Time Series algorithm in data mining?

Explain Association algorithm in Data mining?

What is Sequence clustering algorithm?

What are algorithms provided by Microsoft in SQL Server?

How does data mining and data warehousing work together?

What is XMLA?

What is Discover and Execute in XMLA?

Integration Services/DTS

What is Integration Services import/export wizard?

What are prime components in Integration Services?

How can we develop a DTS project in Integration Services?

Replication

What's the best way to update data between SQL Servers?

What are the scenarios you will need multiple databases with schema?

How will you plan your replication?

What are publisher, distributor and subscriber in "Replication"?

What is "Push" and "Pull" subscription?

Can a publication support push and pull at one time?

What are different models/types of replication?

What is Snapshot replication?

What are the advantages and disadvantages of using Snapshot replication?

What type of data will qualify for "Snapshot replication"?

What's the actual location where the distributor runs?

Can you explain in detail how exactly "Snapshot Replication" works?

What is merge replication?

How does merge replication works?

What are advantages and disadvantages of Merge replication?

What is conflict resolution in Merge replication?

What is a transactional replication?

Can you explain in detail how transactional replication works?

What are data type concerns during replications?

Reporting Services

Can you explain how can we make a simple report in reporting services?

How do I specify stored procedures in Reporting Services?

What is the architecture for "Reporting Services "?

Database Optimization

What are indexes?

What are B-Trees?

I have a table which has lot of inserts, is it a good database design to create indexes on that table?

What are "Table Scan's" and "Index Scan's"?

What are the two types of indexes and explain them in detail?

What is "FillFactor" concept in indexes?

What is the best value for "FillFactor"?

What are "Index statistics"?

How can we see statistics of an index?

How do you reorganize your index, once you find the problem?

What is Fragmentation?

How can we measure Fragmentation?

How can we remove the Fragmented spaces?

What are the criteria you will look in to while selecting an index?

What is "Index Tuning Wizard"?

What is an Execution plan?

How do you see the SQL plan in textual format?

What is nested join, hash join and merge join in SQL Query plan?

What joins are good in what situations?

What is RAID and how does it work?

Transaction and Locks

What is a "Database Transactions "?

What is ACID?

What is "Begin Trans", "Commit Tran", "Rollback Tran" and "Save Tran"?

What are "Checkpoint's" in SQL Server?

What are "Implicit Transactions"?

Is it good to use "Implicit Transactions"? 315

What is Concurrency?

How can we solve concurrency problems?

What kind of problems occurs if we do not implement proper locking strategy?

What are "Dirty reads"?

What are "Unrepeatable reads"?

What are "Phantom rows"?

What are "Lost Updates"?

What are different levels of granularity of locking resources?

What are different types of Locks in SQL Server?

What are different Isolation levels in SQL Server?

What are different types of Isolation levels in SQL Server?

If you are using COM+ what "Isolation" level is set by default?

What are "Lock" hints?

What is a "Deadlock"?

What are the steps you can take to avoid "Deadlocks"?

How can I know what locks are running on which resource?

Project Management Interview questions

Basics

Define project?

Who is a stakeholder?

Can you explain Scope triangle?

Can you explain what's a vision and a goal?

What is ROI?

Can you explain project life cycle?

You have people in your team who do not meet there deadlines or do not perform what are the actions you will take?

Are risk constant through out the project?

Explain SDLC (Software development Life Cycle) in detail?

Can you explain waterfall model?

Can you explain big-bang waterfall model?

Can you explain phased waterfall model?

Explain Iterative model, Incremental model, Spiral model, Evolutionary model and V-Model?

Explain Unit testing, Integration tests, System testing and Acceptance testing?

What's the difference between system and acceptance testing?

Which is the best model?

What is CAR (Causal Analysis and Resolution)?

What is DAR (Decision Analysis and Resolution)?

Can you explain the concept of baseline in software development?

What is the software you have used for project management?

What does a project plan consist?

When do you say the project has finished?

Can you explain what a PMO office is?

How many members in your team you have handled?

Is GANTT chart a project plan?

Two resources are having issues how do you handle the same?

What is a change request?

How did you manage change request in your project?

Can you explain traceability matrix?

What is configuration management?

What is CI?

Define stakeholders?

Can you explain versioning?

Can you explain the concept of sign off?

How will you start a project?

What is an MOU?

What where the deliverables in your project?

Can you explain your project?

Do you also participate in technical activities?

How did you manage code reviews?

You have team member who does not meets his deadlines how do you handle it?

Did you have project audits if yes how was it handled?

What is a non-conformance report (NCR)?

How did you estimate your project?

How did you motivate your team members?

Did you create leaders in your team if yes how?

How did you confirm that your modules are resource independent?

Was your project show cased for CMMI or any other project process standardization?

What are the functions of the Quality Assurance Group (QAG)?

Can you explain milestone?

How did you do assessment of team members?

What does entry and exit criteria mean in a project?

Risk Management

Define risk?

What is risk break down structure?

How did you plan your risk?

What is DR, BCP and contingency planning?

Schedule Management

Can you explain WBS?

Can you explain WBS numbering?

How did you do resource allocation?

Can you explain the use of WBS?

Can you explain network diagram?

What are the different types of network diagram?

What is the advantage of using network diagrams?

Can you explain Arrow diagram and Precendence diagram?

What are the different types of Network diagrams?

Can you explain Critical path?

Can you define EST, LST, EFT, LFT?

Can you explain Float and Slack?

Can you explain PERT?

Can you explain GANTT chart?

What is the disadvantage of GANTT chart?

What is Monte-Carlo simulation?

Costing

Can you explain PV, AC and EV?

?Can you explain BCWS, ACWS and BCWP?

What are the derived metrics from Earned Value?

Can you explain earned value with a sample?

Estimation, Metrics and Measure

What is meant by measure and metrics?

Which metrics have you used for tracking purpose?

What are the various common ways of estimation?

Can you explain LOC method of estimation?

How do we convert LOC in to effort?

Can you explain COCOMO?

Can you explain Intermediate COCOMO and COCOMO II?

How do you estimate using LOC?

Can you explain in brief Function points?

Can you explain the concept Application boundary?

Can you explain the concept of elementary process?

Can you explain the concept of static and dynamic elementary process?

Can you explain concept of FTR, ILF, EIF, EI, EO, EQ and GSC?

How can you estimate number of acceptance test cases in a project?

Can you explain the concept of Use Case's?

Can you explain the concept of Use case points?

What is a use case transaction?

How do we estimate using Use Case Points?

Can you explain on what basis does TPA actually work?

How did you do estimation for black box testing?

How did you estimate white box testing?

Is there a way to estimate acceptance test cases in a system?

Can you explain Number of defects measure?

Can you explain number of production defects measure?

Can you explain defect seeding?

Can you explain DRE?

Can you explain Unit and system test DRE?

How do you measure test effectiveness?

Can you explain Defect age and Defect spoilage?

Software process

What is a Software process?

What are the different cost element involved in implementing process in an organization?

What is a model?

What is maturity level?

Can you explain the concept of process area in CMMI?

Can you explain the concept of tailoring?

CMMI

What is CMMI?

What's the difference between implementation and Institutionalization?

What are different models in CMMI?

Can you explain staged and continuous models in CMMI?

Can you explain the different maturity levels in staged representation?

Can you explain capability levels in continuous representation?

Which model should we use and under what scenarios?

How many process areas are present in CMMI and in what classification do they fall in?

What the difference between every level in CMMI?

What different sources are needed to verify authenticity for CMMI implementation?

Can you explain SCAMPI process?

How is appraisal done in CMMI?

which appraisal method class is the best?

Can you explain the importance of PII in SCAMPI?

Can you explain implementation of CMMI in one of the Key process areas?

Explanation of all process areas with goals and practices?

Can you explain the process areas?

Six Sigma

What is six sigma?

Can you explain the different methodology for execution and design process in SIX sigma?

What does executive leaders, champions, Master Black belt, green belts and black belts mean?

What are the different kinds of variations used in six sigma?

Can you explain the concept of standard deviation?

Can you explain the concept of fish bone/Ishikawa diagram?

What is Pareto principle?

Can you explain QFD?

Can you explain FMEA?

Can you explain X bar charts?

Can you explain Flow charting and brain storming?

Agile Development

What does Agile mean?

Can you explain Agile modelling?

What are core and supplementary principles in Agile modeling?

What is the main principle behind Agile documentation?

What are the different methodologies to implement Agile?

What is XP?

What are User Stories in XP and how different are they from requirement?

Who writes User stories?

When do we say a story is valid?

When are test plans written in XP?

Can you explain the XP development life cycle?

Can you explain how planning game works in Extreme Programming?

How do we estimate in Agile?

On What basis can stories be prioritized?

Can you point out simple differences between Agile and traditional SDLC?

Can you explain the concept of refactoring?

What is a feature in Feature Driven Development?

Can you explain the overall structure of FDD project?

Can you explain the concept of time boxing?

When to choose FDD and when to choose XP?

What is SCRUM?

What does product owner, product back log and sprint mean in SCRUM?

Can you explain how SCRUM flows?

Can you explain different roles in SCRUM?

Can you explain DSDM?

Can you explain different phases in DSDM?

Can you explain in detail project life cycle phase in DSDM?

Can you explain LSD?

Can you explain ASD?

Software Architecture Interview Questions

Basic architecture Interview questions

What is the definition of software architecture?

Can you explain your current project architecture?

Which design pattern have you worked with?

Which UML diagram have you used in your project?

What things do you include in the technical document?

Can you explain different software development life cycles?

What is a definition of enterprise architecture?

What is TOGAF?

Can you explain OOA and OOD?

What is the concept of load balancing?

Can you explain stateless load balancing?

Can you explain stateful load balancing?

What is round-robin?

Can you explain least connections, weighted distribution and response time?

OOP

What is OOP?

What are the advantages of using OOP over functional programming?

What are the characteristics of OOP?

Can you explain interfaces?

Can you explain aggregation and composition?

What are abstract classes?

What's the difference between abstract classes and interfaces?

Can we create a object of a class whose constructor is private?

UML

Define UML?

Can you explain use case diagrams?

Can you explain primary and secondary actors?

How does a simple use case look like?

Can you explain 'Extend' and 'Include' in use cases?

Can you explain class diagrams?

How do we represent private, public and protected in class diagrams?

What does associations in a class diagram mean?

Can you explain aggregation and composition in class diagrams?

What are composite structure diagram and reflexive association in class diagrams?

Can you explain business entity and service class?

Can you explain System entity and service class?

Can you explain generalization and specialization?

How do we represent an abstract class and interface UML?

How do we achieve generalization and specialization?

Can you explain object diagrams in UML?

Can you explain sequence diagrams?

Can you explain collaboration diagrams?

Can you explain activity diagrams?

What is state chart diagram?

Can you explain stereotypes in UML?

Can you explain package diagrams?

Can you explain component diagrams?

Can you explain deployment diagrams?

Can you explain how UML flows in actual project?

Design Patterns

What are design patterns?

Which are the three main categories of design patterns?

Can you explain factory pattern?

Can you explain abstract factory pattern?

Can you explain builder pattern?

Can you explain prototype pattern?

Can you explain shallow copy and deep copy in prototype patterns?

Can you explain singleton pattern?

Can you explain command patterns?

What is Interpreter pattern?

Can you explain iterator pattern?

Can you explain mediator pattern?

Can you explain memento pattern?

Can you explain observer pattern?

Can you explain state pattern?

Can you explain strategy pattern?

Can you explain visitor pattern?

What the difference between visitor and strategy pattern?

Can you explain adapter pattern?

What is fly weight pattern?

Can you explain bridge pattern?

Can you explain composite pattern?

Can you explain decorator pattern?

Can you explain Façade pattern?

Can you explain chain of responsibility (COR)?

Can you explain proxy pattern?

Can you explain template pattern?

Can you explain MVC?

What is aspect oriented programming?

What is Inversion of control?

What is OR mapping?

SOA (Service oriented architecture)

What is SOA?

In SOA do we need to build systems from scratch?

Can you explain business layers and plumbing layers in SOA?

What's the difference between services and components?

Can you describe the complete architecture of SOA?

Can you explain a practical example in SOA?

What are ends, contract, address, and bindings?

Are web-services SOA?

What is SOAP?

What is WSDL?

Can you explain UDDI?

What is BPEL?

What are WS-* specifications?

Can you explain SOA governance?

Estimation, Metrics and Measure

What is meant by measure and metrics?

What are the various common ways of estimation?

Can you explain LOC method of estimation?

How do we convert LOC in to effort?

Can you explain COCOMO?

Can you explain Intermediate COCOMO and COCOMO II?

How do you estimate using LOC?

Can you explain in brief Function points?

Can you explain the concept Application boundary?

Can you explain the concept of elementary process?

Can you explain the concept of static and dynamic elementary process?

Can you explain concept of FTR, ILF, EIF, EI, EO, EQ and GSC?

How can you estimate number of acceptance test cases in a project?

Can you explain the concept of Use Case's?

Can you explain the concept of Use case points?

What is a use case transaction?

How do we estimate using Use Case Points?

JAVA Interview questions

OOPS and CORE JAVA

What is JVM (Java Virtual Machine)?

What is JIT (Just-in-Time) Compilation?

What is Object Oriented Programming?

What's a Class?

What's an Object?

What's the relation between Classes and Objects?

What are different properties provided by Object-oriented systems?

How do you implement inheritance in Java?

How can we implement polymorphism in Java?

What's an interface and how will you go about implementing an interface?

What is an Abstract class?

What are Abstract methods?

What's the difference between "Abstract" classes and "Interfaces"?

What's difference between Static and Non-Static fields of a class?

What are inner classes and what's the practical implementation of inner classes?

What are packages?

What is a constructor in class?

Can constructors be parameterized?

Can you explain transient and volatile modifiers?

What is the use if "instanceof " keyword?

What are Native methods in Java?

Explain in depth Garbage collector?

How does the garbage collector determine that the object has to be marked for deletion?

Can you explain "finalize()" method?

How can we force the garbage collector to run?

What's the main difference between "Switch" and "If " comparison?

What's the use of JAVAP tool?

What are applets?

In which package is the applet class located?

What are native interfaces in Java?

What are Class loader's?

What is Bootstrap, Extension and System Class loader?

Can you explain the flow between bootstrap, extension and system class loader?

Can you explain how can you practically do dynamic loading?

How can you copy one array in to a different array?

Can you explain the core collection interfaces?

Can you explain in brief the collection classes which implement the collection interfaces?

What's the difference between standard JAVA array and ArrayList class?

What's the use of "ensureCapacity" in ArrayList class?

How can we obtain an array from an ArrayList class?

What is "LinkedList" class for?

Can you explain HashSet class in collections?

What is LinkedHashSet class?

What is a TreeSet class?

What's the use of Comparator Interface?

How can we access elements of a collection?

What is Map and SortedMap Interface?

Have you used any collection algorithm?

Why do we use collections when we had traditional ways for collection?

Can you name the legacy classes and interface for collections?

What is Enumeration Interface?

What's the main difference between ArrayList/HashMap and Vector/Hashtable?

Are String object Immutable, Can you explain the concept?

What is a StringBuffer class and how does it differs from String class?

What is the difference between StringBuilder and StringBuffer class?

What is Pass by Value and Pass by reference? How does JAVA handle the same?

What are access modifiers?

What is Assertion?

Can you explain the fundamentals of deep and shallow Cloning?

How do we implement Shallow cloning?

How do we implement deep cloning?

What's the impact of private constructor?

What are the situations you will need a constructor to be private?

Can you explain final modifier?

What are static Initializers?

If we have multiple static initializer blocks how is the sequence handled?

Define casting? What are the different types of Casting?

Can you explain Widening conversion and Narrowing conversion?

Can we assign parent object to child objects?

Define exceptions?

Can you explain in short how JAVA exception handling works?

Can you explain different exception types?

Can you explain checked and unchecked exceptions?

Can we create our own exception class?

What are chained exceptions?

What is serialization?

How do we implement serialization actually?

What's the use of Externalizable Interface?

Threading

What's difference between thread and process?

What is thread safety and synchronization?

What is semaphore?

What are monitors?

What's the importance of synchronized blocks?

How do we create threads?

What's the difference in using runnable and extends in threads?

Can you explain Thread.sleep?

How to stop a thread?

What is wait() and notify()?

Can you explain how Scheduling and Priority works in threads?

Can you explain Yielding in threading?

What are daemon threads?

JDBC

How does JAVA interact with databases?

Can we interact with non-relational sources using JDBC?

Can you explain in depth the different sections in JDBC?

Can you explain in short how you go about using JDBC API in code?

How do you handle SQL exceptions?

If there is more than one exception in SQLException" class how to go about displaying it?

Explain Type1, Type2, Type3 and Type4 drivers in JDBC?

What are the advantages and disadvantages of using JDBC-ODBC bridge driver?

What are the advantages and disadvantages of using Native-API/Partially Java Driver?

What are the advantages and disadvantages of using Net-Protocol/All-Java driver?

What are the advantages and disadvantages of using Native-protocol/All-Java driver?

Define meta-data?

What is DatabaseMetaData?

Can you explain "ConnectionFactory" class?

I want to display tables of a database how do I do it?

Define "ResultSetMetaData"?

What is the difference between "ResultSet" and "RowSet"?

Can "ResultSet" objects be serialized?

Can you explain "ResultSet", "RowSet", "CachedRowset", "JdbcRowset" and "WebRowSet" relation ship?

What are the different types of resultset?

Explain the concept of "PreparedStatement "statement interface?

What's the difference between "Statement" and "PreparedStatement"?

How can we call stored procedure using JDBC?

Can you explain "CallableStatement" interface in detail?

How do you get a resultset object from stored procedure?

How can we do batch updates using "CallableStatement" Interface?

Define transactions?

What is ACID in transaction?

What are the four essential properties of a transaction?

Explain concurrency and locking?

What are different types of locks?

What are the different types of levels of resource on which locks can be placed?

Define lock escalation?

What is Table level and Row level locking?

What are the problems that can occur if you do not implement locking properly?

What are different transaction levels?

Twist: what are different types of locks?

What is difference between optimistic and pessimistic locking?

What are deadlocks?

How can we set transaction level through JDBC API?

Can you explain transaction control in JDBC?

What are Savepoints in a transaction?

Servlets and JSP

What are Servlets?

What are advantages of servlets over CGI?

Can you explain Servlet life cycle?

What are the two important API's in for Servlets?

Can you explain in detail "javax.servlet" package?

What's the use of ServletContext?

How do we define an application level scope for servlet?

What's the difference between GenericServlet and HttpServlet?

Can you explain in detail javax.servlet.http package?

What's the architecture of a Servlet package?

Why is HTTP protocol called as a stateless protocol?

What are the different ways we can maintain state between requests?

What is URL rewriting?

What are cookies?

What are sessions in Servlets?

What's the difference between getSession(true) and getSession(false)?

What's the difference between "doPost" and "doGet" methods?

Which are the different ways you can communicate between servlets?

What is functionality of "RequestDispatcher" object?

How do we share data using "getServletContext ()"?

Explain the concept of SSI?

What are filters in JAVA?

Can you explain in short how do you go about implementing filters using Apache Tomcat?

Twist: Explain step by step of how to implement filters?

What's the difference between Authentication and authorization?

Explain in brief the directory structure of a web application?

Can you explain JSP page life cycle?

What is EL?

how does EL search for an attribute?

What are the implicit EL objects in JSP?

How can we disable EL?

What is JSTL?

Can you explain in short what the different types of JSTL tags are?

How can we use beans in JSP?

What is <jsp:forward> tag for?

What are JSP directives?

What are Page directives?

What are include directives?

Can you explain taglib directives?

How does JSP engines instantiate tag handler classes instances?

What's the difference between JavaBeans and taglib directives?

What are the different scopes an object can have in a JSP page?

What are different implicit objects of JSP?

What are different Authentication Options available in servlets?

Can you explain how do we practically implement security on a resource?

How do we practically implement form based authentication?

How do we authenticate using JDBC?

Can you explain JDBCRealm?

Can you explain how do you configure JNDIRealm?

How did you implement caching in JSP?

EJB

What is EJB?

What are the different kind of EJB's?

You are designing architecture for a project how do you decide whether you should use session, entity or message driven bean?

Can you explain "EJBHome" and "EJBObject" in EJB?

Can client directly create object of session or entity beans?

Can you explain the concept of local interfaces?

What are the limitations of using Local object?

Which application server have you used for EJB?

Can you explain step by step practically developing and deploying EJB component?

What is Passivation and Activation in EJB?

Can beans who are involved in transaction have "Passivation" process?

How does the server decide which beans to passivate and activate?

In what format is the conversational data written to the disk?

Can you explain in brief Life cycle for Stateless and Stateful beans?

Struts

What's MVC pattern?

Define struts?

Can you explain the directory structure for a struts folder in brief?

Can you give an overview of how a struts application flows?

> **Twist:** *What are action and action form classes in Struts?*

XML and WebServices

What is XML?

What is the version information in XML?

What is ROOT element in XML?

If XML does not have closing tag will it work?

Is XML case sensitive?

What is the difference between XML and HTML?

Is XML meant to replace HTML?

Can you explain why your project needed XML?

What is DTD (Document Type definition)?

What is well formed XML?

What is a valid XML?

What is CDATA section in XML?

What is CSS?

What is XSL?

What is element and attributes in XML?

What are the standard ways of parsing XML document?

In What scenarios will you use a DOM parser and SAX parser?

What is XSLT?

Define XPATH?

What is the concept of XPOINTER?

What is a Web Service?

What is DISCO?

What is SOAP?

What is WSDL?

Can you explain UDDI?

Can you explain JAXP?

What is a XML registry?

What is JAXR?

What is JAXM?

Can you explain how JAXM messaging model works?

Can you explain JAX-RPC?

Internationalization

Can you explain i18n and l10n?

Can you explain internationalization and localization?

What is Locale?

How do we display numbers, currency and Dates according to proper Locale format?

What are resource bundles?

How do we load a resource bundle file?

How can we do inheritance in resource bundles?

JNI

What is Native Interface in JAVA?

Can you say in brief steps required to implement Native interfaces in Java?

Can JNI be used for VB6, C# or VB.NET directly?

What are JNI functions and pointers?

How does the garbage collector know JNI objects are no more used?

Twist: What are the different types of references JNI supports?

Twist: How to do you delete global objects?

How does the native language C or C++ understand data types in JAVA?

Can you explain exception handling in JNI?

What are limitations for "JNIEnv" pointer in multi-threading scenarios?

What are the advantages and disadvantages of using "JNI"?

Architecture

What are design patterns?

What is the difference between Factory and Abstract Factory Patterns?

What is MVC pattern?

Twist: How can you implement MVC pattern in Servlets and JSP?

How can we implement singleton pattern in JAVA?

How do you implement prototype pattern in JAVA?

Twist: How to implement cloning in JAVA? What is shallow copy and deep copy?

Can you give a practical implementation of FAÇADE patterns?

How can we implement observer pattern in JAVA?

What is three tier architecture?

What is Service Oriented architecture?

What is aspect oriented programming?

Project Management

What is project management?

Is spending in IT projects constant through out the project?

Who is a stakeholder?

Can you explain project life cycle?

Twist: How many phases are there in software project?

Are risk constant through out the project?

Can you explain different software development life cycles?

What is triple constraint triangle in project management?

What is a project baseline?

What is effort variance?

How is normally a project management plan document organized?

How do you estimate a project?

What is CAR (Causal Analysis and Resolution)?

What is DAR (Decision Analysis and Resolution)?

What is a fish bone diagram?

Twist: What is Ishikawa diagram?

What is pareto principle?

Twist: What is 80/20 principle?

How do you handle change request?

What is internal change request?

What is difference between SITP and UTP in testing?

What is the software you have used for project management?

What are the metrics followed in project management?

Twist: What metrics will you look at in order to see the project is moving successfully?

You have people in your team who do not meet there deadlines or do not perform what are the actions you will take?

Twist: Two of your resources have conflicts between them how would you sort it out?

What is black box testing and White box testing?

What's the difference between Unit testing, Assembly testing and Regression testing?

What is V model in testing?

How do you start a project?

How did you do resource allocations?

How will you do code reviews?

What is CMMI?

What are the five levels in CMMI?

What is continuous and staged representation?

Can you explain the process areas?

What is SIX sigma?

What is DMAIC and DMADV?

What are the various roles in Six Sigma implementation?

What are function points?

Twist: Define Elementary process in FPA?

What are the different types of elementary process in FPA?

What are the different elements in Functions points?

Can you explain in GSC and VAF in function points?

What are unadjusted function points and how is it calculated?

Can you explain steps in function points?

What is the FP per day in your current company?

Twist: What is your company's productivity factor?

Do you know Use Case points?

What is COCOMO I, COCOMOII and COCOMOIII?

What is SMC approach of estimation?

How do you estimate maintenance project and change requests?

UML

What is UML?

How many types of diagrams are there in UML?

Twist: Explain in short all types of diagrams in UML?

What are advantages of using UML?

Twist: What is Modeling and why UML?

What is the sequence of UML diagrams in project?

Twist: How did you implement UML in your project?

Just a small Twist: Do I need all UML diagrams in a project?

Give a small brief explanation of all Elements in activity diagrams?

Explain Different elements of a collaboration diagram?

Explain Component diagrams?

Explain all parts of a deployment diagram?

Describe the various components in sequence diagrams?

What are the element in State Chart diagrams?

Describe different elements in Static Chart diagrams?

Explain the different elements of a Use Case?

Twist: *What is the difference between Activity and sequence diagrams?*

Notes

